W9-DIY-587

Rabbi In The Strike Zone

A Decade in the Big Leagues

RABBI IN THE STRIKE ZONE

A Decade in the Big Leagues

Rabbi Barry Konovitch

Ktav Publishing House, Inc.
Jersey City, NJ

Published by
KTAV Publishing House, Inc.
930 Newark Avenue
Jersey City, NJ 07306
Email: info@ktav.com
www.ktav.com
(201) 963-9524
Fax (201) 963-0102

Contents

PART B
THE SEASON

PART B
MR. OCTOBER

Dedication

Dedicated to my good friend Irwin Edelstein whose support and encouragement has been invaluable.

Acknowledgments

A good batter is not born that way; he is the product of proper mentors, good coaching, first class teammates, and loyal fans.

My parents, Saba Si and Savta Sara, played for many seasons in the big leagues and it only remained for us to observe them carefully. My dear wife Aileen taught me to keep my eye on the ball, disregard all distractions, and hit away. Jonathan, Jordanna and Gideon read the signs and signaled me home. Together we put the runs on the board. And all my fans in the congregation sat in the grandstands week after week and cheered me on.

The season will eventually draw to a close, but the "stats" will remain prominently in the record books.

The Prologue
THE BIG LEAGUES

For the past ten years I have been playing in the "big leagues." The Aventura-Turnberry Jewish Center is a major congregation in South Florida where people have gravitated from all over the hemisphere and beyond.

But no one can bat 1000; even the greatest hitter of all time, Ted Williams, finished his career a bit over .400. And major homerun hitters, Babe Ruth and Mark McGuire included, were also the ones who accumulated the most strikeouts. The important thing is to swing straight and true with all your power and all your might. Revel in the ball disappearing over the left-field fence; do not dwell on the called third strike. You will come up to bat again; just be ready. Do the wind sprints, take batting practice, build your muscles, hone your eye, study that pitcher; and then watch that fast ball coming straight across the plate. And when the moment comes, stride into that ball with self-assuredness and a mental calmness that comes with being totally prepared, physically and psychologically.

The cheering of fans is a wonderful elixir. The upward movement of the numbers measuring RBI's or ERA's or hitting averages is a validation of effort, concentration and brilliance. But in the end, your real standing depends not on the fans, but on self-validation. You have to live with yourself, your conscience, and your personal expectations a lot longer than you will live with anyone else's. Please yourself and you may please others. Impress yourself and you will probably impress others.

And if not, there are the New York Yankees who are always looking for an experienced hitter. Just ask George Steinbrenner.

A. SPRING TRAINING
Sports as Metaphor for Life

TOO FAST TO SEE

Brian Robinson, a computer engineer, age 40, just completed the longest, fastest hike in American history: 7,371 miles in 10 months. He traversed America's three national scenic trails, the Appalachian, Pacific Crest, and Continental Divide Trails. That means he hiked the length of the Sierras, the Rockies, and the Appalachian Mountains, through snow, rain, and heat. Through it all, he was fueled by 6,000 calories a day including 900 Snickers bars. "Flyin Brian," as he is called, would get off the trail every now and again to binge eat, whole chickens, cheesecakes and two quarts of ice cream for desert.

He met a number of attractive women en route, but he was moving too fast to take careful notice. The only thing he concerned himself with was the logistics of the trip, where to pick up the 95 packages of food, and, most important, how to maintain his pace of 30 miles a day. Needless to say, it took months of serious preparation, both physical and mental; and it took more than physical toughness, it took an iron will to persist through such difficult terrain.

Standing atop Mt. Katahdin in Maine at the northern terminus of the Appalachian Trail, Brian Robinson allowed himself a moment of exultation. He had achieved what no other person had ever achieved. He wore out seven pairs of hiking shoes and almost wore out his 40-year-old body, but he made it. He covered 7,371 miles, but I doubt that he can tell you much about the terrain or the natural beauty he was surrounded with or the interesting people he met on the way. Because Brian was interested in only one thing, actually obsessed about one thing: speed.

The landscape passed in a rush, born of the determination to stay on a tight schedule. The journey was of secondary importance, only the end mattered.

Brian Robinson had it all wrong. He should have been focused on the journey. If everything passes in a blur, without making an imprint on our "mind's eye," then what is the purpose of the journey? We will all come to an end, sooner or later. We will all stand on the mountaintop after taking our last step. But what of all the steps that brought us to that final moment?

So many of us cannot live in the moment. Life passes us by in a rush of meaningless activity. We are making great speed but we don't know where we are. We confuse speed with progress. The point of it all is not to come to the end, but to enjoy the trip.

The end will come soon enough—we might as well enjoy the ride.

I wonder what Brian Robinson is thinking now?

THE BRONX BABY BOMBERS

When you speak of the Bronx, the last thing that comes to mind is a green, manicured field with four evenly spaced bases and a pitcher's mound. This is an image of Scarsdale or Great Neck. The Bronx conjures up a vision of dilapidated tenements, raucous streets, and kids playing stickball with a pink "spaldeen" that flies over two sewers if the hitter is any good. Where would a Bronx kid ever get a leather mitt or a genuine Louisville Slugger, even if he had access to a real ball field?

Yet, the Rolando Paulino Little League All-Stars made it all the way to the Little League World Series, and had it not been for "the scandal," they probably would have taken home the winner's trophy.

I must say that I was rooting for them to win. It seemed so unfair that a Florida team might win again. After all, they can practice all year round; they don't have two feet of winter snow to contend with, or the spring slush that turns the city streets into a sloppy mess. They have the warm sun, not cold rain. They play in tee shirts, not in gloves and wool hats.

And I surely didn't want the Japanese to win again. I always suspected that inside those twelve-year-old bodies lurked the machinery of those robots that I played with as a boy. If you pulled off the rubber mask, you might find Arnold Schwarzenegger.

So I rooted for the kids from the Bronx, who spoke more Spanish than English, whose parents came to America from the Dominican Republic and points south, who cleaned floors, waited tables, ran elevators, and worked at any job available until they could work themselves up the economic ladder.

And they ate and dreamt and lived "beisbol." They saw the great American pastime as a way out of the "barrio" and out to the trees and parks of Long Island. A way out of the dilapidated apartment houses near Crotona Park and along Bruckner Boulevard, and into a neat little house with a backyard and a garage in Mineola.

The Bronx Baby Bombers, as they were called, recruited Danny Almonte to pitch for them. Danny was a fabulous pitcher; he seemed to overwhelm the little batters in the box one after another. He was bigger and stronger than most of them, and he was downright intimidating up on the mound at Williams Port, Pennsylvania.

There was a good reason that Danny was superior to the rest of his compatriots; he was two years older, too old to be playing Little League ball. After a great deal of fudging, and a few documents from the Dominican Republic, Danny's father finally admitted that he had tried to pass his son off as a 12 year old, forged birth certificates and all.

The team was disqualified, the manager fired (he happened to be Danny's father), and Danny was sent back to public school in the Bronx where he had been playing "hookey" for the better part of the year.

But the fans in the Bronx didn't really care about the scandal. They gave Danny and the Rolando Paulino All-Stars a big parade through the borough, as if they were the conquering heroes of the Little League World Series. After all, Danny had thrown 46 strikeouts in 18 innings. A big sign along the route read: "12 or 14, so what."

Danny represented to his people the ticket to the American

dream; a way up and out of the daily misery of slum life. Surely a few digits on a birth certificate shouldn't make any difference. It shouldn't hold a kid back from his American dream. The kid is a great pitcher; one day he'll take the mound for the Yankees.

Of course, the point of baseball is that it has it's clearly defined rules. You run out of the baseline, the umpire calls you out. You have too many players in the dugout, you forfeit the game. It's called a level playing field; everybody plays by the same rules and everyone gets an even chance.

Danny and his father chose to ignore the rules. The rewards were just too tempting. The result was a Bronx mini-tragedy.

But the kids from the Dominican Republic will be back next spring as soon as the snow is cleared from their field in Macombs Dam Park, right near the Yankee Stadium. Hopefully, they will be a little bit wiser.

The Bronx Baby Bombers will make it back to the World Series; you mark my words. Danny will have his tryout with the Yankees in a few years. He will be terrific. Only this time everyone will be playing by the rules. It's the American way no matter what country you come from, or what language you speak. It is what makes us all Americans.

SUCCESS COMES FROM FAILURE

I always block out time to view the Olympics, this year being broadcast from Sydney, Australia. (I finally found the shtetl where my father-in-law, Sydney Brenner, came from; and I thought he was from Poland.) Because so much media time is being reserved for the games, we get to see many of the preliminary heats instead of just the finals as in years past.

I watched in horror as the Australian women's gymnastic team flew off the pommel horse only to fall in a twisted heap in the attempt to complete each maneuver. These were young girls, barely entering their teens, and here they were flying through the air in body-wrenching, awkward positions. Each imperfect landing produced a grimace of pain indicating a possible torn rotator cuff, a twisted ankle, or a broken femur. I wonder why

such pain has to be inflicted on young girls who are still growing, both physically and psychologically. Surely, the Olympics
could wait until they are a bit stronger and more mature.

But these concerns aside, I must admit that I was very
impressed when each young lady got up off the floor and calmly (at least outwardly) returned to the starting line for her next
attempt. And the next attempt was usually successful.

One of my favorite sports events is the triathlon, which this
year, for the first time, was added to the Olympics. Simon
Whitfield was cycling along in the peloton at top speed. After a
grueling swim of almost one mile in Sydney Harbor, he was
fighting to maintain his position on the second leg of the com-
petitions. Suddenly, two wheels touched, a rider went down,
and the ten surrounding cyclists went down in a heap. The
unscathed leaders increased their lead and seemed to remain
untouchable. Simon Whitfield climbed onto his bike and slowly
and laboriously began turning his gears. He was behind and I
didn't expect to see or hear of him again.

As the bikes were put aside and the competitors set out on
the 10 kilometer run around the Sydney Opera House, the pro-
jected winners seemed to be comfortably in the lead. Suddenly,
out of the back of the pack came Simon Whitfield. One by one,
he passed the leaders until only a lone runner remained; a powerful churning machine from Germany. Incredibly, Simon
increased his already amazing pace, passing his competition
just 200 yards from the finish and winning the first gold
triathlon medal in Olympics history.

More incredible, and much more amazing, was the fact that
just 45 minutes before, Simon Whitfield was lying on the
ground in a tangled heap of riders and bicycles. But he got up,
got moving, and won the race. To me, that's a real winner!

We all occasionally fall. We stumble; we are bruised. We fail,
we are discouraged. We are hurt, physically and psychologically. But the difference between winning and losing is that
unquantifiable ability that some of us have, to get up, shake off
the pain, and get moving again. It is called character. Nobody
really wants to know why you faded before the finish. No one is
really interested in your pulled muscle or your torn tendon.

With God's help we pray that the New Year 5761 will be a healthy, meaningful and successful one. But often the difference between our success and our failures, our achievements or our disappointments, depends on our ability to reach down and find that extra gram of determination to get us across the finish line. It is the difference between the winners and the also rans.

MULLIGAN

On Rosh Hashana, we ask the good Lord for another chance to do better, to do mitzvas, to be helpful, to do positive things for our synagogue and the community.

In golf, this is called asking for a "mulligan."

Our wonderful friend and founder of our congregation, Sol Schenck (A.H.) was a dedicated golfer. Notice I didn't say good golfer, I said dedicated. Sometimes the rest of his foursome would come by shul and describe their weekly game. They called it playing by Sol's rules. Anything Sol hit that went into the rough came out of the rough before the next shot. Because Sol said so. Any shot that Sol didn't like, he took another, a mulligan. He could always do it over. Take another shot. Try again.

I noticed President Bill Clinton was on vacation on Martha's Vineyard. He spends a lot of time on the golf course. He must have taken lessons from Sol because whenever he doesn't like a shot, he yells mulligan and takes another one. He never asks permission of his foursome; he just does it. Presidential prerogative I suppose.

Bill Clinton played a round with Gerald Ford back in 1993. Gerald Ford is not only an avid golfer but an honest one. Clinton told reporters that he shot an 80. Jack Nicklaus who was also playing with them, leaned over to President Ford and whispered in disgust, "80 with 50 floating mulligans."

Clinton's life has been full of mulligans. The voters put this comeback kid back in office in Arkansas, granting him a mulligan. The Senate refused to convict him after his impeachment by the House. Another mulligan. Hillary Clinton continues to stand by him. Another mulligan or two.

We all need a mulligan now and again. Our shot goes into the rough. We have to get back on the straight and narrow fairway. We have to fly true. We would like to be on target with our lives. We just need another shot, a second chance.

And that's why we are here in the synagogue. Asking God not to mark our score card, not just yet. Give us another stroke or two to get our game going. A spiritual mulligan if you will. Another chance. Just one more chance to make the cut. Before the end of the game, before Neilah, before the lights go out.

GROUND BALL TO THIRD

The young men are running around the outfield trying to work out a winter of stiffness. The infielders gather around the diamond to field grounders from the coach's bat. Slowly and gingerly at first, tentative and unsure. Slowly but surely, more fluid and sure as the afternoon wears on. Only one month remains until the season opens, and decisions need to be made: who stays on first and who goes to the grapefruit league for more seasoning. Who shows the promise of a future star and who needs to catch the next bus back to Iowa.

A particularly loud crack of the bat draws my attention. The speeding ball careens right at the third baseman and hits the grass directly in front of him. He plants his two feet, drops into his crouch, and extends hand and glove; a simple play he has already made dozens of times during the sunny afternoon. But this time the ball takes an unexpected bounce. Instead of meeting the palm of his glove, the ball ricochets off of his thigh and into the outfield. In a real game, runners would advance; perhaps the go-ahead run would cross the plate. A quick shake of an annoyed head, and he sets to try again. The coach is watching carefully.

So it is in our daily lives. We can deal with the expected. We know the right moves from years of practice. We analyze, we make decisions, we bend and move as we react to whatever is hit our way. We don't even have to think about it. The stimulus enters through our pupil, smacks into our retinal capillaries, and enters our neural system. Almost instantaneously, a hand extends or a leg flexes. It's all over in milliseconds and the task is done, and done properly.

But when the stimulus is out of the ordinary, everything stops until the brain can sort it out. But it takes too long; the reaction is too slow or the reaction is the wrong one. The ball is bobbled, we let a run score.

So we need to go back to basic drills. Practice for the bad bounce. Do it over and over. Cover the possibilities of every eventuality; and then we will be prepared for whatever comes flying at us. And if we miss, and we will miss from time to time, just shrug it off and try again.

A DIFFERENT PERSON ON ROSH HASHANA

A friend came by my office to visit. He was dressed in his gym clothes and he was still sweating from an obviously strenuous workout. But it wasn't the sweat I noticed, (or "perspiration" as it is known in more polite circles) or even the obvious post workout odor. Rather the color of his face and the sag of his body as he flopped down in the seat caught my attention. Before I could say another word, he commented rather ruefully, "I am not the man I used to be." I quickly quipped; "maybe that's good."

After I had wiped and sprayed away all traces of his visit, I began to reflect on our conversation. None of us is the same person we used to be. Time marches on and as every second passes, we move closer to our maker. The body we had yesterday is not the same body we have today. We are missing a few million cells, which include several thousand gray cells from various sections of our cerebrum and cerebellum.

We don't move the same and we are reminded of this fact by the creak in our knees where the cartilage is supposed to be, by the twinge in our shoulder where the bursa is inflamed, and by the search for our car keys exacerbated by those missing memory banks.

Rosh Hashana and the advent of a new year is a time for taking stock of our lives. We are not the same people we used to be, and maybe that's good. We may be slower, but we are wiser, more compassionate, more sympathetic, and a whole lot more patient. The process we go through annually called penitence (*teshuva*) is supposed to remind us that it can't be business as usual. We can't remain the same person we used to be. We are supposed to redirect ourselves, improve our lives, and become better people. And if at some point during the New Year we look ourselves in the mirror and say, "we are not the same people we used to be," then wonderful. We have improved our lives, we have grown closer to the ones we love, and we have increased our concern for our people and our heritage. We are better people, we are better Jews, and we are better Americans. We aren't the people we used to be, and that's just fine!

A HOMERUN

The mighty Mark McGuire ended his baseball season with 70 homeruns, not only breaking Roger Maris's record (61), but surpassing all expectations. He also posted one of the biggest strikeout records of the year. Obviously, if you don't swing for the fences, you won't hit it out of the infield.

McGuire was under tremendous pressure. A few months ago, he said he felt like "all eyes in America were on him." Every time he came to bat, the fans expected him to blast one into the upper deck. A double was not good enough, a walk was certainly not good enough. The fans expected to see that ball rocketing out into the bleachers every time.

No human being can hit a homerun every time, not even McGuire, with those arms the size of an average man's thigh. And yet, he maintained his composure, remained almost Zen-like in his focus, and did the very best that he could; and his very best was terrific.

I have been a bit bored by baseball since Mickey Mantle retired, and since "George S." keeps threatening to take the Yankees out of the Bronx. But as with so many people, I have been elated by "Big Mac;" not because he is some kind of role model for youngsters, and not because he is some new moral force in the universe, but simply because he was able to do so well under so much pressure; with a certain "grace" as Hemmingway might have put it.

I can relate to that, being no stranger to large audiences with great expectations, who are only interested in the "home-run." Every person is allotted only so many "at bats." We prepare ourselves to be in the best physical shape and mental state possible. And then, we take a mighty cut at the ball as it comes speeding at us. Everything is reduced to milliseconds and millimeters. Sometimes we connect in awesome fashion and sometimes we just get on base. But it all counts for the final score.

So hail to all of us who get up at the plate, dig in our spikes, and prepare to hit. The fans are screaming for a homerun; and when the ball stays in the infield, they have the chutzpa to boo. How quickly they forget. It takes a great deal of confidence and concentration to shut out all the noise and concentrate on a smooth, powerful swing. And if we are well conditioned, and if we are well prepared mentally, and if we have mazal, everything goes right; and the fans leap to their feet cheering wildly, the last strikeout suddenly forgotten.

It doesn't always work that way, but when everything goes right, what a day in the park it is!

OLYMPIC DISAPPOINTMENT

As with millions of people around the world, I am transfixed by the phenomenal display of athletic prowess at the Nagano Olympics. Couch potatoes and weekend warriors alike are amazed at what young athletes from around the world can accomplish as they go "faster, higher. and farther" on the snow and ice. However not everyone can win the gold;

but everyone who is invited to participate in the games is truly a champion.

Many Olympians brought their parents and families along, and the close-up cameras would reveal their agonizing faces, their jubilation, and their despair. It was a reflection of what was going on in the skating rink or at the skiing venue even before we heard the decision of the judges. When Hermann Maeir crashed during the downhill, his parents back in Flachau were heart broken. When Nicole Bobeck fell during the short program, her mother, in the stands, groaned and covered her face. And when dozens of athletes came down with the flu and many had to withdraw from the events, we sympathized with them. They train for years, for most of their young lives, and everything comes down to minutes on the snow or ice, and suddenly they are too sick to even buckle on their boots. Imagine the disappointment. Words could never begin to describe the horrible feeling of coming so far and then being denied even the chance to approach the starting line.

Being a parent or a grandparent entails similar experiences. We rejoice in our children's triumphs and we are saddened by their failures. We have to sit nervously in the stands as they get ready to compete. The SAT's for college, the GRE's for graduate school, the LSAT's, for law school, the MCAT's for medical school, and a host of other ABC tests and hurdles each one has to overcome. We can all remember holding our breaths as our children opened the university acceptance letter or the medical school letter, hoping against hope that it was acceptance and not rejection. And if the news was good, we immediately ordered the appropriate decal for the car window and we had bragging rights for months.

Sometimes our expectations for our children are so high that the pressures become unbearable. We all want the best for our sons and daughters but sometimes it is best to sit patiently on the sidelines and to cheer them in victory, console them in defeat and, continually remind them that they are always our champions, no matter what the game and no matter what the score.

YOM KIPPUR FROM A BRONX PERSPECTIVE

The World Series (baseball, of course) always coincided with the High Holydays when I was young. Messengers keep on arriving from the corner candy store in the north Bronx, updating us from "unesaneh tokef" to "neila." Once when the Giants lost a game, the Rabbi got up and read a part of the Bible relating to the story of David and Jonathan: "Aich Naflu Gebborim." We didn't need the translation to know it meant the Giants had lost the game. ("How the Giants have fallen," was the rough translation, referring to the death of Saul and Jonathan on Mount Gilboa, as well as the fortunes of the teams at the Polo Grounds.)

Lately, I am not so enthusiastic about my old Bronx team. My Yankees have deserted Fort Lauderdale for Tampa and I am not about to drive four hours just to see pitchers and catchers, not even the great Roger Clemens, George's latest acquisition.

Speaking of George Steinbrenner, the man Yankee fans love to hate; perhaps you noticed that last January the Yankees owner did something so totally out of character that we began to worry about the health of his gray matter: He traveled from his home in Tampa all the way to Little Falls, New Jersey, for the opening of the Yogi Berra museum on the campus of Montclair State University. He made the trip to meet the great Yankee catcher Yogi Berra and to apologize for firing him 16 games into the 1985 season. Berra then vowed never to set foot in Yankee Stadium as long as Steinbrenner owned the team.

Here was George to make a public apology, so out of character for the Yankee's dictator. He took Berra's hand, looked him in the eye, and said: "I know I made a mistake by not letting you go personally. It's the worst mistake I ever made in baseball."

Yogi's wife, Carmen, said she believed Steinbrenner's visit had to do with clearing his conscience. "With the year 2000 coming, everyone is thinking about peace, about making things right. Yogi's son, Dale, told his dad that 14 years was long enough to hold a grudge."

I like to think that Yom Kippur is a time of renewal. We mark the day by a process of introspection, "cheshbon hanefesh." It is a time of forgiveness: We forgive those who have offended us, and God hopefully forgives us. It is a time for spiritual growth and personal renewal. To achieve this we have to leave the past behind and turn our faces into the Florida sunshine. It is the time to divest ourselves of old grudges and annoyances.

If Yogi can forgive George, then surely we can forgive our brothers and our friends. Yogi used to say, "It ain't over 'til it's over." Yom Kippur is a time to say, "it's over," time to start fresh, time to enjoy the new season. If we wait for Neila, it might be too late.

THE GAME MUST GO ON

Whenever Paul O'Neil comes up to bat, I expect the ball to fly. He takes that odd step forward as he prepares to swing and anything can happen. Unfortunately, he seemed preoccupied toward the end of the World Series, and rightly so. His father was seriously ill; and before the last game began, the senior O'Neil passed away.

For me, the biggest Yankee story was not how quickly they would win the series. Rather it was all about Paul O'Neil: Would he take his place in the outfield and help his magnificent teammates sweep the championship, or would he retire and mourn the passing of his father?

I didn't have long to wait. Paul was in his accustomed place when the last ball was popped into the outfield and the Yankees raucously celebrated their third championship in four years.

Paul O'Neil was crying. He quickly left the clubhouse to make funeral arrangements and to contemplate a future without his father, who was perhaps the most important influence in his life. His greatest fan would henceforth be missing from the stands, and life would never be the same.

But the game must go on. How difficult it must have been for Paul O'Neil to concentrate on his swing as his dad lay dying in the hospital. Mayor Rudy Guilliani commended him and a few of his teammates who had the courage to go on even in the face of great personal adversity. In the venerable tradition of the Yankees, the game went on, and the game was won.

In the popular American culture, the game must go on. The game is the most important thing in life. Health and sickness, life and death; all take a backseat to the "game." But not in my culture.

The fifth commandment reads: "Honor your father and mother." It applies in their lifetime and in their death. No game takes precedence over the fifth commandment. There are times in a person's life when the game has to stop because there are more important things to attend to. There are moments when we have to remind ourselves that our priorities do not, and cannot, center around the game. There are issues of the soul that cannot be addressed by a bat and a ball.

I still remember the famous stories of Hank Greenberg in Detroit and Sandy Koufax in Brooklyn and Art Shamsky in Queens who declined to play in crucial series games because Rosh Hashana and Yom Kippur were more important to them. Sometimes, there are more important things in life than the game. Imagine going through life, coming to the end, and never figuring this out. That would be the real tragedy; not just failing to reach first base.

TEAM WORK

Mark McGwire and Sammy Sosa continue to "whale the tar" out of the baseball. It seems as if every time I turn on the sports news, I see a picture of these muscled giants rapping the ball out into the upper deck of Busch Stadium or over the wall in Wrigley Field. They have surpassed Babe Ruth and Roger Maris; they are in a league of their own.

But ironically, the St. Louis cardinals and the Chicago Cubs are not in contention for the championships, not even for a "wild-card spot."

Last I looked, it takes a team of nine players (or is it now ten with the designated hitter?) to play baseball, emphasis on "team." If the pitcher can't cut the inside corner of the plate, or if the left fielder can't snag a long fly ball, or if the third base-man can't knock down a sizzling grounder, then the team can't win. And if the clean-up man can't send his teammates around the bases and across home plate, then the numbers on the score board won't move up.

McGuire and Sosa are two stars, two magnificent ball play-ers, but they can't carry a whole team on their shoulders. In order to win a pennant, a team has to be just that: a team. All nine men (or ten) have to do their share. All nine men have to work together. All nine men have to trust one another, support one another, and encourage one another. Mighty Mark has 62 homeruns as of this writing. But during this same period, his team lost some 38 games. Even if Mark hits twice the amount of "four baggers," and even if the ball flies all the way to the Missouri River, nothing will change in the team's standings. Because one man, even a mighty man, can't carry a whole team.

I have noticed that the most successful organizations are those that can field a first-class team, where each of the mem-bers can make a significant contribution and where each of the members works closely and respectfully with his compatriots. Bill Gates, Jr., is certainly the moving force behind Microsoft but I have seen a videotape of his corporate meetings, with his executives sitting together in their jeans and denims sharing ideas, concerns, and plans. The energy of Microsoft seems to be a synergy of combined brainpower, instead of the nuclear fusion of one cerebral mass.

It takes a long time to put together a top-notch team that can work together. But once such a corporate team comes together, there is no limit to the energy they can radiate and the power they can produce.

So it is with the "minyan," the quorum of ten people needed to begin the daily prayers. There is no "tenth man"; every indi-vidual is the tenth man, because only ten people constitute a bonafide prayer community. If the Lubavitcher Rebbe himself came into the "Bais Midrash" and sat down to pray with us, and we only numbered nine, we could not pray as a minyan. The great Rebbe would only count as one, no different from you or me. Not Rabbi Akiva, not Hillel, no one individual, no matter how great he may be can carry the entire prayer community. Even if Yossele Rosenblatt or Richard Tucker stood at the cantor's table and began chanting the liturgy, they still could not substitute for the required ten. It takes a minyan; it takes a "team" effort if you will.

Stars are for the outer galaxies; teams are for the planet earth.

SAMMY AND "EL DUQUE": HEROES WITH NO EXCUSES

The Yankees just won Game Two of the World Series, and Orlando Hernandez was the winning pitcher. El Duque was superb: Pitching in the first world series of his life, literally just off the boat from Cuba, he terrorized the Padre batters into submission. As he winds up, he lifts his foot high into the air in that trademark movement that allows him to hide the ball from the hitters until it is almost too late to see his sinking fast ball approaching the plate. Before each pitch he tugs his cap up and down, chews determinedly on his gum, and lets loose one of his "shot from canon" pitches. He never seems to become flustered or nervous; as if he has been pitching for the Yankees his entire career. No one is really sure how old he is, but we know that he pitched in one of the world's toughest leagues, communist Cuba under the glaring eye of Big Brother Castro. The Cubans are fanatic baseball players and fans, perhaps one of the few things they like about the United States, along with every 1950s' car ever manufactured in Detroit. Orlando was the greatest baseball star in Cuba, a man of considerable talent, but it took audacity and not a little desperation for him and his brother to cross the gulfstream in a rickety raft in order to realize their dream of playing in America.

Sammy Sosa grew up in the Dominican Republic, where the people are also avid baseball fans. As a child, he used a glove made of cardboard, and a ball of rags to practice. He came to America with many of his compatriots, who make their home in Washington Heights, Manhattan, and listen to every crack of

Sammy's bat. And when he surpassed Roger Maris's mark of 61 homeruns, the fans in upper Manhattan went wild. Mark McGuire might be the "man" for Sammy, but Sammy is the "man" for all the Caribbean people.

Both of these fine athletes came from humble beginnings. No manicured little league diamonds, shiny aluminum bats, and new leather gloves. They couldn't afford to buy even a shoelace in the Sports Authority. Yet they persevered, and single-handedly pursued their dream. And most refreshing of all, they never used their poor, deprived backgrounds as an excuse for failure. Giving up a homerun is never attributed to that cardboard glove; striking out is never blamed on the empty stomach of childhood. In an age where it becomes convenient to avoid responsibility and blame it on "bad genes" or a deprived environment, Sammy and Orlando are refreshing in their genuineness.

The Nike Company, which is tenaciously pursuing our new heroes, uses the motto "just do it." As Sammy and Orlando are quickly transformed into multimillionaires, I hope that they continue to present themselves as the genuine article, taking responsibility for their performance on and off the field and never offering extraneous excuses for occasional failure. May they continue to "just do it" without agents, lawyers, publicists, and spin-doctors.

I can't wait for the next game!

MOSES AND MOE: A PASSOVER DELIVERANCE

When President Harry Truman decided to use the atomic bomb, World War II came to a terrifying and devastating end. Instead of sending an invasion fleet to the shores of Japan, the "Enola Gay" delivered the coup de grace from some thirty thousand feet in the air over Hiroshima, and in one fiery flash of flame, tens of thousands of American soldiers were spared. Never mind the revisionist historians who prefer to remind us of the hundreds of thousands of Japanese incinerated in several seconds: "What ye reap, so shall ye sow."

Had the Manhattan project at Los Alamos been completed just a year or two earlier, several million Jews would have been saved from the crematoria and untold thousands of allied soldiers would have returned home to their families. There would have been several tons less of ashes at Auschwitz and the forest of crosses and stars at Omaha Beach would have been considerably reduced.

The allies were in a race with Germany to perfect the atom bomb. Leading the Nazi effort was Werner Heisenberg, and the Americans were terribly worried that a bomb would be headed to New York before Robert Oppenheimer and Albert Einstein could complete their work out in the New Mexico desert.

So we sent a spy to Zurich in 1944, where Heisenberg was lecturing, to determine if the Nazis had the bomb. The Danish Nobel Laureate Niels Bohr was also present and these two leading physicists tried to feel each other out on the bomb project. The spy in the audience was under orders to shoot Heisenberg if it became clear that the Nazis were about to complete the first atomic bomb.

The name of the spy was Moe Berg. A Jew. A baseball catcher. He was ready to execute Heisenberg, the 1939 Nobel Prize winner for quantum mechanics, and save the world from the Nazis.

In the end, it was clear that Heisenberg and the Nazis didn't have the bomb. They misunderstood some of the basic physics involved. But Moe Berg was ready to sacrifice his life, if need be, to save the free world.

Passover is a time of the year when we celebrate our deliverance. Some 3500 years ago, Moses saved the Israelites from the destructive environment of Egypt. And we read in the Hagada that each of us should consider that redemption in very personal terms. Not only were our ancestors delivered, but we were also delivered. Had Moses not led us through the Red Sea, we would still be slaves in Cairo.

So we should remember and celebrate Moe Berg, whose Hebrew name was probably Moshe (Moses). In every generation, God sends His deliverer to us. Sometimes we recognize him and sometimes we don't. Sometimes he is recorded for posterity in our historical annals, and sometimes he is just a foot-note. Let us raise one of the four cups to the memory of Moe Berg, a Jewish hero.

LOYALTY

David Wells was a star of the 1998 World Series, propelling the New York Yankees to a magnificent championship. A few weeks ago he got a call from the front office: Pack your bags, you have been traded to the Toronto Blue Jays. Not only was Wells devastated, which was obvious even through his brave smile and despite his many zeroed salary, but his Yankee teammates were also demoralized. If George could do it to David, then he could do it to any pinstriper.

George has no loyalty, and without loyalty, you really can't build a solid team that will perform with any longevity. This year's champion team can quickly become next year's cellar dwellers without that all important ingredient that holds a team together and encourages them to give 100 percent of their effort. Nothing motivates like the feeling of being needed, want-ed, and cared for. It is bad enough that George picked up the team and moved them ball, bat, and gloves to Tampa, leaving me to watch the Baltimore Orioles in Ft. Lauderdale stadium. The great green field spread out in the Florida winter sunshine beckons, and who can resist spring training fever. But it grates on me when I am constantly reminded of George's ficklemind-edness. Maybe that is the formula for making money, but it surely can't be the formula for building a great institution for the long haul.

We all need to feel valued, the beneficiaries of a sense of loy-alty, nations as well as individuals. The story of the Exodus of the Israelites from Egypt as recounted in our celebration of Passover reflects this concern to feel wanted and needed. God continues to perform his wondrous miracles for His people: the ten plagues, the splitting of the Red Sea, the trek through the desert to the Promised Land. On several occasions, an exasper-ated Lord almost stretches out His hand to crush His constantly complaining people. But He keeps his temper. Perhaps, He realizes that through constant encouragement, motivation, and the obvious loyalty to His people, the Israelites will finally see the light. It becomes so apparent that God will never forsake his people; that no matter what they do, no matter how terribly they try the Lord's patience, He will continue to be loyal to them. Perhaps, this is the true definition of loyalty. And that is why the people of Israel have never failed to be loyal to God.

What do you say we invite George to our Seder and teach him a thing or two about loyalty?

LANCE ARMSTRONG: CHAMPION

The greatest story of the summer had to do with a young man in a yellow jersey riding on a bicycle through the French countryside. Lance Armstrong of Austin, Texas, became the second American in history to win the famous Tour de France cycling race. Three weeks of grueling 150-mile days, up mountains and across back roads at incredible speeds test even the world's greatest athletes. Just to finish the Tour is an accomplishment; winning is an extraordinary event. But wearing the coveted yellow jersey of the champion on the podium in Paris after undergoing cancer surgery and chemotherapy is the most amazing thing that ever happened in the 80 year history of the race.

Not yet out of his twenties, Lance Armstrong became the American Road racing champion. Then a chance medical check-up revealed he had widespread cancer.

He never once complained, he never gave up, he never stopped fighting. After two years of extensive treatment, he began his comeback. And the rest is racing history.

I have followed his career for a number of years. We even prayed for him in our synagogue during his cancer surgery. I gave him a Hebrew name for this purpose and only a few aficionados realized who he was. I wrote to him regularly offering our prayers and support. He appreciated our concern, and the concern of thousands of well-wishers across the country.

And he recovered; and he got back on his bicycle; and he won the Tour de France. Tremendous determination; an unfaltering positive attitude; a will to do anything necessary for survival and recovery.

Many of us will be tested this year. We will wonder how to keep going. We will consider crawling into a corner and giving up. We will grow tired and weary both in body and spirit.

But keep in mind the young man in the yellow jersey from Texas. Take heart; keep fighting; the battle can be won. With God's help, with grit and determination and a positive, focused attitude and a little mazal we can achieve the miraculous.

At least we can try, which is infinitely more satisfying than giving up.

JOE DIMAGGIO: AMERICAN HERO

The newspapers have been filled with glowing tributes to Joe Dimaggio, one of the greatest baseball players who ever swung a bat. But he wasn't a god; he was just an athlete who had the extraordinary hand-eye coordination to hit the ball consistently well for 56 straight games in the 1941 season. And he had the good sense to keep his mouth closed most of the time, so people grew to think of him as wise. In actuality, he never gave people an opportunity to consider his intelligence; he never said enough to be criticized. The only time we heard him say more than a few words was as "Mr. Coffee" in a series of advertisements on television.

By no means am I commenting on Joe's intelligence or denigrating his greatness as a champion baseball player, or even as an icon of American culture. Rather, I am considering the nature of our society where a baseball player is elevated to demigod status, known and recognized by almost every citizen, while a Nobel Prize winner for medicine is unknown outside his immediate academic circles. Which one contributed more to the progress and improvement of American life?

Yes, you will trot out the discussion about "heroes" and the need for the "hero" in an age of anxiety and depression. Indeed,

Joe Dimaggio was a hero, and a lift, even a spiritual lift for those who went through the Great Depression and were anxious about the coming world war. But what does it say about our society when the most intellectually stimulating moment in the year comes when a great Yankee outfielder marries the Hollywoood sex symbol that every male over puberty dreams about. Joe and Marylin were the royal couple of the United States (albeit for less than a year) instead of that year's greatest schoolteacher or that year's finest physicist.

And you will repeat that "he had class." I certainly agree that compared to present-day athletes with foul mouths, roiling hormones, inflated egos, and much too much money to spend, with no value system to direct their rather conspicuous consumption, Joe D. had class. He carried himself regally, quietly, with some dignity (except when he took after Marilyn), and almost humbly. Or was it that he had an uncanny sense of self-marketing. He never overexposed himself, doling out his royal presence at carefully scripted events. Joe's presence was always a great event and he knew it.

I am amazed that I am saying all this, a Yankee fan from the getgo with a warmed seat in the grandstands of the Bronx stadium. I, who worshipped Mickey and Whitey and Phil and Yogi. (Joe was more part of my father's youth than mine.) I, who sent regular letters of protest to George about his latest catastrophic decision. Why not just say Joe D. was the classiest guy who ever played baseball and let it go at that? Why not just add my voice to the chorus of the faithful?

I have chosen these words not because I don't admire the Yankee clipper, rather, because I am pained by the shallow worship of athlete demigods in our society, people who without that team number on their uniform would probably cause us to cross to the other side of the street in an attempt to avoid their menacing presence.

In those days, when Dimaggio patroled the outfield at Yankee stadium, athletes were looked upon as role models, and the "splendid splinter" did not disappoint. Thousands of kids across the country remember worshipping at his Bronx shrine, held in thrall by that smooth graceful swing with not an ounce of wasted energy.

Yet, no one remembers that Joe had a son. His son showed up at the funeral in San Fransisco; he hadn't heard from his father in two years. Joe's son lives in a trailer in a junk yard, and no funeral suit can disguise the fact that as a father, as a family man, Joe struck out.

So before we designate our gods, before we worship idols, before we crown our role models, best we consider carefully. As wonderful and captivating as an athlete may be, surely he can not wash the feet of the man who discovered the Polio vaccine, or the woman who will discover the cure for cancer. Yet, every adolescent in America will remember the name McGuire and the number 70, as their fathers remember Dimaggio and the number 56. Yet, very few fathers or sons will recognize the names of Waxman or Pasteur and the millions of lives they saved. How sad.

SLOWING DOWN

A few years ago, at the Seattle Special Olympics, nine contestants, all physically or mentally disabled, assembled at the starting line for the 100-yard dash.

At the gun, they all started out, not exactly in a dash, but with a relish to run the race to the finish and win. All, that is, except one little boy who stumbled on the asphalt, tumbled over a couple of times, and began to cry. The other eight heard the boy cry.

They slowed down and looked back. Then they all turned around and went back. Every one of them. One girt with Down Syndrome bent down and kissed him and said, "This will make it better." Then all nine linked arms and walked together to the finish line.

Everyone in the stadium stood, and the cheering went on for several minutes. People who were there are still telling the story. Why?

Because deep down we know this one thing: What matters in this life is helping others, even if it means slowing down and changing our course.

B. THE SEASON
Getting Through the Year
1. Israel Fights On

FIGHTING TERRORISM:
THE SIN OF MORAL EQUIVALENCE

Throughout the year of the so-called Arab "Infitada," the international media have equated the murder of Israeli civilians and the deaths of Arab terrorists. No distinction is made between an Arab suicide bomber blowing up Israeli teenagers in a nightclub and the Israeli Army shooting a Kalashnikov-toting member of Hamas. No distinction is made between Arab terrorists machine-gunning Israeli women waiting for a bus and a Jihad mastermind shot by the Israeli Army on the way to murder Israeli citizens going about their daily business. The violence committed by the Palestinian Authority has no relationship whatsoever to the tactics adopted by the Israeli Army in self-defense.

The achievement of peace is not such a complicated issue: The day the Arab Palestinians lay down their arms and stop sending their children to throw rocks at Israeli soldiers and stop training their young men as suicide bombers, that is the day all the violence will stop. Israeli soldiers were never sent to murder innocent men, women and children. Israeli soldiers never blew up a civilian bus in Nablus; Israeli soldiers never exploded teenagers in a Ramallah nightclub. Israeli soldiers never machine-gunned children in a Gaza restaurant. All this is perpetuated only by Arabs; all this is called terrorism; all this is called murder. Israeli soldiers fire only in defense of their lives and their country.

In years past, when the Palestinian Arabs wanted to accuse Israel of an atrocity they would always trot out "Deir Yasin," where in 1948, Israeli irregulars from the Irgun got into a fire-fight with local villagers after being fired upon. Israel could present a list of hundreds of Arab atrocities from Hebron to Ma'alot through Sbarro's. When Arafat's Fatah wished to accuse the Israeli Army of murder, they would trot out the picture of a young boy dying in the arms of his father during a Gaza confrontation. It was only later that the truth became known: Right behind the stone-throwing boys were Arab terrorists trying to machine-gun Israeli patrols.

There is no moral equivalence between firing to murder and firing to defend yourself. Neither can the term "freedom fighter" be conveniently substituted for "terrorist" as the western world has done for years. Since September 11, with the leadership of the United States, all terrorist organizations have been recognized as such: Al Quaeda, Hamas, Hizbolla, Fatah, and dozens of others around the world. As President Bush rightly observed, if you are with the free world, then you are against terrorism in any form; and to harbor or aid terrorists is to become a terrorist yourself.

Some try to remind us that the "Irgun" and "Lechi" organizations that struggled for Israel's independence in the 1940s also called themselves freedom fighters, but were labeled terrorists by the British Mandate authorities. However, the Israeli underground never attacked British or Arab civilians. They never set out to murder innocent men, women, and children just to terrify the population. They always fought against soldiers of the British Army or Arab irregulars; and if in the process, civilians were harmed then, to use the American term in vogue, it constitutes collateral damage that sometimes is unavoidable in a war theater.

In the end, an Arab Palestinian state will not be born of terrorism against Israeli civilians. It will only come about through peaceful negotiations. Until that time, it would be helpful for the world media to report the truth and it would certainly help to resolve the real issues: the right of Israel to exist as a free and independent state, recognized by all belligerent Arab states, and the right of the Israeli people to a safe and secure existence.

JERUSALEM AGAIN, JERUSALEM ALWAYS

As I write this article, we have just celebrated "Yom Yerushalayim," the thirty-second anniversary of the reunification of Jerusalem at the end of the Six-Day War in 1967. The Israelis have held elections for Prime Minister and Parliament, the only free election in accordance with democratic principles in the Middle East. Each of the candidates has been heard from on the subject of Jerusalem and each has the same declaration of "united and forever." During the past year, several Israeli leaders from the left and the right have been in our community and each seems to be of the same mind regarding Jerusalem. They profess a unified Jerusalem, capital of Israel. Everyone cheers; and we think the issue is resolved.

But do not be fooled by pre-election rhetoric. The darling of the left, Dr. Yossi Belin, with his counterpart in the Palestinian congress, Abu Mazen, have agreed and proposed that a suburb of Jerusalem, Abu Dis, be incorporated into the city proper and that it be designated the Palestinian capital of Jerusalem. Others have suggested the suburb of Ramallah.

Hanan Ashrawi reported a few days ago that an agreement had been reached with Shimon Peres during the Rabin Administration to, in her words, "share Jerusalem as the capital of both Israel and Arab Palestine." During the same interview, she attempted to rewrite history by telling her audience that all of Jerusalem was always an Arab city until 1948, when the Jews took over the western sector. And she suggested that there was no validity in quoting "holy texts" from 2000 years ago to assert modern claims. Rather, the fact that Arabs have lived in Jerusalem for "centuries" (her word) is geo-political fact enough to honor their claim to Jerusalem. Of course, she quoted a United Nations resolution that made Jerusalem a "corpus separatum" a separate entity not attached to any country (read: Israel).

I believe that the obstacle to peace is not Jerusalem, or even a Palestinian state in Judea and Samaria, however dangerous and odious as the prospect may be. The real obstacle to peace in Arab eyes is the presence of the State of Israel, a western Jewish entity in the midst of the Muslim oriental Middle East. One way or another, either through military, terrorist, or diplomatic means, the Arab states will continue to attempt to remove the foreign infidel presence (Israel) from their midst. The only way to ensure quiet, if not peace, is to make it very clear, through military preparedness, diplomatic initiative, and plain old stubbornness that Israel is here to stay, that a united Jerusalem is capital of Israel and only Israel, and that any proposed Palestinian state will have to be structured to insure the security and integrity of Israel and its citizens. Only when the Arab states in general and the Palestinians in particular give up their strategies of reducing and eventually eliminating Israel will a real peace process begin.

PRESIDENTS

The State of Israel has chosen a new President, Moshe Katzav; and in a few months, the United States will choose a new President. (The biggest news, of course, is the possibility that a "member of the tribe" [M.O.T.] may become the Vice-President for the first time in American history.)

The President should be the President of all the people, not merely the representative of special interests. He should carry out a policy of inclusion, which means that all segments of society should be carefully considered and included in the American dream of social, political, and economic progress. And this policy of inclusion should be much more than just a slogan or a staged show for the media. It should be reflected in the Presidential appointments, policies, and political platform.

President Moshe Katzav is the first Israeli of Persian decent to hold this highest office. Although mostly ceremonial in nature, the President can be a strong moral force in the national life of the people. Since the rise of modern Zionism and the

pioneering movement to rebuild Eretz Yisrael, the power structure has always been controlled by the Eastern European intelligentsia. This Ashkenazic elite often looked down their noses
at their oriental brothers from Yemen and Arabia as backward
and primitive. As the Yishuv became a State and the political
system changed from socialism to capitalism and the economy
changed from agrarian to high technology, the gap between the
Ashkenazim and the Sefardim grew larger. In an effort to rem-
edy the situation, the Sefardim organized into a political vot-
ing block (Shas) and began to demand a greater share of the
economic and political pie. This ongoing tug of war within the
body politic threatens to tear the very fabric of Israeli society
apart.

President Moshe Katzav can be a force for reason and unity.
He will give the Sefardim a great deal of pride and a feeling of
political power and vindication. How wonderful that a member
of one of the Israeli "minorities" has been elevated to the presidency. It reconfirms the democratic nature of the State of Israel.
(Not something you might see in Baghdad or Damascus or
Amman).

But the test of a great President is not how well he represents his own constituency, but how well he represents all the
people. President Katzav has the sacred opportunity to unite
the Jewish people in Israel and around the world. We pray that
the "Rock of Israel" will give him the wisdom and the courage to
carry out his mandate.

May the New Year 5761 bring peace, security, and dignity to
our people.

LETTER TO PM NETANYAHU AND
STATE OF ISRAEL

Dear Prime Minister Netanyahu and Brothers and Sisters of
the State of Israel:

I am horrified at the news from the Machneh Yehuda marketplace and the Ben Yehuda shopping mall: dozens killed and

hundreds wounded by Arab terrorists. This past Shabbat, we read the names of the dead as we recited a memorial prayer, and we prayed for the wounded whose lives will never be the same. The important thing is never to lose hope and faith. If we take the historical perspective, Arab terrorists have exploded bombs on Ben Yehuda since the day the Balfour Declaration was issued in 1917 in an effort to eliminate any Jewish presence in Israel (what was then called Palestine). The cost of Jewish independence in our ancient homeland has always been the blood of its citizens, because our freedom is never free.

I do not wish to sound like an armchair general from the distance. After all, I could have purchased a one-way ticket on El-Al Israel Airlines at any time during the last 50 years and added to the strength of the nascent state. Yet, I chose to remain in the relative safety of America. (Although sometimes I wonder about which society is indeed more secure). I am not a citizen of Israel, nor do I vote for its leaders, nor do I have any say in its polices, yet as the poet Yehuda Halevi wrote some 900 years ago, "my heart is always in the East."

My heart and the hearts of the several thousand members of my community go out to you. Whatever you decide to do, we are with you.

I would respectfully remind you that the State of Israel is supposed to be the one place in the world where a Jew doesn't have to worry about anti-Semitism, the next pogroms or "final solutions." Whatever it takes to achieve this security for our people must be done.

It would appear that more drastic measures are needed to deal with the situation. It is clear that Arafat and his henchman are either incapable or unwilling (or both) to deal with Arab terrorists. It suits his purpose to use the bombers for his own agenda. Prime Ministers Rabin and Peres hoped that Arafat would be a suitable peace partner, but their hope was naïve and their faith misplaced. The man who kisses the leader of the Hamas unashamedly in front of the whole world has clearly indicated where he stands. It is therefore time for Israel to recognize the reality of the situation and begin to take matters into its own hands.

When I say it is time for drastic measures, I mean as follows (there are only several alternatives for peace):

1. Take down the flag, pack up and go back to Poland or Germany or Yemen or America.

2. Give the Palestinian Arabs everything they have demanded: all the land of Judah and Samaria and half of Jerusalem. Allow them an international port, an air terminal, and free access between Gaza and the West Bank. And then hold our breath and hope that they don't begin to ask for Haifa and Jaffa and half the Gallilee while at the same time importing major shipments of armament from North Korea and China and a host of western nations who are just waiting to do business.

3. Realize that the Israeli government represents 2000 years of hopes and dreams of so many generations of Jewish people. Therefore, the State may not gamble away our future existence on the empty promises of proven murderers. Israel must do what is best for Jewish people; and most of us have had more than enough of blood and suffering. We have concluded that the utopian concept of coexistence with the Arabs and a shared economic enterprise is "pie in the sky."

Therefore, separate completely from the Palestinian Arabs. Put a security wall around their West Bank enclaves and around Gaza and seal the border to Israel. Gaza may do business with Egypt, and Nablus can do business with Jordan; and encourage political confederation. Let the Palestinian Arabs decide their own political fate, but completely separated from Israel, because it is apparent that they cannot live in peace.

With the coming of Rosh Hashana and New Year 5758, we extend to you and the people of Israel our best wishes for shalom. With God's help, and Jewish perseverance and courage, it will surely come to pass. As the Torah says, "do not be afraid," because surely God did not bring us to the Promised Land to abandon us now.

Sincerely,

Rabbi Barry J. Konovitch

COMPENSATION AND THE RIGHT OF RETURN

Consider the following figures on Jews expelled from Arab lands and the seizure of over $11 billion worth of Jewish property and assets: (Figures provided by the Israeli Consulate)

Algeria	130,000 Jews
Egypt	60,000 Jews
Iraq	150,000 Jews
Libya	40,000 Jews
Morocco	300,000 Jews
Syria	15,000 Jews

In total, approximately 700,000 Jews were brutally expelled from Arab countries and their property stolen. Israel took in these Jewish refugees and gave them a new life.

Several hundred thousand Palestinian Arabs left Israel after the "catastrophe" as they call it (the creation of the State of Israel). Their leaders promised them they would return to a "Judenrein" Israel. But Israel was established and it survived. The Arab refugees were never resettled and integrated into Arab countries. Instead, they were forced into squalid refugee camps and used as political pawns and terror cadres against the Jewish State.

I would suggest that any talk of compensation should include compensation for the 700,000 Jews who were ejected from Arab lands, just for being Jewish.

The terrible injustice done to the Arab refugees by their own people should not be placed on the shoulders of the Jewish State. It should be placed at the doorstep of the palaces in Saudi Arabia, Egypt, Jordan, Syria, etc., where it belongs. The billions of dollars in yearly oil revenue could have properly resettled these people decades ago.

It is fashionable for Jews to feel guilty, especially Jews from the old liberal, socialist school. But the guilt this time needs to be borne by the real perpetrators of this crime, the brutal and callous regimes of the Arab dictatorships. Israel took in several million refugees; let the Arab states do the same.

EARTHQUAKE IN TURKEY

During their six days in Turkey, the 385-member Israeli team rescued 12 people, including a nine-year-old Israeli girl visiting the country, and uncovered 146 bodies that were buried beneath mounds of rubble. By Tuesday, one week after the earthquake struck northwestern Turkey, the Turkish government said that 12,500 people had been killed, 42,000 injured, and 200,000 left homeless. Turkish media put the number still missing at between 30,000 and 35,000.

Leading one of the Israeli rescue teams in Golcuk was Capt. Ariel Blitz, 24. One of his most memorable moments occurred when Turkish family members summoned him to the ruins of a building where a father and two young boys could be heard trapped in the rubble. "I went there and actually heard the man," said Blitz. "I think he was 50 or 55 and he was buried on his bed and there were three floors on him. His leg was trapped."

He said the Israeli team worked seven hours before freeing the man and that they were also able to free the two young boys.

Liebovitz, 47, said one of his most memorable moments was while he was working with the rescue team on Monday in the town of Cinarcick at about 10 A.M. Suddenly, a Turkish rescue team nearby called them for help.

"They had been digging and digging and suddenly they heard a voice," Liebovitz said. "They didn't have any mechanical or technical equipment, or any instruments, and so they approached our team for help."

The Israeli team rushed to the site and listened for the voice to "decide the position of the person, the depth of the noise, and in terms of mechanics how best to get the patient out as quickly as possible," said Liebovitz. "It took only some 20 minutes."

The person trapped in the rubble for some 170 hours was a four-year-old boy, Ismail Cimen.

Before leaving, Israeli and Turkish rescuers held a moving memorial service in Cinarick for 11 Israeli tourists and thousands of Turks killed in the disaster. The event was broadcast on Turkish television. The Israeli team was the first from a foreign nation to arrive in Turkey and it was among the last to leave.

THE SAME OLD SONG

Once again, the United Nations, in knee jerk fashion, condemns Israel for trying to defend its citizens. Even after the savages in Ramallah stabbed and beat to death two Israeli reservists who lost their way, the "civilized governments" represented in the U.N. have decided that they would rather see Jews murdered in the streets than Israeli tanks trying to protect them. The retreat from Lebanon was applauded; the vulnerability to terrorist attacks in the northern Galilee was "pooh-poohed." Even the kidnapping of three Israeli soldiers from northern Israel was not discussed or condemned by the U.N. But once Jews refuse to roll over and die, it again becomes a "cause celebre," a good reason for the anti-Zionists (read anti-Semites) in the Security Council to condemn the Israeli government.

It remained for the Israeli security forces to penetrate the Palestinian Authority territories and arrest the savages responsible for the Ramallah lynching. Those who threw a dead Israeli out of the window of the police headquarters, those who stomped on the body, those who dragged him through the streets as the mob cheered, and especially the one who stuck his hands into the poor man's guts and showed his bloody hands to the world.

The Italian news team who filmed the whole barbaric scene has apologized to Arafat for embarrassing him in front of the world. They are afraid they will be barred from filming the next murder. Notice, no one is embarrassed by what the Arab mob did.

It is not the first time that Jews in Israel have been savagely massacred by Arab mobs; and it may not be the last unless Israel finally takes off the gloves and begins to deal seriously with Arab violence. As Prime Minister Barak pointed out, "in the Middle East there is no mercy shown for weakness."

At the same time, Arab terrorists have murdered several dozen young sailors aboard the destroyer *Cole* in the port of Aden. Our government has vowed to punish the terrorists, when and if they are found; the FBI has been dispatched to Yemen to head the investigation.

So far, the United Nations has not condemned the United States for using excessive force: too many battleships, too many guns, to protect American interests and citizens. Perhaps America should be called upon to appease Arab terrorists by granting them independent territory in Yemen or Saudia Arabia, or maybe a few square miles of Arizona. Let them have Phoenix, as their capital, arm them with machine guns, and allow them to control the area.

Most governments represented in the U.N. regularly use intimidation, torture, and murder to keep their civilian population in line. Never have we seen the U.N. condemn such outrageous behavior. Only Israel is condemned, regularly and consistently. And this same U.N. is called upon to investigate and render an "even-handed" opinion.

As long as the Arabs continue to put their children in the streets to shield the militia machine-gunners crouching behind them, the tragedy will continue. The callous disregard for the life of their children underscores the fact that a civilized people (read: Israel) finds it very hard to deal with such barbarism. What 18-year-old Israeli soldier wants to kill an eight-year-old Arab child?

Golda Meyer's famous statement comes to mind: We can never forgive them for forcing us to kill their sons. She meant, of course, that it was tragic enough that young Israeli soldiers had to die in the process of defending themselves by killing the enemy.

Perhaps we will now recognize that the goal of the Israelis and the civilized world was peace; but the goal of the Arab world was the ultimate elimination of the infidel Jews from the Middle East, either by bad-faith negotiation or violent confrontation. Compromise in the Arab world is seen as a sign of weakness and concessions are an indication that the "enemy" is in retreat.

And so we go back to square one and begin again. Perhaps we will learn from past mistakes.

A PURIM "SHPIEL"

I have heard that the children in Israel are already planning their costumes for the annual street parades in honor of the Purim holy day (March 12, Adar 14). This year some new characters have been added: Queen Esther is being protrayed as Monica Lewinsky, King Achashverosh as Bill Clinton, Haman as Arafat, and Mordecai as Binyamin Netanyahu. And herein lies the most amazing spin on the ancient Megilia story:

Last month, Prime Minister Benjamin Netanyahu prepared to visit President Clinton. The American President had already expressed publicly his dissatisfaction with the pace of the "peace process" and his personal annoyance with the Israeli Prime Minister whom he accused of foot dragging on the Oslo accords. The Israeli proposals for withdrawals from Judea and Samaria were considered minuscule, and Clinton was preparing to lean on Netanyahu in order to force Israel to relinquish more territory to the Palestinian Arabs. The issue of Israeli security was being brushed aside in favor of courting favor with the Arab world in preparation for the united coalition of "Desert Thunder" gearing up to bomb Iraq. By forcing Israel to cede territories to a future Arab Palestinian state, the United States would be perceived as pro-Arab, thereby solidifying Arab support and cooperation for the imminent attack against Sadaam Hussein. The fact that the Iraqi threat most immediately affects the surrounding Arab states of Saudia Arabia, Jordan and Kuwait seems to have been ignored by these governments—who backed away from helping the United States to defend their own Arab sovereignty in the region, trotting out their convenient anti-Israel excuses. Imagine: In certain Arabist circles in the State Department and across the Arab Middle East, Israel was being blamed for the problems caused by Saddam Hussein. It would be well for all concerned to remember that when Baghdad first built a nuclear reactor at

Osirak, to threaten the world, (a gift of French largesse), no one had the courage to do something about it. It was three F-16 Israeli fighter bombers that did the job to the condemnation of the United Nations but to the relief of all free nations.

Prime Minister Menachem Begin was eventually hailed as the savior of the free world.

France and Russia, along with several other governments working through third-party corporations, have continued to greedily sell Iraq all the necessary equipment and material to manufacture weapons of mass destruction. Only American military power provides the threat that heretofore has kept Saddam Hussein in his box. And America's only support in the Middle East comes from Israel; and at the last minutes President Clinton stopped short of strategically weakening America's only ally in the area. He hesitated (they say in Israel) because he was pre-occupied with a young Jewish woman.

So it happened in Jewish history more than 2,000 years ago, when a young Jewish woman convinced the leader of the Persian Empire to save the Jewish people from the clutches of the contemporary version of Hitler. If this is the way the children of Tel Aviv choose to interpret recent events, than so be it. Stranger things have happened in Jewish history and it isn't the first time that we find that "someone" is watching over us.

LAND AND PEACE

As Israel marks its forty-eighth year of Independence and prepares for the most important national election in decades, a debate rages on the issue of "the people versus the land." At first blush, most of us would conclude that the safety and security of the people is of paramount concern, and if it can be secured at the expense of a few hundred square kilometers of land, then so be it. The exchange of land for peace would be well worth it. On this subject, I reprint an article from the *Jerusalem Post* written by Jonathan Blass titled, "Real Estate Versus Human Life."

The IDF has left Nablus and Bethlehem, and the rag of a foreign nation lies over the cities of my homeland.

The bitter prophecy of Isaiah (1:7) "your land, strangers devour it in your presence," has been fulfilled yet again in an age when the armed might of the Jewish state has made foreign military conquest of Israel's cities a near impossibility.

Once more relevant is the talmudic teaching of Rabbi Elazar (reaffirmed by Maimonides and the Shulhan Aruch) requiring Jews who see the cities of Judea under foreign domination to rend their garments in mourning.

Why mourn a land? Why cry over rocks and mud, pine trees and barren hilltops? Aren't these just "real estate," less important than the life of a single soldier called upon to risk himself in their defense?

Commonly heard is the thesis that the issue dividing right and left in Israel is the relative importance of land and human life. But that this is even seen as a question calls into doubt the vitality of Jewish nationalism.

This is because all nationalism subordinates the life of the individual to the national interest, not least of which is the nation's territorial integrity.

There can, for example, be no English national identity without England, no French national identity without France. A nation's land has never been a function of security alone. It is essential to its self definition. Land is an organic part of the national identity, much as the human body is an indispensable element of the identity of the individual man. Neither is just spirit alone.

Recognizing the truth, Yosef Trumpeldor, echoing the cries of American patriot Nathan Hale and of other patriots throughout history, declared as he lay dying in Tel Hai, felled by the bayonets of Arab marauders: "It is good to die for our land."

Zionist pioneers implicitly acknowledged the same principle when they came to settle malarial swamps, risking their lives to reclaim the land of Israel for the Jewish people.

What motivated them to self sacrifice was more than the feeling that they were jeopardizing the lives of the few to guarantee the lives of many. It was also their sense that they were building a nation.

For them, as for any patriot, the question, "What is more important, life or land?" could bear only one answer: The life of the individual is more important then his private home or field, but it is less important than the life of the nation, and that life includes a territorial dimension, worth fighting for and, if need be, dying for. That this is no longer clear here in Israel means that Jewish nationalism is in crisis. It should come as no surprise.

A recent issue of *Newsweek* reported that secular schools in Israel taught their students that Israel's significance to Jews is as a "haven."

Is the English claim to England or the French claim to France based on the need for a "haven" for Englishmen and Frenchmen? Are only Jews not entitled to a land of their own, except as a place of escape?

Israelis regularly hear that Jewish nationalism is racist, that it is wrong for there to be even one small place on the globe that is particularly Jewish, where only the Jewish people is sovereign to determine national direction. To be democratic, it is contended, Israel must belong to all of its residents, Jewish and Non-Jewish, equally.

The argument most often raised is: What if Jews were deprived in other countries of their right to vote on national issues—wouldn't that be unfair racial discrimination?

The answer in most cases is no. As long as I can determine the policy of my country if I choose to live there, I am not the victim of unjust discrimination, if, opting to reside outside my nation's homeland, I am not allowed to participate in deciding the direction of the foreign country in which I live.

Though not the American "melting pot" mode, it is appropriate for a nation loyal to its sense of common destiny and national purpose.

And as Hamlet put it, "there's the rub." Lowering the Star of David in Bethlehem—the city of King David's birth, and touting individual life as more important than Jewish sovereignty to the Jewish homeland are symptoms of a still greater problem that ultimately must be addressed: the loss of our sense of national purpose. Until it is rediscovered, and barring a miracle, we will continue to watch "strangers devour our land" through no fault but our own.

ISRAEL AT 50

I listened carefully to the woman discussing the events that brought her to Israel. Her parents were Bulgarians who miraculously survived the Shoah, and made their way to Israel after the allies liberated Europe. They were given a house to live in after the War of Independence in 1948. It was an old stone house with a little garden in the town of Ramleh, about half way between Tel Aviv and Jerusalem. The house was empty because the Arabs who built it had fled during the fighting.

Some twenty years later, she answered a knock on the door, and was surprised to see a Palestinian Arab who asked if he could see the house and the garden. "Was the lemon tree still growing?" asked the blind man with him, the patriarch whose ancestors had lived in this ancient town for many generations. After many hours of conversation and visits, the Israeli family decided that the house wasn't really theirs. They moved out and asked that a community center for the local Arabs and Jews be created.

And oh yes, the visiting Arab turned out to be a terrorist who spent several years in a Israeli jail for murdering Jews. But he was now a writer and professor, an intellectual leader of his people, presumably rehabilitated.

As Israel celebrates its fiftieth anniversary, the press and media is filled with Israeli accounts of guilt, self-flagellation, and self-doubt. Under the guise of honest soul searching, the moment is being turned into a maudlin exercise in the old "galut mentality." The underlying sentiment is "we don't deserve a state of our own because we displaced the Palestinian Arabs who are the rightful owners of the land." The unexpressed conclusion is "we should go back to Poland and Germany where we Jews came from so that peace will come to the Middle East."

The Israeli lady from Bulgarian ancestry conveniently forgot that the Arabs in Ramleh as well as in Jerusalem and Jaffa and Haifa would have slit the throats of the infidel Jews if they had gotten the chance, just the way they did in the Arab riots of the 20s and 30s. And she suffers from short-term memory loss regarding the history of the Jewish people in Arab lands. From Baghdad to Damascus to Isfahan. From Cairo to Tripoli to Sa'na, the Jews were deprived of basic human rights, hung in the public squares as Zionist spies and ejected from the countries where they had lived for more than a thousand years. No one speaks of this horror. What of the homes and businesses and real estate that were stolen from them. Why is there no call for compensation? Why do the journalists of the world call only upon Israel to remove themselves from Arab lands? Why is it that only the Jews have no right to a secure and peaceful life? Why is it that the Palestinian Arabs have a very clear idea of who they are and what they want, but the Palestinian Jews are beset by angst, guilt, and doubt?

If we Jews don't understand our place in history, if we aren't clear about our connection to Israel, then we don't deserve our state.

So it was with our ancestors who left Egypt in the great Exodus some 3,500 years ago. The Promised Land was ready for them but they weren't ready for the Promised Land. They would die in the desert, paralyzed by self-doubt and self-incrimination, and a new self-assured generation would rise to transform Jewish history.

The Israeli government accepted the United Nations Partition Plan in 1947. David Ben-Gurion was ready to live with a truncated Jewish nation so that the Palestinian Arabs would also have a state. But the Bulgarian Jewish family in Ramleh seems to have forgotten that Israel was attacked in 1948 as soon as the British Mandate authority pulled down the Union Jack. The avowed Arab purpose was to "push the Jews into the sea." In case the "poetic" Arabic language was unclear to Jews from Europe, it meant that the Arabs would attempt to exterminate every Jew in Palestine, and this just three years after the Holocaust. If it wasn't for the miraculous valiant struggle by the Israel Defense Forces, Ramat Gan would be an Arab olive orchard today and Jerusalem would be a Judenrein Muslim city, free of any trace of Jewish history.

The Jewish people of Palestine always wished to live in peace with their Arab neighbors; but when the Yishuv (Jewish community) was attacked on all fronts, they fought back as fiercely as they knew how. Civilian populations are often casualties of war, which is why civilized people always try to settle accounts peacefully. When the Arab leaders refused peace and went to war with the tiny Jewish state, they sacrificed their own civilian populations. The terrible consequences were on their heads, not the heads of the Jewish people who defended themselves.

And about our Bulgarian lady, who felt so guilty about living in an Arab house that she moved out: perhaps she should inquire about her parent's home in Sofia. I doubt that the neighbors who moved in after the Nazis deported the Jews would immediately move out and give it back. So she certainly isn't going back to her home in Bulgaria and neither is the government going to compensate her. Maybe she could move into a tent in the middle of the Negev wilderness, just the way Moses took his sheep into the desert to be sure they weren't feeding on anyone's land. Such a wonderful person deserves sainthood, but not statehood. We, on the other hand, have to live in the real world.

Fifty years later, we have so many things to be proud of. If the state isn't perfect, then we will keep working on it. But in the meantime, it would be well for us to remember that Israel is the one place in the world where Jews don't have to apologize for living, where we don't have to worry about the next pogrom, where we are masters of our own fate. It is the only state that we have and best we take good care of it. This inability to celebrate 50 years of statehood brought on by a perverse epidemic of self-doubt will sap our strength and undermine our will to continue the struggle for existence. The future of Israel is not guaranteed; it depends on the undiminished determination of the Jewish people to survive and prosper. New Zealand is more peaceful, Sweden is more liberal, Tibet is more exotic, India is more spiritual, America is richer; and Israelis who have lost the Zionist dream are adrift in the world. But Israel is our homeland and without our homeland, we would once again be blowing in the wind of every political climatic change.

I am not sure if the teeth-gnashers, nay-sayers and chest-beaters that have been ferreted out by the journalists are representative of Israeli thinking today. I suspect it reflects their own prejudiced picture of the society. I hope that most Israelis and Jews around the world still hold the Zionist dream in esteem and have not lost the faith and hope in its power to transform the Jewish people.

ISRAEL AT 50, PERLMAN AT 53

The State of Israel's fiftieth birthday was celebrated with a gala concert at the Jackie Gleason Auditorium. As we rose to sing "Hatikva", my eye was fixed on the Israeli flag covering the wall of the concert hall, and my ear rehearsed the familiar words of hope for a free people in our national homeland.

For us, the privileged generation, it is no longer a hope but a reality, and our only transgression would be to take it all for granted. We are no longer the accursed people wandering the face of the earth at the mercy of every despotic government. We are a free people, in an independent state, quite capable of defending ourselves and defending the rights of Jewish people around the world. We are proud, we are secure, and, with God's help, we will live in peace.

Itzhak Perlman was born in Israel in 1945. He is the perfect ambassador of the State, projecting a sophisticated culture that is the product of 2,000 years of contact with every major civilization in history. We have distilled every significant concept and imparted our own unique Jewish interpretation. We have been the leaders of every important literary and artistic movement precisely because we have always been urbane cosmopolitans throughout the generations of our exile, absorbing, analyzing, filtering, and transducing every significant new idea. Add to this an unfortunate history of pain and suffering and you combine a high degree of intellectual activity with a heightened sensitivity, the perfect ingredients for "great artistry."

And so we return to Mr. Perlman. The door to the stage opens and he appears, literally dragging himself across the floor. His face registers the grimace connected with legs encased in iron braces and crutches that support his body weight. He heaves himself into the chair and throws down his crutches. They hit the floor with a crescendo signaling his arrival. The violin is tucked under the chin, the conductor waves the orchestra to attention, and the music begins. And Itzhak Perlman is transformed, and in turn, he transforms the audience. We are drawn inexorably into the centrifugal force of his musical genius. We are no longer separate electrons flying about in our individual orbits; rather we merge and fuse into one adoring entity.

Mr. Perlman is on the way home to celebrate Passover with his family in New York. It is the holiday of freedom ("zman cheruteynu"). As Itzhak is bound by the iron bars of his infirmity, so are we all imprisoned by the iron bars of our illnesses and heartaches. Yet, the great violinist casts down his crutches and is immediately transformed into a free soaring spirit. So must we cast down our aches and pains and proceed with our lives as free spirits.

It's not so easy, you say. It's easier said then done, you say. Then think of Itzhak Perlman. How easy is it for him to overcome the crippling effects of polio to the point that when you listen to him, you don't even remember those iron bars. Think of Perlman the next time you are about to complain. Throw off your chains; the holy day of our freedom is at hand.

ONE UNITED PEOPLE

Peter Bergson passed away in Israel a few weeks ago. Perhaps you remember the rally to save the Jews of Europe in Madison Square Garden in March 1943. Forty thousand people came to proclaim, "We will never die." Edward G. Robinson, Marlon Brando and Stella Adler were among those who took part in the proceedings organized by Bergson and the writer Ben Hecht. Their Emergency Committee to Save the Jews of Europe tried to overcome the feeble "official" efforts on the part of the American government and on the part of the Jewish establishment to respond to the murder of Europe's Jews. By 1942, the *New York Times* had already reported (page 10) that two million Jews had been killed in Europe.

The Bergson Committee took out full-page advertisements in the major newspapers in 1943: "For Sale to Humanity: 70,000 Rumanian Jews, Guaranteed Human Beings at $50 a piece." Jewish leaders were outraged and Rabbi Stephen Wise, head of the American Jewish Congress, quickly condemned the ads as a hoax.

Two days before Yom Kippur, October 1943, Bergson brought 400 Rabbis, mostly Orthodox, to march in Washington to protest the indifference of the Roosevelt administration to the plight of the European Jews. Roosevelt did not receive the marchers because he was told by his "Jewish advisors" that they (the Emergency Committee to Save the Jews in Europe) did not represent the mainstream of American Jewish opinion.

Even so, Congress was prompted to hold its first public hearing on the "issue." It probably led to the creation of the Government War Refugee Board in 1944. Of course, it was too little, too late.

It is fashionable in Jewish historical circles to blame the Roosevelt Administration and his State Department for the callous indifference that allowed the Nazis to go forward with their final solution. But perhaps the larger issue was the political silence of the Jewish community and the cowardice of the American Jewish "leadership." An apparent lack of unity, courage, and vision allowed the issue of the European Jews to be swept under the carpet until it was too late.

Some 60 years later, I wonder if we have learned the lessons. The State of Israel remains in a state of war, her civilians constantly under brutal attack by Palestinian Arab terrorists who think nothing of sending their children to blow up Jewish children. And we in America sit and discuss the issues, unable or unwilling to come together in a unity of opinion and purpose. I wonder what it will take before the Jewish people unite as one behind the people of Israel. When will we put aside our differences of opinion and realize that the future of the State of Israel is on the line? And our future is bound up with theirs.

May the new year, 5762, bring security and peace to our State of Israel.

ORDE WINGATE: 55 YEAR ANNIVERSARY

A. Captain Orde Wingate, a British officer, was posted to Palestine in September 1936. The British government was backing out of its promise to create a Jewish homeland in Palestine as mandated by the 1917 Balfour declaration.

 1. The British were trying to appease the Arabs. Why support a handful of Jews when the world's oil reserves were under Arab sands? Wingate was a graduate of the London School of Oriental and African studies. He was fluent in Arabic and Arab history. He was fascinated by Arab culture; and influenced by his famous cousin T. E. Lawrence, who led the World War I Arab revolt against the Turks on behalf of the British. They both had ice-blue eyes and they had as a relative Sir Reginald Wingate, former governor of Egypt and Sudan. He could pull political strings for them.
 2. T. E. Lawrence was one of the great heroes of the Arab world. He led the Arab armies into Baghdad; and total Arab independence would likely have been achieved had not the colonial powers double crossed the Arabs and divided up the area into spheres of control: French Syria, British Palestine and Trans-Jordan, etc.

    Orde Wingate was the T. E. Lawrence of the 1930s. And it is truly amazing that a British Arabist, coming from a line of pro-Arab English military officers, and trained politically to sympathize with the Arab cause, could become such a strong pro-Israel Zionist.

A. The answer begins with his parents. They were fervently religious adherents of the fundamentalist Plymouth Brethren in England. Orde Wingate's father was a cavalry officer in India before becoming an evangelist. His grandfather led the English mission to convert the Jews of Hungary. The Wingates knew and studied the Bible. They had an appreciation for the Jewish people, their role in history, and their historical and religious connection to the holy land.

1. When Orde was posted to the Middle East, he wound up in the Britishled Sudanese Defense Force. In the Sudan, he began to develop his unique tactical concepts that later became the SNS, "Special Night Squads," in Palestine.

   He needed a force that could operate for long periods of time in hostile territory far from home base. They would have to be properly trained and motivated: self-contained elite ranger units. He was assigned to hunt down outlaw poachers. It was his first encounter with death.

2. He also exhibited his strange behavior, his eccentricities that would become famous later on in Palestine—eccentric even by English standards: He ate raw onions, strained tea through his socks, strutted naked around camp, and scoured his body with a rubber brush.

   He tried crossing the Libyan desert on a camel with only water and dried dates like his famous cousin T. E. Lawrence. He gave up and hitched a ride on a Ford truck owned by a British surveyor.

A. In 1936, he was posted to Palestine. Orde knew the Bible by heart. After transferring to British Intelligence, he spent weeks in a Haifa hotel room studying Zionism and learning to speak Hebrew fluently.

   1. When he inspected the kibbutzim, he wrote back to Sir Reginald how the Jews made the desert bloom; that they had such energy, faith, and inventiveness as the world has not yet seen. He was sure that the young Jews would become better soldiers than the British themselves. We only have to train them. If we help the Jews, we will secure Palestine for the British Empire. If we put our trust in the Arabs, we will harm ourselves in the end. Let us do something just and honorable. Let us redeem our promises to the Jews and shame the devil of Nazism, Fascism, and our own prejudices.

   2. No wonder the Jews of Palestine called him Hayedid, the friend. Our friend.

He contacted the Hagana leadership and explained to them to give up their policy of "havlaga," restraint, and to go on the attack against the Arab terrorists.

Wingate spoke at length with David Hacohen of the Hagana, Moshe Shertok (Sharett), and eventually Weizmann and Ben-Gurion. They naturally suspected the motives of a British officer. But he and his wife won them over with their ardent Zionism. The British high command was even more annoyed, but he got his plan approved by General Wavell, commander of British forces in Palestine. He did it by stepping in front of his car, getting in and presenting his report.

A. The plan was to set up in the Galil a special unit called the "night squads." He applied the lessons he lhad earned in the Sudan. Small groups of highly trained, lightly equipped men moving silently and quickly at night, attacking the enemy by total surprise in his own backyard.

The formal mission was to protect the TAP line, the Trans-Arabian Pipeline of the Iraq Petroleum Company. But Captain Wingate had an ulterior, messianic motive. He was out to create the nucleus of a Jewish army that would one day defend the Jewish state. He saw himself as a modern-day Gideon, and he headquartered at the well of Ein Harod, precisely where Gideon headquartered to fight the Midianites.

He was obsessed by his vision and he drove himself and his men relentlessly. Yigal Alon, Zvi Brenner, and Moshe Dayan paid close attention. He wasn't interested in military manners. He commanded by yelling Acharai, after me. He led from the front of the attack.

1. The SNS succeeded beyond all expectation. Sabotage on the pipeline stopped. In a series of pitched battles through 1938 the Arab irregulars were roundly defeated. He was fearless in battle, and seemed to be indifferent to the bullets.

But finally he was wounded at Daburiya near Mt. Tabor in July by a British machine gunner. A grenade tossed into his car didn't explode. Chaim Sturman, leader of Ein Harod, was killed by an Arab bomb. And the British issued the 1939 White Paper ending Jewish immigration to Palestine.

Orde Wingate's mission was over. The SNS was disbanded. A propaganda post card printed at the time said it all:

The Sword of the Lord and of Gideon.

On the opposite side was the picture of Major General Orde Wingate.

A. Wingate went on to fight for the liberation of Ethiopia from the Italian fascists. He was a close friend of Emperor Haile Selassie, who called himself the Lion of Judah after the Queen of Sheba and Solomon. Wingate once again trained guerilla bands of British officers and mountain tribesmen. He sent for his trusted lieutenant Avraham Akavia from the SNS. The force was called the Gideon force. In May 1941, the allies marched into Addis Ababa and, at the emperor's insistence, Wingate headed the column on a white horse.

B. Wingate's last campaign took place in the jungles of Burma. He was sent to organize a commando force to fight the Japanese in Burma. The Japanese were threatening India. The commando unit was called the "chindits," Burmese for Lion. He marched hundreds of miles across the southern Himalyas, across the Irrawaddy and Chindwin Rivers, with 3,000 men and completely surprised the Japanese. They stopped Tokyo's plan for invading India. Wingate became a national hero. Lowell Thomas who made T. E. Lawrence famous interviewed him. He met with Churchill and Roosevelt. He was promoted to Brigadier General.

1. But he remained vitally concerned about Israel. He exchanged letters with Weizman and Shertok, with his hope for "seeing the fulfillment of Hatikvah."

2. During the second chindit expedition, Wingate's chindits were supplied by the U.S. First Air Commandos under Col. Phil Cochran, an American hero, and former child actor Jackie Coogan. On March 24 Wingate's plane went down and his body was never identified. Just his pith helmet was found.

   The news of his death stunned the world. Churchill called him a man of genius who might have become a man of destiny.

3. As a token of appreciation, his name appears on the Wingate Institute and the Yemin Orde Academy in Israel. My son attended the 50th Anniversary. Leading the proceedings was Avraham Akavia, his old assistant from the SNS. Akavia is now an accountant in Haifa.

4. Wingate's old Bible is on display in Ein Harod. There was a story that Lorna Wingate dropped it from an Israeli Air Force plane over Ramot Naftali when it was besieged by Arabs, to inspire the settlers who belonged to the Wingate organization.

5. Wingate's tomb is located in Arlington. The fragments of the nine Americans killed in the Mitchell B25H bomber were interred there, probably with whatever was left of Wingate after the crash. In keeping with British custom, soldiers are buried where they died. Wingate's family protested. The United States allowed bodies to be brought back for burial in the United States.

   On March 24, 1974, on the thirtieth Yahrzeit, a new headstone was placed in Arlington. It was dedicated by Captain Jonathan Wingate of the British army. He was conceived aboard the *Queen Mary* as the Wingates were on the way to meet with President Roosevelt after his successful first campaign in Burma.

6. Yechi Hayedid. Long live the memory of one of Israel's greatest friends.

THE CIA AND CABERNET SAUVIGNON:
THE GOLAN HEIGHTS QUANDARY

Suddenly, the Syrians, led by that fossil from the cold war era who bullied the Israelis from behind the skirts of the Red Army, has finally decided to allow Israel to return the Golan Heights, in exchange for recognizing the Jewish people as a legitimate Middle East nation. The Golan Heights was never populated much by Syrians. It was an empty, barren area with a few scattered Druze villages, where the latest in a long line of Jewish *chalutzim* (pioneers) came after 1967 to build the land.

Today, it is a thriving agricultural showcase, dotted by avocado fields, apple orchards, cow farms, and vineyards. In ancient times, especially in the period of the Mishna (200 CE), it was well populated by Jewish people: witness the dozens of ancient synagogue ruins, some rather elaborate and ornate testifying to the wealth of the Jewish traders astride the main route to Damascus and beyond. The Golan is an exceedingly beautiful place to hike through and explore, filled with verdant valleys, thundering water falls in the rainy season, and all kinds of mysterious ancient runes and ruins.

A great deal of Jewish history unfolded here, from the great battle against the Romans at Gamla led by Flavius Josephus (who went on to write his famous history of the Jewish people, *Antiquities*, and *Wars of the Jews*), to the great tank battles in 1967 and 1973, General Avigdor Kahalani being just one of the heroes of that period. Eli Cohen, another hero, was executed in Damascus in 1965 as he gathered intelligence on behalf of the IDF. He gave his life to help our people drive the Syrians off the Heights and secure once and forever the Israeli settlements in the Hula Valley. For years, Israeli children in the northern kibbutzim slept in bomb shelters because of the murderous Syrian shelling from the Heights.

All this seems to be fading into past history as the Israeli government prepares to negotiate with Hafez Assad.

But what about the wine? The Golan Heights winery produces the finest wine in Israel, and one of the finest wines in the world. And in the field of kosher wine, where there isn't exactly a great deal of competition, the wines of the Golan are superb. There was many an erev Shabbat when we raced over to the Supersol to buy a bottle of Yarden or Gamla to share with friends over kiddush. Shabbat will never be the same if the vineyards are uprooted and the vinters go home to Burgundy and the Napa Valley. Somehow I can't see myself buying a bottle of wine with a Syrian-Arabic label, with who knows what in the bottle.

I don't know if the CIA operatives sitting alongside the Mosad agents atop the Mt. Hermon listening post are wine connoisseurs. And I doubt they are allowed to drink on the job as it would cloud their view of Damascus and points east, all the way to "ayatollah land." But I do know that they aren't climbing down from their perch above the Golan so quickly. The final deal remains to be seen. In any case, I for one would be saddened to leave the Golan to Syrian tanks who would quickly turn it to a wasteland once again. I would be very apprehensive as the Syrians take control of the main water sources of the entire Israeli population, blind the Mt. Hermon listening post, and move their artillery into deadly range, a demilitarized zone notwithstanding.

And I would surely miss the fruity taste, rich aroma, and palate-pleasing bouquet of that great 1985 Cabernet.

HEBRON REVISITED

The bus runs every hour from Jaffa Road in Jerusalem, stopping at the Gush Etzion block via the Bethlehem bypass road, proceeding to Kiryat Arba and Hebron in about an hour. The driver is protected by a wire shield screening his windshield and the passengers look out through Lexan windows. These materials will stop rocks, but won't do much to repel bullets. I begin to wonder about the sanity of this bus trip as the passengers file aboard: a handful of soldiers toting the ubiquitous M-16 or Galil automatic rifle, a group of youngsters in little knitted wool kippas weighed down by huge book bags, and a few mothers with their little babies returning from a shopping trip. I begin to relax as I realize that life is normal aboard the bus to Hebron, or as normal as life can be in the State of Israel.

By the time I get to the suburb of Kiryat Arba, I am feeling down right comfortable, a lot more comfortable than I feel in certain sections of Miami. Kiryat Arba sits on the edge of Hebron. Little children run and jump and play; their older brothers and sisters get on and off the bus on the way home from school; mothers push baby carriages on the street; and this Hebron suburb of some 7,000 people resembles, in parts, some of the nicest neighborhoods in Jerusalem. It is not surrounded and isolated by barbed wire and machine gun towers. Rather, it is an impressive modern expansion of Hebron where Jewish people live a normal life.

The last stop for the bus is in front of the Cave of Machpela, where I get off to spend some quiet time at the graves of our ancestors Abraham, Sara, Jacob, and Leah, Isaac, and Rebecca. However, to my chagrin, half of the Machpela is now off limits to Jews except for ten days a year. It is the half that includes the most beautiful part, where Isaac and Rebecca are buried and where you can see through a glass window in the floor to the original cave underneath.

I sit and meditate for the better part of an hour, daven mincha (recite the afternoon prayers), and go out to find my guide from the Hebron Public Relations office. The Israeli guards engage me in conversation after they determine that I am not a Christian, and that I speak fluent Hebrew. The first thing they want to know is where I got my new Nike boots and how much they cost in America. Eventually, I notice that the only other civilian in the vicinity of Machpela is a young woman with two long braids, a long denim skirt and sandals. She turns out to be my guide, Sara Nishkin, a volunteer from Miami Beach. This "Heidi of Hebron" starts walking toward the city center and obviously I am expected to follow and listen.

I first came to Hebron in 1970, just a few years after it was liberated by the Israeli army in 1967. During the years, I limited my visits to the great Herodion precinct of Machpela, reluctant to move beyond the security of the army guards. Now, I found myself following a girl, unarmed, who smiles and waves at everyone, Arab and Jew alike as we make our way towards the Jewish neighborhoods of Hebron.

I referred to the Jewish "enclaves," but she preferred to call them neighborhoods. And, indeed, there is no separation between them and the surrounding Arab buildings. Each of the three neighborhoods are built around an inner courtyard. The construction is relatively new, and thus stands out from the surrounding buildings. They are more "condominiums" or housing projects than whole neighborhoods. And the most amazing thing about them is that the children play freely in the street and the mothers push their carriages, and no where can you find a bolted gate, a curtain wall, or even a strand of barbed wire. In other words, the neighborhood and the people are an integral and nondifferentiated part of Hebron. And in Avraham Avinu, Kiryat Hadassah, and Tel Rumeida (the three Jewish neighborhoods), they are determined to live as nearly a normal life as possible. They refuse, as they adamantly told me, to live in a ghetto behind barbed wire and machine gun posts, which is exactly how I envisioned them before I came to see for myself.

It bears repeating that everything we know of Hebron comes from the media, and the media are filled with distortions and sensationalism that often borders on the down right anti-Semitic. If we were to believe the *New York Times* or the *Miami Herald*, we would think that the Jews of Hebron walk around with huge .45 pistols in their ammunition-laden belts, with machine guns slung over their shoulders, with handlebar mustaches drooping under their wild-eyed faces, just looking for Arabs to kick around and threaten. Nothing could be farther from the truth. The only guns I saw all day were held by the Israeli army on patrol. I must say I would have felt more comfortable if Sara had been carrying an Uzi, but she insisted on making a point: The Jews of Hebron will live in peace with their Arab neighbors even at the cost of Jewish blood.

I was curious to ask about the Baruch Goldstein incident. Everyone referred me to the Shamgar commission inquiry which confirmed that the Arabs had been hiding weapons in Machpela for a planned pogrom against the Jews on Purim. The Army turned a deaf ear to the rumors, and the result was that

Baruch Goldstein took the matter into his own hands, ostensibly saving Jewish lives, but leaving a dark stain on future relations between Jews and Arabs in the State of Israel.

At the end of the day, I sat drinking Turkish coffee with David Wilder, chief spokesman of the community. He came to Israel a few decades ago, the product of a minimally Jewish American home. He moved his family to Hebron because he chose to be an urban "chalutz" (pioneer). Hebron is one of the holy sites, second only to Jerusalem, for those of us who come with the requisite intellectual background and the historical-religious underpinnings, who believe that the Jewish connection to the land of Israel begins with the Bible and not with His Majesty's Mandate government. It is the reason why Jews wish to live there, at least Jews who are imbued with the words of our ancient prophets and who care little for the vicissitudes of contemporary Middle Eastern politics. The Hebron Jews are not a bunch of wild-eyed fanatics attempting to ignite an explosion. Rather, they are living the Zionist-religious dream of the return to the holy places of Eretz Yisrael. When my cousin in Tel Aviv wants to know why "these crazy people insist on disturbing the Hebron Arabs by living right in their face," I can only respond by telling him that I haven't found a single reference to Tel Aviv or Ramat Gan in the Bible, but I certainly find Hebron, where Abraham recorded the purchase of Machpela and the adjacent land. And now his descendants have come back to Abraham's land. That has to be one of the most exciting developments in 2,000 years of Jewish history. The city may be divided, more than half of the territory might belong to the Palestine Arab authority, but you would never know it sipping coffee in the Hebron Jewish Community. As they say in Israel, "Kol Hakavod," all the more power to them!

B. THE SEASON
Getting Through the Year
2. The Arts

JASCHA AND ME

Jascha Heifetz was one of my boyhood idols along with Mickey Mantle and Joe Namath. I began taking violin lessons at an early age at the behest of my mother who sang to me an old Yiddish ditty, "Yiddle Miten Fiddle" before I knew the difference between the "frog" and the "horse hairs."

I reached the peak of my "brilliance" during my high school years when I studied regularly at the Silverman studio in the Bronx. Professor Silverman had been a student of Leopold Auer, the great teacher who had taught Jascha Heifetz himself. I dreamed of being as perfect as the great Heifetz, strolling onto the stage without so much as a hint of a smile, disdain for the audience, and totally immersed in the concerto at hand. Heifetz never made a mistake, ever. He had the most perfect technique since Paganini. I was in awe of him.

Every June, the studio gave a concert at Carnegie Hall. Nothing ever frightened me more than this annual torture. Preparations went on for months: committing the music to memory, refining the technique, and adding a veneer of interpretation. I listened to Heifetz's "Bruch" for hours to pick up some hints, but to intimate that my playing had any semblance to the great man is to mislead my public.

The appointed hour came; it was always on a Saturday evening in June when Shabbat is over at 9:00 P.M. The concert was well underway when I arrived backstage. My Uncle Louis was designated to get me to Carnegie Hall before the next-to-the last performer took his last bow. I was the last one scheduled to play because I had to wait until Shabbat was over before heading down West Side Highway. Uncle Louis always managed to get me there in the nick of time without getting a speeding ticket. Over the years, he had acquired three driver licenses, New York, New Jersey, and Connecticut. This way, when one was suspended for speeding, he had two others.

I would rush backstage where Dr. Silverman was nervously waiting. I took out the violin and caught my breath. The Professor tuned me up, wished me luck, and pushed me out on stage. The bright lights mercifully blocked out the faces of the audience. The pianist signaled my start. A down bow and off I went, playing as if the devil was after me. I didn't remember a thing until the audience politely broke into applause. My fingers moved of their own accord and my brain seemed to be disengaged. I took a bow or two, tucked the violin under my arm, and exited stage left. I could breathe for the first time in 20 minutes. Until the annual concert was over, I wasn't on vacation. Classes were over, the infamous high school Regent's exams were finished but I was never on vacation until the last down bow of the concert. Nothing in my life ever frightened me as much—not speaking to two thousand people on Rosh Hashana; not negotiating the ice crevasses of Mount Blanc; not taking the Graduate Record Exam for admittance into the doctoral program. Nothing made my knees shake and my mouth go dry like the annual concert.

In retrospect, I am glad that I underwent the experience. I left the violin in its case all through college and didn't pick it up again until years later. But I never lost appreciation for the sublime music of the violin. On a visit to Lithuania, I made a pilgrimage to the recital hall in Vilna where Jascha Heifetz made his public debut at age seven. I posed for a picture next to the brass plaque, the closest I could ever get to his playing. When he taught at the University of Southern California toward the end of his life, I wrote to him indicating my admiration for his play and my appreciation for his inspiration albeit at distance. He died soon after without ever answering. I always wanted to ask him how he was able to stand in front of a discerning audience of thousands without betraying the slightest discomfort.

It is one hundred years since the great Heifetz was born. There have been many brilliant violinists during this century: Kreisler, Elman, Francescatti, Stern, Perlman, and dozens more. But none equaled Heifetz. And for me, nothing equaled that moment in time when I stood alone inCarnegie Hall, knees buckling, ready to crumple to the stage floor were it not for the presence of Jascha Heifetz holding me up by the armpits and directing the course of my bow. At least this is the way I always imagined it. How else did I manage to walk off stage alive and well?

SOUNDS OF SILENCE

Luciano Pavarotti was scheduled to sing at La Scala in Milan. He has performed there many times during his illustrious career, yet the Italians can never get enough of his magnificent voice. And the Italians are not alone in their adoration; the world of opera cognoscenti, as well as countless people who are untutored in the finer points of classical music, know a great voice when they hear it.

But the great Pavarotti had to cancel. He had a bad cold. The concert was postponed for a future date, and thousands of disappointed opera lovers just had to wait. Perhaps one of Luciano's adoring fans sneezed just as she was giving the "great one" a kiss. Maybe he shook hands with a devotee who was just coming down with the flu. Whatever the cause, a bacteria managed to make its way via the great singer's fingers into his nose and from there right into his most sensitive place, his vocal chords.

Pavarotti's vocal chords are surely insured by Lloyd's of London for more than the value of the entire La Scala. He is very careful of his health, avoiding situations that could compromise his voice box. But nothing could prevent that germ from sneaking through his defenses; and the sniffles were quickly followed by a croaking laryngitis. Poor Luciano, frustrated and annoyed to the extreme, had to bow out and retire to his villa for total vocal rest. That means he was not allowed to speak to anyone for a week until the infection subsided.

I can surely empathize with Luciano. I, too, depend on the health of my vocal chords in my profession as a Rabbi. I am, after all, a communicator, a teacher, a preacher, a lecturer, a conciliator; and everything depends on two slender chords. As with all muscles, they can become overworked and tired; and even worse, they are subject to invasion by germs when the body's resistance is lowered due to high stress combined with a host of other factors including poor diet, "the cold season," change of climate, fatigue, etc.

I can certainly empathize with Pavarotti, having been reduced to vocal croaking every now and then. The difference is that Luciano can postpone his concert but I don't have the authority to postpone Rosh Hashana. The High Holidays are the Jewish *La Boheme*, World Series, and La Scala all rolled into one. So it is not very pleasant, to say the least, when a virus lays me low, as it did a year ago on Rosh Hashana. Just try directing a service through hand signals. Luckily, I have good associates who can immediately step in and help out, and, coincidentally, my son Jonathan was available on a few minutes notice to deliver my sermon. But it was certainly a traumatic experience for me, one that I would not want to repeat.

People reacted in different ways: some were amused and some were annoyed and probably wanted the services rescheduled or their money back. The Rabbi is not allowed to get sick, certainly not for Rosh Hashana. But most people were sympathetic and commiserated with me even as I could only smile wanly and nod my head.

John Glenn, who is about to blast off into outer space for the second time in his life, said recently that his only worry was that he would catch a cold, and be forced to abort the mission. NASA officials said that even if he catches a cold, they would wait for him to recuperate. Imagine that huge rocket idling on the landing pad, waiting for John Glenn to complete taking his coricidin pills, or his keflex.

Every year I also worry that some well meaning congregant will give me a great big kiss and transfer that bacteria with my name on it and I will come down with the flu. Only my rocket ship won't wait and the "show must go on."

So, comes the end of August, I start taking double doses of vitamin C. I finish bottles of echinacea, I drink tea with lemon and honey, I wear a red bendel, and I go into semiquarantine. Most of the time, with God's help, it works and I take off into the spiritual stratosphere. And when it doesn't work, there is always next year, as the Brooklyn Dodger fans would chant miserably at this time of the year.

B. THE SEASON
Getting Through the Year
3. The Environment

IT'S A BIT EARLY FOR PASSOVER

It's about three o'clock in the morning and I am suddenly wide awake. What is that infernal noise outside? By six A.M., after repeated attempts to fall back to sleep, I get in the car and start circling the neighborhood to track down and pinpoint the source of the noise. It sounds like a machine, actually like a machine gun, firing short bursts, on and off, on and off. I have the feeling that it is a water pump, regulating the level of the canal behind the house, especially active after the recent heavy downpour. If I find that infernal machine, I will switch it off. Failing that, I could pour some sand into the moving parts. That should silence the beast and give us some nocturnal peace.

But I can't locate it. It seems to be moving from one end of the canal to the other, the sound resonating between the unfinished construction, confusing and angering me at the same time. As I am standing in the back of someone's house, who I am sure will call the police on the unknown intruder trespassing around his property, I see a man who is unloading his tools. "Do you hear that," I ask. "What the heck is that?" Without hesitation he answers, "Frogs." No pump, no exotic machine, no conspiracy to keep the neighborhood from sleeping. Just frogs.

After a heavy rain, the frogs come out to sing and dance. It is their mating ritual, I suppose. And the spin-off is total sleep deprivation for the neighborhood.

Now I begin to appreciate the ten plagues, especially the second one, "frogs." (tzfardea). What was the big deal about frogs jumping around Pharoah's palace? So they jumped into his bed and in his soup, and were a colossal nuisance, particularly if you don't like frog's legs.

But now I know. Try going without sleep for a few nights due to the frog symphony and you will understand why Pharoah finally said, "let those bloody Jews go as long as they take the frogs with them." To this day, some Jews commemorate that moment in history by eating frog's legs. Most traditional Jews, however, have the opposite custom: we never eat frog's legs, because kashrut problems aside, we hold dear the memory of those little rascals who saved our people.

NOISY NEIGHBORS

My backyard neighbor put in a hot tub, and I was very happy for him, until he gave a hot tub inauguration party, along with music—very loud music—Saturday night—very late Saturday night. So, at three in the morning, after tossing and turning for several hours, I went out into the backyard and shouted some expletive deleted in the direction of the hot tub party. Of course, nothing happened because it is impossible to make yourself heard over a hot tub party, fueled by copious amounts of Jack Daniels and deafened by the thinly disguised noise called " techno music."

The next morning, I took a walk around the block, knocked on the door, and calmly explain how excessive noise blocks the ability in humans to experience rapid eye movement in the deep sleep segment. In other words, it is impossible to fall asleep when a bunch of rowdy drunks are splashing about to the rhythms of a monstrous boom box set on maximum volume. My neighbor was chastized and duly chastened by my remarks, and I headed back assured of some peace and quiet in the neighborhood.

The next Saturday afternoon, just as I was about to take a traditional Shabbat afternoon nap, the boom box reminded me that obviously I wasn't speaking their language. Or maybe I am living in the wrong society. I always thought that quiet was something to be valued and protected, especially when most of us are subjected to constant electronic noise during our working day. Telephones ring, cellular phones buzz, faxes whine, air conditioners whir, microphones blast, until we literally can't hear ourselves think. I would think that normal human beings would welcome a respite from all that nerve jangling noise. But obviously I am wrong; or I am abnormal. Most people seem to enjoy being surrounded and drowned out by noise.

I can't engage in a conversation with my table partners at a Bar Mitzva party without shouting until I am hoarse. People wait until the band takes a break in order, hurriedly, to have a few words with their friends. We begin to hope that the wires to those monstrously huge speakers will mysteriously become separated so that we can eat our chocolate mousse in peace, and guarantee its digestion.

A fellow in our congregation has the perfect solution: he turns off his hearing aid, especially when he disagrees with his wife. He also turns it off when the guest speaker goes beyond our attention span of 20 minutes, uses four syllable words when two will do, becomes overly verbose in an attempt to make a two-minute point in ten (as if he was being paid by the word), seems to lack terminal facilities, or otherwise begins to verbally torture his audience with his personal brand of noise pollution. I call it selective hearing, but maybe at the entrance table for all Bar Mitzvas, along with your place card and yarmulke, should be earplugs.

How interesting that we greet each other with "Shalom." It means hello and goodbye but it also means peace, as in "peace and quiet." Primitive tribes greeted each other with pulsing drum beats and rhythmic stomping and clapping. Quiet was viewed with alarm and suspicion, as if an attack was imminent. Obviously, my neighbors don't belong to my tribe; and you should know that when I greeted them with "Shalom," as they moved in last year, they looked at me quizzically. I should have known then that we weren't speaking the same language and that our disparate cultures were about to clash.

The police department assures me that there is an ordinance against excessive noise, but I feel guilty bothering the cop on the beat when he is occupied with more pressing and significant crimes. I would hate to find out that a robbery took place in our neighborhood because the assigned policeman was too busy checking out a complaint about a radio.

The only solution I can think of, at the moment, is to have repeated noise offenders locked into a room with gigantic speakers booming out techno music, day and night. I hear the Israelis have used this system quite effectively to neutralize terrorists and force them to confess. If it works on terrorists, surely it would work on my neighbor.

Shalom.

TU' BESHVAT AND THE AVOCADOS

Winters are chilly and dreary in Jerusalem, but February brings a refreshing warm breeze and the trees begin to bud. It is time to celebrate Tu' Beshvat, the new year of trees. In Florida, one season seems to blend into another and it is hard to distinguish between November and April. No matter what the date, we live in summer—fall—winter—spring. (Sounds like the Indian Princess in the *Howdy Doody Show*.) The sun always shines, it is always a good day to golf, and before we know it, the year flies by.

The only thing that reminds me of the passage of seasons (except for the atrocious August humidity) is the avocado tree in my back yard. I cut it in half just before Hurricane Andrew because I didn't want it visiting me in my living room. But it came right back with a vengeance and it now covers the entire corner of my roof. When the wind blows, its branches make eerie noises scratching on my facia board, prompting me to dial 911. In the winter, it covers my yard with fallen leaves that prompt a surcharge from my gardener; and in the fall, it gives fruit—giant, pear-shaped avocados, the likes of which can not be found in the supermarket.

Avocados are good for you. They are a bit high in calories, but they lower your HDLs and raise your LDLs (or is it the reverse?). And my avocados are delicious. We eat them in guacamole, or straight from the peel, with lemon, with pepper, with mayonnaise, with salads, or any way we can think of. Either way, they taste wonderful.

But it isn't possible for two people to eat 200 avocados. All right, so I exaggerate: 175 avocados. We give them away to relatives, to friends, to neighbors, to fellow Rabbis, to fellow teachers, to the postman, to the garbage man, to anyone who will take them. We have avocados coming out of our ears; we need help to finish them.

Mind you, Aileen and I are not ungrateful. Having our own fruit trees and picking our own fruit allows us to play kibbutznik, but without the real work. We don't water the tree, or fertilize, or prune, or spray. In short, we have a perfect arrangement with our tree: We leave it alone and it gives us fruit. Once in a while, it drops an avocado on our roof. It lands with a thud and shakes the house, much the way a B-17 bomber would unload on Germany. The purpose is to remind us not to take our tree for granted. I go out to pick up the green missile, being careful not to step directly under the tree for too long. An avocado meeting your head from 20 feet up will put you in the hospital emergency room with a concussion.

All in all, we have a good working relationship with our tree.

Each morning as I leave the house for the minyan, I find the avocados on the ground, waiting to see if the squirrels will get them before I do. It must be similar to the experience of the Israelites who found their daily dose of manna on the Sinai desert floor. And it is on Tu' Beshvat that we take the time to say "thanks for the avocados," which is more than our ancestors ever did. And maybe that's why they died in the desert without ever having seen the promised land.

WHAT IS JEWISH FOOD?

Bagel:

The Yiddish word *bagel* was first mentioned in the ordinances of the Cracow community in 1610, which stated that they could be sent as gifts to women about to give birth and to midwives. The bagel was a ringlike roll of South German or Austrian origin, as the term bagel is said to be derived from the German word *Bugel*, meaning a bow-shaped piece of metal or wood, or *Steibigel*, meaning a stirrup. Hence, the round shape of the bagel with a hole in its center.

Kneidlech:

In the winter, big dumplings (*kneidlech*) were made from potato dough and were often filled with oatmeal, chopped onions, and goose or chicken fat. The Yiddish kneidel was almost certainly derived from the South German *Knodel*, meaning dumpling.

Lokshen:

The Yiddish word *lokshen* (noodles) is derived from the Persian word for noodles, *lakshah*, meaning to slide. An Arabic cookery book from the tenth century described how the dough was rolled "with a rolling pin and cut with a knife into strips," much as the East European Jews were later to prepare noodles.

Cholent:

It was universal to eat *schulet* or *cholent* on the Sabbath in Eastern and Central Europe although it varied in both name and form in different areas. Cholent, which is a one-dish hot meal, consisting of a variety of meats, grains and vegetables all cooked together for a long time in one pot was also called schulet in Bohemia (Czechoslovakia), whereas in Poland it was called cholent (Eastern Yiddish). The latter name preserved the designation by which the dish had been known since the 13th century, when first mentioned by Rabbi Isaac of Vienna (1180–1250), the author of *Or Zarua*, who regarded himself as a citizen of Bohemia.

Kugel:

Different types of pudding cooked with cholent were called *kugel*, a Yiddish word derived from the German for ball or sphere, *Kugelhoph* as it was called. The prototype for kugel, called *weck schalent*, in the 1870s was made from softened rolls, flour, fat, raisins, eggs, ground almonds, grated lemon peel, pepper, and salt. The Polish kugels also included the traditional kugel made with flour and breadcrumbs, a matzah kugel and a lokshen (noodle) kugel.

Latkes:

In order to remember the miracle of the oil in Chanuka, Jews in Poland enjoyed donuts fried in oil (*paczki*) or pancakes (*plazki*) made from potato flour. The German Jewish immigrants to Israel, most whom arrived in the 1930s, encouraged the rest of the population to enjoy munching jelly doughnuts (*sufganiyot*) on Chanuka, the new Hebrew word *sufganiya*, being derived from the Greek for sponge, *spongos*. Jews in Lithuania ate pancakes (*latkes*) made from potato flour, borrowing this culinary invention *kartoflani plaatzki* from the Ukrainians.

Kreplach:

Originally, in Poland and the Jewish community of Prague, kneaded the dough for the *kreplach* with honey and spices, filling them with fruit or preserves. Afterward, it was filled with chopped meat. It seems that the word kreplach originated from the French *crepes*.

Herring:

Herring was so inexpensive and popular in Eastern Europe that practically everybody ate it. For the poor in particular it was often the only kind of fish that was affordable. This was probably the condition that gave birth to the many Jewish jokes to surround the topic of herring over the years.

Gefilte Fish:

The actual recipe for *gefilte fish* grew out of poverty. Fresh fish, in Eastern Europe, was difficult to come by, and whatever was available was very expensive. Yet, even the poorest Jews wanted to have a piece of fish every week in honor of the Sabbath. So a recipe was developed over time as a kind of "fis stretching" in which the meat of the fish was ground together with onions and mixed eggs, seasonings, matzoh meal of crumbs, and maybe even a little grated carrot. In this way, a small quantity of fish could be made to go a long way and create enough food to give everybody a least a taste of fish for the Sabbath.

FOR THE BIRDS

Each spring the swallows return to Capistrano in southern California; and the blackbirds return to the Konovitches in North Miami Beach.

Several years ago, I noticed that the screening that runs along the underside of my eaves was worn away. It took me awhile to determine the proper nomenclature and to distinguish eaves from facia boards. All this I accomplished during an impromptu consultation with Miguel of Home Depot, after I had made one of my bimonthly forays into the plumbing department in an attempt to repair, yet again, a haunted toilet tank. (Haunted, because the unusual flusher valve emits a banshee-like noise every evening around midnight.) Miguel of plumbing didn't know much about screening material, but he was able to explain the difference between a facia board and eaves. But I digress.

It seems that unbeknownst to me the birds had located a worn section of screening under the eaves and had patiently and determinedly opened a hole big enough to squeeze through. They whistled for their whole extended mishpocha and before I could say "four and twenty blackbirds baked in a pie," they were half way finished with a brandnew bird condominium. Working day and night, they gathered every loose twig in the neighborhood onto my garageway, and slowly and methodically hoisted it up into the open eaves.

Now I didn't mind the construction going on without a permit, but my daughter was home from college and it was hard to sleep after sunup, what with all the chirping and related bird racket. Furthermore, I noticed that they were using my car for target practice in their spare time, and even with a regular car wash, the marks remained. So, in my exasperation, I got out the ladder and climbed up to confront the intruders.

They flew away to scream at me from the nearest tree. Construction was still going on so I wasn't worried about eggs in the nest. I reached in and began pulling out the ten pounds or so of twigs and grass that pass for aviary architecture. Most of it fell into my hair and face, but I managed to get rid of it; and I repaired the screen.

I felt guilty, but I needn't have. The very next morning they flew right up to the screen and managed to shake it loose. And the nest building assembly line started up in earnest.

This time I looked into the Talmud for guidance. I didn't want to be punished for not taking a bird's eye view of things. "If you are hunting birds for food and you discover a nest, you must first send away the mother, and then you may take the baby birds", says the Torah. This didn't seem to apply to my situation, especially since we don't eat birds for Shabbat dinner. Chicken, yes, but not birds. Chickens come in frozen packages from the supermarket and you just put the pieces in the oven. Who knows from feathers, or claws, or squawking or blood or ritual slaughtering ("Shechita").

"You may not cause an animal undue anguish," says the Torah. This I could relate to. My old German Shepherd, Sheba (she was black and brown, of course) used to terrify the mailman by trying to bite off his hand when he put the mail in the door slot. We punished the dog by making her stay in her cage during mail time. It was undue anguish for her ("Tzar Ba'aley Chaim"). We eventually let her out to terrorize the mailman. There were no biblical laws for mailmen that I could find.

Getting back to the birds: How could I continue to chase away such persistent and resourceful creatures? Maybe it was a sign of mazal that they always picked our house eaves in which to build their nest. And if you measure mazal by the amount of bird droppings adorning the front of our house, then we were indeed blessed. So we gave up the battle. I left the screen with a gaping hole. I put away the ladder and resolved to allow the birds a home for their new family for one more season.

This Yom Kippur I will be counting up my mitzvahs to set before the good Lord in demonstration of my piety and all-around "good guyness." I expect those blackbirds to come to my rescue as I came to theirs.

B. THE SEASON
Getting Through the Year
4. Time Waits for No Man

AN APPOINTMENT WITH THE PAST

I don't enjoy going to the doctor. I'd rather not know what's wrong with me; and I get very nervous waiting for the results of my fluid tests. I don't even like giving fluids, red or yellow. Worse of all, I flinch when the nurse puts a needle into my arm vein. And speaking of nurses, I certainly don't like sitting around in the presence of a strange woman in a socalled gown that is open in the front and open in the back and is slit down to there, and covers my upper arms and a bit of my back at best. The entire enterprise is rather unpleasant to say the least.

But there is one ray of light in my visit to the netherworld of the HMOs and PPOs and medical "mucky-mucks": my doctor, my personal primary care physician, is an old family friend. His father and uncle were physicians to my parents back in the Bronx, and eventually to me. Years later, after migrating to Florida, we found each other once again, only it was the two "sons of": of the Rabbi and of the doctor. We were now also Doctor and Rabbi respectively, following in the footsteps of our fathers and continuing the old friendship along with the professional care.

So it is that I put up with the poking, prodding, and sticking, the nervous waiting, and endless forms in order to spend an hour with my old friend, Dr. Sheldon Warman.

His uncle taught us both to ski. His family came every year to our Passover Seder. To this day we remember each other around the table, even as we remember the great exodus from Egypt. Our friendship has crossed geographic and sidereal time; it has survived the rigors of medical school and rabbinical school and connects us across two generations.

We sit in the examination room—he dressed in his glistening white lab coat and I in that infernal gown—and we reminisce. Perhaps the nurses wonder at the loud laughter that floats out through the door. It underlines the fact that it isn't just a patient and his doctor sitting knee to knee in the examining room, but two old friends remembering the dog who would only eat on the command "kosher," or the local Italian politician who lived in the big stone house with the ornate lions in the front, who came to the synagogue just as often as he went to church, at least in election years and who spent a few years in the less than luxurious surroundings of a New York jail.

As the years go by, it is increasingly valuable to be able to hold on to the past. There are fewer and fewer links to our childhood as old friends move away and preoccupy themselves with their new lives and careers. The opportunities to reconnect and rediscover lost experiences do not present themselves very often. But when they do, we are privileged to participate in a sacred moment, a moment that brings to life the way we were so many years ago, that rekindles the joy of shared experiences with valued friends. We tend to forget those treasured moments; they are buried in our computer banks until someone hits the correct key to bring them up on our screen.

So it was that the two of us probed our memories and brought forth a host of good stories, one memory triggering the next until we were transported back to the Bronx of our youth a lifetime ago. Only old friends can do this. Only old friends share in common good times and valuable experiences.

Dr. Sheldon's father passed away at a very young age and so did his uncle. The two of them practiced medicine together out of their offices on the Grand Concourse. But when I got sick they were at my bedside, something that is unheard of today in an age of medical specialization. Somehow they seemed to be able to take care of most problems. I believed in them I trusted them and always felt better after their visit. Their bedside manner was the product of a sincere desire to help and to heal, not just as a physician, but also as a close friend of the family.

My friend, Dr. Sheldon, went to the finest schools and accumulated enough degrees to wallpaper his office. But his manner is "genetic," he inherited it from his father. Competence and skill are learned on the wards, but compassion and genuine interest are passed through our DNA. Doctors can be trained but real human beings are born.

I can't say that I look forward to my annual visit to the doctor. But in this case, the anguish is mitigated by the fact that I am visiting with an old friend. It's better medicine for me than any prescription he can write.

ON TIME; OVERTIME

A colleague of mine writes that he is searching for a synagogue without a clock on the wall. "After all, the shul is the sacred sphere of the Timeless One. This is where finite man seeks to enter the infinite world of prayer, of study, and of communion with God." In the quiet of the Bet Midrash (chapel), we contemplate the Eternal and our relationship to Him, Who is beyond time. The last thing we need is a clock on the wall reminding us that we have to be home in time for supper.

But when reality sets in, we realize that even religious life is dictated by the clock. One must pray before the fourth hour of the day, recite the morning Shema before the third hour, Musaf (additional service) on the Sabbath before the seventh hour, "Mincha" (the afternoon prayers) after the sixth hour but before sunset, and the evening Shema before midnight.

So we start our services on time, and we finish on time. I, for one, am always disturbed when someone comes late to an appointment. It means that they don't value my time and can cavalierly ignore the clock. How much more so do we need to respect God's time? Do you think He has all the time in the world for us?

See you on time.

SUIT FOR THE WEDDING. DRESS FOR THE CHUPA.

In the old days, it was much simpler: A few months before the Bar Mitzvah, you went with your mother to visit Gene Lubin, the king of the Bar Mitzvah suits. All the kids in the Bronx went to visit him up in Yonkers at the Cross Country Shopping Center. Until Bar Mitzvah, my friends and I shopped in children's stores where we were treated like little kids. But when we stepped into Lubin's emporium, it was different. He didn't address my parents; he spoke to me, like a real person.

When my son became a Bar Mitzvah, we were living in Miami, and I took him to the local king of the Bar Mitzvah suits. Also a genius with the needle and thread who learned from his father who was a master tailor in Poland. When my son left the store down on Washington Avenue, in what was still Jewish South Beach, he looked smashing.

Now it comes time to celebrate the next great simcha: a wedding. My daughter announced that she has found her intended. The first call is to the grandparents; the second call is to the dressmaker. (The third to the caterer.) No, not the dressmaker; the "couturier." What is a couturier you might ask? A couturier is French for the old Yiddish tailor who made your Bar Mitzvah suit. Only this fellow is 35 years younger, has a headband and earrings, and will take twice as long and twice the gelt to make the wedding dresses.

Now we go for fittings. And the dress is not sewn; it is created. And what a creation it is. It should have been listed in Genesis along with the rest of God's creations. One week before the wedding it still isn't finished. If the good Lord created the world in seven days, I expect that our couturier can complete the gown in that time. He does. It looks smashing. The bride is happy; the "mechutaynesteh" (newly minted mother-in-law to be) is radiant.

They sweep down the aisle rustling in white tulle, gleaming in satin, and smiling nervously as they carefully approach the bimah. I, on the other hand, wear my old double-breasted tuxedo, just to demonstrate that it still fits. I wonder what the old king of the Bar Mitzvah suits could have put together for me. It will wait until my son decides to get married. The styles could be very different by then. I wonder if they let you walk down the aisle in "nursing home white"?

TIME STANDING STILL

Atop the MetLife Tower in Manhattan is a 92-year-old clock. It is 27 feet in diameter; the clock dials are 26 and half feet across, with six-foot bells that chime every quarter hour from 9:00 a.m. to 10:00 p.m. Even New Yorkers need some quiet time at night.

Lately, the clock mechanism began to show the effects of 92 years of New York weather. The works were corroding, the marble face was eroding and the result was that the clock came to a stop. In Manhattan, at Madison Avenue and 24th Street, time stood still.

A complicated restoration project was mounted by the Metropolitan Life Insurance Company Three years and $35 million dollars later, the scaffolding came off and the clock started up again.

Wouldn't it be nice if every now and again we could make time stand still, so we could inspect and repair the workings of our lives. Sometimes we run too fast; sometimes we run too slow. Sometimes we breakdown and don't run at all. We need to fix some of our parts, and rewind our inner clock.

Actually we do this once a year, in the month of Elul, 4 weeks before Rosh Hashana. We do a full inspection of the inner workings of our soul. It is called "cheshbon hanefesh," a spiritual stocktaking. We make the necessary repairs as best we can and we look forward to the smooth movement of our works. We polish out the corroded spots and sandblast the irregularities in anticipation of Yom Kippur, when we stand before the Heavenly Clock Maker. We hope we have corrected the faults and our lives will run more accurately and smoothly in the New Year.

FATHER'S DAY

Dear Dad,

I was out jogging early Sunday morning around the Turnberry golf course. It was one of those rare Sundays that I have to myself without a service to officiate at or a meeting to attend; and as you remember from your 50 years in the Rabbinate, what a treat that is. Whenever I am out running, my thoughts drift to you and the countless hours we spent together in one activity or another. You often reminded me that the Talmud lists the responsibilities of a father, which center on teaching a son how to take care of himself in the world. This includes even learning how to swim. Well, you taught me how to swim, and how to throw a fastball, and how to kick a football, and how to swing a racquetball.

I mention racquetball because a little boy of 6 or 7 crossed the jogging path as I came by. He was clutching an oversized racquet under his arm and holding his father's fingers tightly in his other hand. Our eyes met; I saw myself many years back, holding your hand on the way to the courts, or to the pool, or to the park. Whatever I know, you taught me. It took me many years to beat you on the racquetball court, a few less years to outscore you on the basketball court, and I still can't throw a curve ball the way you can.

But don't worry, there is an "umpire on high" who eventually levels the playing field. Your grandson already beats me fairly regularly on the basketball court. You are not the only one being called "old man."

Through all these years you were teaching me the importance of staying in shape as a prerequisite for good health. Only a healthy body can support a keen mind, and lest I thought you were glorifying Greek philosophy, you would quote Maimonides and the Talmud as supporting a balance between the physical and the spiritual. We lived by the "golden mean," never extreme or fanatic in anything we did, but always committed to principles.

But getting back to my Sunday morning jog. The running path circles the Turnberry golf course, and you should know that I am surreptitiously practicing and preparing to challenge you. I know that I used to scoff at golf as a game for "old men," but I seem to be changing my mind (or is it my age?). I played nine holes with your grandson last month for the very first time. We broke 100 (on nine holes, of course) but we had a great time. He used your old wooden shafts that qualify as antiques. I can still remember the first time you took me out on the golf course at Split Rock on the Bronx/Westchester border. It was a beautiful fall day, and the multicolored leaves were all over the fairway, hiding every drive. We must have gone through a dozen balls that day. And you said that one day I would appreciate the sport of golf. It took 30 years, but "one day" is here.

In our weekly conversations you still remind me to keep in shape, not only physically, but intellectually and spiritually. As the Talmud says: The study of Torah is more important than anything else. Your perennial question "What are you studying today?" prompts me to open the book each day, because I know that I will have to answer your questions. It is good for everyone, myself included, to answer to a higher authority.

By the time I circled the running track, I had decided to write to you in honor of Father's Day. Perhaps I wish to thank you for all the wonderful years, and look forward to many more. There are so many more things I need to learn, and so many more things you need to teach me.

Your son.

IN YOUR HEART

Many years ago, my brother-in-law invited me to watch him perform. His "performance" was in the operating theatre and his instrument was the scalpel, he was a newly minted heart surgeon. I elected to experience it all at the distance. Even a "bris" troubled me. He mentioned that prior to every operation, he always thinks of a prayer in the siddur said early in the daily service reminding us that the body is a mighty complicated vessel, created through God's wisdom. "It is composed of so many tiny vessels and sphincters. If any of them are suddenly blocked, we cannot remain alive." And the prayer ends with the hope that God will care for us; because in the end, even the heart surgeon will tell you that "everything is eventually in the Lord's hands."

A few months ago, one of our eminent heart surgeons invited me to watch a heart operation at Miami Heart Institute. But this time, I would stand right at his shoulder and see every detail of the procedure. I agreed, but with a great deal of trepidation. Did I really want to see it all? How would I react? Would I faint at the first sight of arterial blood?

The appointed morning came. I changed into the green uniform and listened to the briefing on what would happen, step by step. And then, there we were inside, under the glare of the lights and the operating team began.

Five hours later, a ninety-year-old man, who was living on borrowed time, was wheeled into the recovery room with a new lease on life. Three bypasses performed by a brilliant doctor in an extraordinary operation added years of life that was already being measured only in days. I recall the doctor's words as the procedure began, "Rabbi, you pray for him, and I will operate on him, and with God's help, he will be well."

This combination of medical science and spiritual power can work. And when God is good to us, we are presented with a special gift, a longer and healthier life.

On Rosh Hashana and Yom Kippur, we will sit in the synagogue and commune with God. We will pray for health and long life. The word "Chaim" (life) is one of the most repeated words in our prayer book, and we will say it over and over hoping that the good Lord is listening.

And some of us will thank God for allowing us to survive the operating table, including that fellow who was lying in front of me and whose heart I saw literally resting in the hands of the surgeon. And the surgeon said, "It wasn't my hands holding the heart, it was God's hands."

YOU CAN'T GO HOME AGAIN

Prologue:

The search for ancestral roots has become a Jewish obsession some 50 years after the Shoah. So much disappeared in smoke and ash that even a tiny remnant beckons and intrigues. The generation of survivors would rather not revisit the scene of their would-be annihilation. It is too painful to relive those horrifying years, especially when surrounded by those same buildings on those same streets. And to stare into the faces of those very same neighbors who pointed them out to the Nazis is too much to ask of a normal human being.

So the curiosity jumps a generation to the children and grandchildren who want to encounter the past, and who, by virtue of physical and intellectual distances, are strong enough to confront their history. It is the last chance to find the housewife who was looking out the window when the swastika inscribed truck pulled away with its load of Jews; or the farmer who heard the machine gun fire in the woods and peered through the trees to see his Jewish neighbors fall bleeding into the pits. It is the ghosts and spirits we pursue through the forests of Poland. We wish to recover something of the past life and to take it away with us. How can the spirits rest easy when they are still surrounded by the accused murderers? Why should we allow our memories to remain buried beneath shattered gravestones and in moldering barracks surrounded by rusting barbed wire? We have come to claim our past.

So it was that we made arrangements to secure the visas that would allow us to cross into the Judenrein territory of White Russia. The embassy in Warsaw was clearly under orders to make it as difficult as possible. But with it all, on the appointed day, at the appointed hour, we presented ourselves at the border. We had a date with our past.

The borders of Eastern Europe have changed so many times that it is hard to know where you were born. At one time, the Austro-Hungarian Empire, sometimes Poland, occasionally Lithuania, and eventually Russia, but currently Belarus; only the names of the towns remained the same. A different passport, a different flag, but the same problems for the Jews no matter who ruled.

Across the border from Bialystok lies the town of Wolkowysk, some 50 kilometers inside Belarus, and light years away from the Western world. Even Poland is a citadel of enlightenment compared to this vestigial appendix from the Cold War communist era. But there we were, lined up at the border, trying to reach a town that my friend ran away from 55 years ago, just one step ahead of the invading Germans. He was sure he would recognize his little town. Just get him to the railroad station and he would find his way home. The apartment building would still be there, a block or two off the market square and right near the synagogue.

But it wasn't to be. Around we went, from one side of town to the other, desperately searching for familiar landmarks: the river, the train tracks, the cemetery, the synagogue, the quiet street. Nothing seemed to be in the right place. Nothing was familiar, nothing made sense. In a panic we hailed a local policeman. Apprised of our predicament he guided us to some of the oldest townspeople. They remembered: the Jews, the synagogue, the cemetery. They were all gone: the Jews to Treblinka or Auschwitz or to the killing fields, and the buildings razed to the ground. Even the cemetery stones were knocked down and overgrown, the cows chewing the grass over them near the railroad tracks.

One modest mausoleum still stood. He imagined it to be the one covering his great grandparents. The one that hid his newly married mother and father from the wrath of their disappointed parents. Everything else had vanished, just as surely as the sounds of his boyhood had vanished into the forest. The laughter of young boys and girls, the sound of the bicycle on the forest path, the taste of the tiny wild strawberries of summer, the smell of the farmer's haystack shielding them from the sudden rain. Was it real, or was it only a dream?

Homesick and heartsick he began the long road back across the border and back to the present. The town of his boyhood now existed only in his memory. The attempt to return home had failed. "Goodbye Wolkowysk," he whispered. "I lost you forever."

In the shtetls of Eastern Europe there is only the past. And it has all vanished into smoke and ash. And any attempt to recapture it is doomed to disappointment and failure.

Epilogue:

In the middle of the night, five hours after arriving at the border, the guard peered into the car and asked him if he was ill. Indeed. It was a sickness of the soul, from which there is no recovery. A "sickness unto death."

THE CELL PHONE: SYMBOL OF AMERICAN CULTURE

The cell phone is everywhere: before the opera begins, the president of the opera association makes an announcement to turn off all cell phones. By the middle of the first act, the first phone rings. During the synagogue services, I announce that unless you are expecting a direct call from God, the cell phone needs to be turned off unless an emergency is pending. Young women in SUV "tanks" turn the corner with one hand on the wheel and one eye on the road. The other hand and the other eye are occupied with a call to their housemaid to make sure they clean that corner of the oven. Two children are strapped into the back seat, the most precious cargo that could be carried, and attention is distracted by the cell phone.

The ubiquitous cell phone is a status symbol across the country. At one point, cardboard cutouts were for sale so that you could make believe that you were making a call in your car. People seem to be deathly afraid of being out of touch. Being connected, 24 hours a day, is the mark of having arrived, of always being wanted. You are always connected, always in touch, always needed. A cell phone advertises the fact that the world can't get along without you. You are so important that a moment can't pass without your words of wisdom. What a great feeling of omniscience and power. The world will collapse unless you can be reached, unless you can relay those all-important words.

The cell phone further inflates large egos until, like the Wizard of Oz, we think we are all-powerful, until someone looks behind our electronic curtain.

On the other side of the electronic beam is the diminution of our privacy. We can never be alone, to think, to read, to pray, or even to sleep. Someone is always interrupting us and robbing us of our personal time. We no longer belong to ourselves but to everyone else in the world who has our number.

The cell phone is a wonderful gadget to have in case of real emergency. On a dark road in the middle of nowhere it is a godsend to be able to call for help when we have a flat tire. In a medical emergency it is so important to have the police or the fire department or the EMT at our fingertips.

However, when we become addicted to hearing a voice on the other end of the electronic line, and we are disturbed by any interruption of connection, we are in serious trouble. It means we are uncomfortable with ourselves, that we cannot bear to be alone with our thoughts; that our self image is only defined by who communicates with us from the outside, and not what we hear from our own brain.

As I write, the legislature is about to forward to the judiciary a law against the use of hand-held cell phones in the car. At least that time in the car will be ours to use, if we choose, without interruption. And who knows how many lives will be saved by eliminating the distractions of the cell phone.

WHO COMFORTS THE COMFORTER

Many of the firefighters and policemen who died in the explosion of the World Trade Center lived "on the island," which in "New Yorkese" means the towns on Long Island.

The Catholic church in West Hempstead is led by Msgr. Jim Lisante. He has buried seventeen New York firefighters, most in their 30s, all with wives and children.

It is difficult enough to speak about a young person who was in the midst of an energetic and heroic life. Young people who were the protectors and saviors of the larger community. Young people who should have expected so many more years of little league baseball, confirmations, school graduations, and wedding anniversaries.

But even more difficult for the spiritual leader of the parish, was the attempt to comfort the young widows and the parents and the little children. What can you say that will bring solace to a woman married for only five or six years? How can you offer a spiritual word to a father who just saw his son turn into ashes and dust in the inferno of the Twin Towers? How do you explain the ways of God to a nine year old who found out on September 11 that his father was never coming home again?

When an old person dies, it is sad, but it is the way of the world. When a young person dies, it is a tragedy, and it turns our world upside down.

The monsignor. feels he is in a "low grade depression, a blueness that's hard to shake". He is running out of spiritual energy and doesn't have much more comfort in him to give. People ask him how he holds up and he usually answers "God or faith or prayer." But the truth of the matter is he is burning out, and needs a place to go to recharge his spiritual batteries. And he needs someone to talk to—someone to give him a little solace and comfort. He goes to talk to his parents. He has no one else.

I can identify with the monsignor. One week before Rosh Hashana, my rabbinic world was turned upside down. Everything I had prepared for four months was suddenly inadequate. People came up to me all week in shock. They looked to me for the answers: "We are waiting to hear what you will say to us. Comfort us, console us, tell us that everything will be all right."

I had four days to find the appropriate ideas and the right words. I had the hopes and prayers of 2,000 people on my shoulders. I had to be the one to express their anxieties and fears, and I had to be the one to offer comfort, and I had to be the one to picture a better future.

If I was able to achieve my goal, it was certainly with God's help and support, and with the support of my family. I, too, was shocked, and I too was worried, and I too was depressed by the attack on America. But I was the one on whom everyone else leaned and depended. Who was I to lean on? From whom do I take comfort and solace?

I immediately understood what the monsignor in West Hempstead was going through.

The spiritual leaders of congregations across the country are probably going through the same thing. The people who give the comfort also need someone or something to give them comfort. Often, the usual avenues are not enough.

The monsignor presented the finest eulogies, in the most eloquent manner possible. Yet he had to deal with the criticism of family members who were unsatisfied or annoyed, who reflected their own guilt and inner turmoil over unresolved internal family matters. And the monsignor, a human being with his own feelings, often went away hurt and disappointed. His comments on the terrible catastrophe of September 11 were met by some in his parish with unwarranted criticism. They would rather not hear about it in church. It was enough that they read about it in the paper. It was enough to have seen the brutal images on television. Their idea of spirituality was to put their head in the proverbial sand and turn inward; hide from the reality of the outside world. Reject the notion that religion has something to say about dealing with a life than can become harsh and brutal. Again, the monsignor went away as if stabbed in the heart.

The shoulders of a spiritual leader have to be wide and strong to carry the weight of an entire congregation. Occasionally they weaken and sag under extraordinary weight. This weight was placed on our shoulders on September 11, and we are still trying to recover. Some will make it easier for us by their kindness and support. Some will make it more difficult for us by their selfishness and callousness. But with God's help, we, too, shall overcome, because we have so much important work to do.

SUCCESS

In 1923, a very important meeting was held at the Edgewater Beach Hotel in Chicago. Attending this meeting were nine of the world's most successful financiers:

- The president of the largest independent steel company
- The president of the largest utility company
- The president of the largest gas company
- The greatest wheat speculator
- The president of the New York Stock Exchange
- A member of the president's cabinet
- The greatest "bear" on Wall Street
- The head of the world's greatest monopoly
- The president of the Bank of International Settlements

Certainly, we must admit that here were gathered a group of the world's most successful men. At least, they were men who had found the secret of making money. Twenty-five years later, let's see where these men were:

- The president of the largest independent steel company—Charles Schwab—died bankrupt and lived on borrowed money for five years before his death.
- The president of the largest utility company—Samuel Insull—dies a fugitive from justice and penniless in a foreign land.
- The president of the largest gas company—Howard Hopson—is insane.
- The greatest wheat speculator—Arthur Cutten—died abroad, insolvent.
- The president of the New York Stock Exchange— Richard Whitney—was released from Sing Sing Penitentiary
- A member of the president's cabinet—Albert Fall—was pardoned from prison so he could die at home.
- The greatest "bear" on Wall Street—Jesse Livermore— died a suicide.
- The head of the world's greatest monopoly—Ivar Krueger—died a suicide.
- The president of the Bank of International Settlements—Leon Fraser—died a suicide.

All of these men learned well the art of making money, but not one of them learned how to live.

This piece is a "bit" harsh and judgmental. Because one had money and loses it—or that he went insane—does not mean he did not know how to live. Commiting a crime and suicide *do* show a lack of appreciation and understanding of life.

Perhaps the real lesson to be learned from this is that there is more to life than making money. We tend to look at wealthy people as successes because of their economic success. The real success in life is the person who understands what life is all about—that there is a God, that He gave us values to live by (the Torah) and goals for our life (to perfect ourselves and the world).

TALKING TO YOURSELF

I have a Rabbi friend who was trained in the public relations business, who always speaks in hyperbole and superlatives. When it becomes a bit too much, I remind him that he is talking to me, his long-time friend, not to one of his clients. To me he can speak like a normal person, I don't have to be constantly impressed or flattered.

We all know people who take fifteen minutes to make a 30-second point, who never let you get away without telling a story that never seems to end, that always underscores how wonderful or how great the storyteller is. After a while, we tend to run the other way when we see such a "bombast" coming our way. There are only 24 hours in the day, and who needs to be bored to death by someone who is always promoting himself or his own "thing"? I would prefer to talk to someone who listens occasionally to what I have to say, instead of constantly enjoying his/her own voice. After all, a discussion or a dialogue implies two people speaking to one another as well as listening. Often, I have spoken with a person whose eyes reveal that they are not listening, rather that they are in the process of formulating their next sentence and care not a wit for what I am saying.

Such people are easily distracted by someone passing who is considered more "important" as well as a better target for self-promotion. Suddenly, you find yourself talking to the thin air, or to the wall, or to yourself. As soon as such a person rudely interrupts the discussion to look for "greener pastures," I leave. Perhaps they will get the message that I don't intend to wait around until they finish promoting.

The Talmud has a wonderful comment on such a person describing him as a "coin dropped into an empty barrel making a big noise," but signifying nothing.

BE HAPPY

I met a fellow who was retired. I know that he recently sold his business for a rather tidy profit. I figured that he would be beaming with joy. He wasn't. He almost seemed depressed. I asked him if he still has an office. No. I was curious to know how he spent his day. After more than 50 years of getting up and going to work, day after day and week after week, what did he do with his time?

His answer was, "I go to doctors. I am supporting the medical profession. On Monday, I went to my internist, on Tuesday, I went to my cardiologist, on Wednesday I went to my gastroenterologist, on Thursday, I went to my urologist, on Friday, I went to my ophthalmologist, and on Saturday, I went to my psychiatrist." I was taken aback for a moment. So I said, "if you came to shul on Saturday, I could have done a better job than your psychiatrist and it would have been a lot cheaper."

The point is that for so many of you, it is downright difficult just to get up in the morning. That's why we say *modeh ani*, thank you Lord that everything still works, more or less. Thank you God for giving me one more day.

Our People spend their days waiting in doctor's offices. They memorize *People* magazine and *Sports Illustrated*. They spend hours to put their pills in order, figuring out in which order to take them. Some life. No wonder people get depressed.

So may I make some suggestions? Don't wait for the doctor to tell you if you should feel good or bad. You decide. When I see you during the day and I ask you "how are you feeling," you can give me the list of what hurts; my knee hurts, my hip hurts, I can't grip my golf club because of my arthritis, I can't see well, I can't hear your announcements. Or you can say, as one of our friends always says to me, "I'm doing the best I can with the little that I have."

You and only you can decide your attitude, your frame of mind. You can obsess about what bothers you, or you can be thankful that you are alive and well. You can be annoyed that you suffer pain, or you can be happy that you can still feel anything. The only people that have no pain, the only people that are at perfect peace are the people who are living in the next world, not in this world.

Surely, it is important to be under the care of good doctors. And, surely, it is encouraging to be able to swallow a pill and feel better. And we should all be so thankful that modern medicine is so amazing. But we need more. We need a spiritual dimension to our lives. We have to believe that no matter what, life is good. It is often just a question of how we want to look at things.

Do we dwell on the pain? Or do we dwell on the blessings?

When you ask a traditional Jew, Reb Yid, "how are you," what does he answer? He answers in two words, Baruch Hashem. Thank God. Because there is always something to thank God about. We try to focus on what's good in our lives, not what's bad. Yes, everybody has their little "peckel" of "tzuris." But all of us also have some brochas, some blessings in our lives, some good things to be thankful for.

The Talmud says that whatever mitzvah we do during our day, we should do it with joy, with a full heart. Simcha shel mitzvah. But you can't be happy if you are depressed. You can't be happy if you are always obsessing about your problems. If you lose all hope that things will get better, then you can never be happy.

Now, surely, everyone has something to be thankful for. Your son was accepted to medical school. Your granddaughter passed the Bar. Your grandson is getting married. Your cholesterol count dropped below 200. You lost 25 pounds. Your MRI shows there's nothing wrong with you that a good vacation won't cure. Your whole family is coming down to celebrate your birthday. The whole shul liked your new hat.

Something makes you happy. Something brings a smile to your face. Something gives you hope that tomorrow will be a better day.

You want to feel better? Automatically, immediately? Go help somebody else. Go visit your friend in the hospital. Call your son and tell him how wonderful you think he is. Take your neighbor to the grocery store—the one who can't drive anymore because his children tore up the license after the third time he hit the car in the next parking spot. Tell your buddy a good joke. Tell the cantor you loved his davening. Tell the Rabbi you loved his sermon. Tell the choir they could sing for the Czar. Put a smile on someone's face and I guarantee you will feel better. I guarantee it will put a smile on your face. This is the power of a mitzvah. It helps someone else and it helps you.

Dante's Hell had a sign on the door. Abandon hope all ye who enter here.

But we Jews have a different sign on our door. Hatikva. Hope. We made it the national anthem of our State of Israel. No matter how bad things get, we pray and we hope that tomorrow will be better. And we take ourselves by the back of the neck, and we march forward and we make it happen. We never lose faith, we never lose hope. And it brings a smile to our faces.

In his book, *The Power of Hope*, Rabbi Maurice Lamm speaks of a man in his middle seventies who was left all alone in a shtetel in Poland before the Second World War. All his children had immigrated to America. He had a hard time securing shelter and food. Every morning he would pick up sticks and put them in a burlap bag and just before sunset, he would take this bag to the wood merchant who would buy it for a kopek or two and sell it to the villagers. One hot July day, he trudged from morning to night picking up sticks. As he was putting the last stick in his bag, the burlap broke and all the sticks fell to the ground. Tired, frustrated, and disgusted, he looked up to heaven and said: "God, what do I need this for? Send me the malach hamoves, the angel of death." Instantly the angel of death appeared at his side. The angel looked at the man and asked, "Did you call?" The man said, "Yes" The angel asked, "What can I do for you?" The man looked at the angel of death and replied, "Help me pick up these sticks."

Hope is a great gift from God. None of us should reject it. "Hatikva" is not only the national hymn of the Jewish people, but should also accompany every Jew during his or her lifetime.

So, on this Kol Nidre, I wish for you hope. May it bring you a feeling of joy. May it brighten your eyes, bring a smile to your face, and let you enjoy every precious moment that God will grant you in the new year.

GOOD AND EVIL: ADAM AND EVE, CAIN AND ABEL

The two stories seem to have little in common. One recounts the primordial sin of Adam and Eve in eating of the fruit of the tree of knowledge of good and evil; the other records the death of Abel at the hand of his brother Cain. But is there a deeper connection that might illuminate a deeper truth about man and his weakness?

When God forbids Adam and Eve to eat of the forbidden fruit, no particular reason is offered, no moral calculus, no logic other than obedience to God's will. Man is commanded to obey, to accept God's dictate, while making his own will subservient to God's higher authority. But man fails the test, and in consequence is not only expelled from paradise, but also acquires the "knowledge" of good and evil that flows from his act, a knowledge which the sly serpent had compared to that of God Himself. Significantly, the very next reference to knowledge gained, occurs when the Torah tells us that Adam "knew" his wife, and as a consequence, she bore a child, Cain. Cain, therefore, could be said to be the epitome or fulfillment of man's "knowing."

If we turn to the crime of Cain, we find ourselves on a completely different plateau. This time the act is not merely a rejection of God's word and will, it is also morally horrendous; a man kills his brother in cold blood, whether out of principle, passion, or personal gain. And while few would justify such an act on moral grounds—it is clear that Cain somehow considered this act, at least at the time that he committed it, to be "good," or "necessary," or desirable, or somehow justifiable. Here, we encounter then a critical consequence of man's new knowledge of good and evil, as it results from his rebellion against the will of God: He uses his new-found moral reasoning to kill his brother.

The Torah thus understood seems to suggest the following lesson: When man rejects the authority of God's word, when he substitutes or relies upon his own judgment of good and evil rather than the revealed word of God, he runs the real risk of moral depravity, albeit one that he rationalizes or justifies through reason, or "common sense," or logic. In matters of morality, human reason can all too easily become but a tool of human passions, instincts, or impulses. When man in his arrogance challenges God's moral dictates, by substituting his own, anything can happen, every depravity becomes not only possible, but justifiable, and possibly even proper and correct. Evil can be redefined as good, the victim be treated as aggressor, depravity perverted into virtue, injustice institutionalized as equity, right and wrong reversed. Does not human history, most especially in our own century, repeatedly confirm this observation as true?

That I would submit, is the real lesson of raising Cain.

GALILEO

A series of coincidences brought Galileo Galilei (1564–1642) and the telescope together, and brought down upon him the wrath of the Church.

"We are certain," Galileo wrote in 1623, "the first inventor of the telescope was a simple spectacle-maker who, handling by chance different forms of glasses, looked, also by chance, through two of them, one convex and the other concave, held at different distances from the eye; saw and noted the unexpected result; and thus found the instrument."

The most likely story puts the crucial episode in the shop of an obscure Dutch spectacle-maker named Hans Lippershey, in Middelburg about 1608. Two children who happened into Lippershey's shop, we are told, were playing with his lenses.

They put two lenses together and when they looked through both at the same time toward a distant weather vane on the town church, it was wonderfully magnified. Lippershey looked for himself and then began making telescopes.

In July 1609, Galileo himself, who happened to be in Venice, had heard rumors that there was such an instrument as a telescope and at the same time heard that a foreigner had arrived in Padua with one of them. To satisfy his curiosity, he immediately returned to Padua, only to find that the mysterious foreigner had already left for Venice. Having learned how the foreigner's telescope had been made, Galileo at once went about making one for himself. Before the end of August, Galileo returned to Venice where he astonished the senate. His nine-power telescope was three times as powerful as the one offered by the stranger. Galileo continued to improve the instrument until at the end of 1609, he had produced a telescope of 30 power. This was the practicable limit for any telescope of the design then in use—a plano-convex objective and a plano-concave eyepiece—and it came to be known as the Galilean telescope.

For some reason, however, Galileo would not leave it at that. Early in January 1610, he did what now seems most obvious— he turned his telescope toward the skies. Today, this would require neither courage nor imagination, but in Galileo's day, it was quite otherwise. Who would dare use a toy to penetrate the majesty of the celestial spheres? To spy out the shape of God's heavens was superfluous, presumptuous, and might prove blasphemous. Galileo was no better than a theological Peeping Tom. But with this one move he proved Copernicus correct. The sun was indeed the center of the universe. The cosmic revolution was on. The world was heliocentric.

The Pope was disturbed with Galileo for disturbing the traditional biblical model of the universe. He was charged with heresy. At his trial, Galileo answered: The Bible is not supposed to tell us how the heavens go; rather, how we go to heaven. His answer is as cogent today as it was some 400 years ago.

ERATOSTHENES

On a recent visit to New York, I couldn't find my way from 96th Street in Manhattan to Brooklyn Heights. I couldn't even measure the distance on my map. I thought of Eratosthenes.

Eratosthenes (276?–194 B.C.?), perhaps the greatest of ancient geographers, is known to us mostly by hearsay and by the attacks on him from those who owed him the most. In Alexandria, he served as the second librarian of the greatest library in the Western world.

Eratosthenes noticed that at noon on June 21 the sun cast no shadow in a well at Syene (modern Aswan) and was thus directly overhead. He knew that the sun always cast a shadow at Alexandria. From knowledge available to him he considered Syene to be due south of Alexandria. The idea occurred to him that if he could measure the length of the shadow of the sun in Alexandria at the time when there was no shadow in Aswan, he could calculate the circumference of the earth. On June 21, he measured the shadow of an obelisk in Alexandria and by simple geometry calculated that the sun was 7° 14' from overhead. This is one-fiftieth of the 360 degrees that make a full circle. This measure was remarkably accurate, for the actual difference in latitude of Aswan and Alexandria by our best modern calculation is 7° 14'. Thus the circumference of the earth was fifty times the distance from Syene to Alexandria. But how great was this distance? From travelers he learned that camels needed 50 days to cover the trip and that a camel traveled 100 stadia in a day. The distance from Syene to Alexandria was thus calculated at 5,000 stadia (50 x 100). He then calculated the circumference of the earth to be 250,000 stadia (50 x 5000). We are not sure about the conversion of stadia (originally 600 Greek feet), into modern measures, but the best estimates put the Greek stadium at about 607 English feet. The Greek "stadium," from which we take our modern name was a footrace course of precisely that length. By this calculation, Eratosthenes arrived at a figure for the circumference of the earth of some 28,700 miles. (He was only off by 15 percent.)

And I can't find my way to Brooklyn Heights.

B. THE SEASON
Getting Through the Year
5. The Holy Days

PASSOVER 1945: THE ITALIAN FRONT

Since the start of World War II, the Jewish people in Palestine (what was called the Yishuv; since "Palestine" was a colonial name imposed by the conquering Romans in 70 of the common era and continued through the British Mandate) watched the German Army march across North Africa with great alarm. It appeared that Rommel could not be stopped and the tiny population of Eretz Yisrael would be threatened with annihilation.

Rommel was finally defeated at El Alamein. The British and American forces destroyed the Afrika Korps and prepared to invade Sicily and Italy.

Chaim Weizmann's request to the British government to allow the formation of a Jewish Brigade from Eretz Yisrael to fight the Nazis was finally accepted after years of political wrangling. The British were fearful of training Jews to fight, these same Jews would one day fight for an independent Jewish state against the best interests (pro-Arab) of the United Kingdom. But, in spite of it all, the Jewish Brigade was born.

Quickly, they were sent to the Italian front for the last great allied push against the Nazis. Past the beaches of Salerno and Anzio, through the formidable Siegfried Line and up to the Senio River in northern Italy.

It was Pesach 1945. Word got around that there were Jews from Palestine, with the Magen David badge on their uniforms, and they were holding a seder. Dozens of Jewish refugees made their way to the Army base, the first trickle of victims from the Shoah, emaciated and terrorized children among them.

Each soldier took a child on his shoulders. They sang and danced into the night, retelling the ancient story of the Exodus and the liberation of the Jewish people.

Just days later, the Jewish Brigade took up positions at the Senio River, and destroyed the opposing German forces. For the first time in 2,000 years, since General Bar Kochba faced the Romans in ancient Israel, a Jewish army under a Jewish General (Brigadier Benjamin) fought for the freedom of the Jewish people, and, indeed, the entire free world.

ENOUGH WITH THE HAMANTASHEN! PASS THE MATZA

It's been three weeks or so since Purim and I can't seem to make a dent in the hamantashen. Don't get me wrong; these three-pointed "ears of Haman" (dough cakes filled with prune or sesame or what have you) are the best you can get. Every year, we put our order in with the ladies of the Skylake Synagogue, who by now are probably selling these baked goods on the Internet from Patagonia to Denali (Alaska for the Sierra Club-challenged). Everyone knows that for the greatest haman-tashen, you order from the Skylake Synagogue.

But they are so good that we over-order, and we eat them until they are coming out of our ears. Like turkey after Thanksgiving.

Actually, its quite correct to eat them until just before Passover. Starting four weeks before Purim, according to Jewish custom, we are not to eat matza. At the Seder, we are to taste matza "for the first time;" it should be novel and unusual in our mouths, provoking a sensory reaction that stimulates our memory cells to recall the great events of the Exodus from Egypt. Of course, hamantashen, made of dough, are considered "chometz," the bread foods that we do not eat for the duration of Passover in favor of matza, the "unleavened bread."

Jews lead a rather complicated religious life, as you can see. The changing months of the calendar year bring new and exciting visual and sensual delights; new reminders of who we are and where we come from. The year's rituals are a veritable Jewish history book leaping on to our tables and jogging our memories. Just when things begin to become stale, we are presented with new sensory sensations. Just when we can't take another turn of the grogger noise, the sound of the Four Questions permeates the house.

And so it was that I was rescued from those ubiquitous hamantashen. I don't want to see another one until next Purim. I promise to put my order in with those great bakers at the Skylake Sisterhood. But for now, just give me a piece of matza, I can't wait for Seder.

ROSH HASHANA 5760/2000

By now you have made your plans to celebrate New Year's Eve 2000. This frantic and frenetic preparation for the millenium is actually misdirected and misplaced. The millenium doesn't begin until the year 2001, when the last millenium comes to an official end, but who's paying attention to such trivialities?

Furthermore, the millenial celebration is really directed at the Christian world, who is celebrating the two thousandth birthday of Jesus, hence the usage of B.C. and A.D. when writing dates. "Before Christ" and "Anno Domini" (year of our Lord) are obviously foreign to non-Christians, hence the designations B.C.E., "before the common era" and C.E., "common era" on all Jewish documents as well as the New Year celebration on September 11, 1999, which coincides with the first of the Hebrew month of Tishrey and begins the year 5760. According to the Bible, it has been 5760 years since the creation of the world as we know it.

The Muslims have their own way of tracking the years, reckoning from the Hegira of Mohammed from Mecca to Medina. And, of course, the Eastern religious all have their own calendars, as do the Mayans, Incas, Navahos, Hopi, and every other religion and culture on earth. So relatively speaking, the year 2000 is not such a big deal after all when you consider it in the larger cultural context.

Most interesting is the coincidence of New Year's Eve with Friday night this year. For the first time in many years Jewish people will have to reckon with the fact that the holy Sabbath bumps up against their annual celebration of the secular New Year. Compounding the quandary is the matter of Jesus' bris which is the Christian basis of the celebration of New Year on January 1 (he was born on December 25, so count to the 8th day), added to the already heavy Christian baggage that comes with the millennial celebration.

It will be interesting to see what Jewish people elect to do on Friday evening, December 31, before midnight when they realize the interesting dilemma that is facing them. Priorities, values, religion, life in a secular society are just a few issues that will be grappled with. What we decide to do will say a great deal about who we are.

SUNDAY, ONE WEEK BEFORE ROSH HASHANA

My antique car stalls at Ives Dairy Road and Highland. It won't start; I push it across the intersection and call AAA.

Some ten to twelve people stop: one North Miami Beach policeman, a state trooper, Donna and her husband make a U-turn, Phyllis and Abe Bochman, nine whites and three blacks. They offer to get me gasoline, or let me use their cellular phone or give me a lift. The North Miami Beach cop gives me flares and shows me how to use them. A big Harley motorcycle stops. He has a black T-shirt reading "Bad Boys, Bad Girls." He has a long mustache and black boots, a gut spills over his belt. She has short-shorts, a cropped top, and a tattoo on her shoulder. I'm ready to give him the keys, but he only wants to help. He knows these cars. He gets out his tools and checks. Finally, he pronounces, it's the battery, and away he goes.

Are people basically good or bad, kind hearted or cold hearted? Sure, some people stopped because they know me. But most didn't know me. They are the good samaritans.

That same day in New York, a woman fainted in the heat and fell to the sidewalk. Dozens of people rushed up to help her.

One of them, a woman, rushed up and, in the commotion, stole her diamond wedding ring.

While I waited, one driver yelled, "Get that piece of junk off the road." One cursed the AAA driver for blocking the road.

I am so impressed by all the people who care, not the few who are meanspirited. On this Rosh Hashana, I am encouraged and inspired once again by the natural goodness of people. I have little doubt that the Good Lord feels the same, He will forgive our few misfits and take notice of all His good people. If strangers can still come to aid a fellow human being in distress, then there is certainly hope for the human race.

KOL NIDRE: HAVE A HEART

At the beginning of the summer, I was invited to observe an open-heart operation. I wasn't sure if I should accept. I get a bit queasy at a bris.

But I steeled myself to go. And, for five hours, I stood at the shoulder of a brilliant surgeon, watching in awe. The details I won't share with you. You really don't want to know. Suffice to say that I was witness to the miraculous. A surgeon, with God's help and strength, literally rescuing a man from certain death.

I will never forget the doctor's words as the procedure began: Rabbi, you pray for him, and I will operate on him, and with God's help he will be well.

And miraculously, several weeks later, that man was walking around, well on the way to recovery.

At one point in the operation, the surgeon held that man's heart in his hands. Literally. He turned it over, examined it, calculated how best to attach the new vessels.

I found myself looking very carefully at that heart. Here was a man's heart. What kind of heart was it? Did he have a good heart, a kind heart, a generous heart? I was tempted to ask the doctor. But he could only tell me about heart muscles, and heart tissue, and heart valves. Even under powerful magnifying glasses, we couldn't tell anything.

Even the arteriogram we saw before the operation didn't tell me anything. Oh, I could see where the artery was blocked, I could see where the surgeon was going to section in a new piece; I could well understand how a heart that was almost ready to stop would be rejuvenated. But I still couldn't tell what kind of a heart this man had.

About six weeks later, I had a surprise visitor. Our heart patient. I say "our" with all due respect to the brilliant surgeon who is sitting here this evening, because one way or another, I was part of the team, and, in some small way, I was part of the success.

In walked our heart patient. He sat down and thanked me for all that I had done. And then he put out his hand. In it was a fine contribution to the synagogue. It was his way of giving thanks for the miracle of his new life.

And in that one moment, I knew everything about his heart. At that moment, I knew more than I could ever learn from his arteriogram, or the binocular magnifying glasses, or careful observation of that naked and exposed mass of muscles and valves called a heart. Because the only way to really know a man's heart is by his hand. The hand that reaches into his pocket to give. The hand that fulfills the mitzvah of zedaka.

So my friends, once a year I ask you about your heart. Of course, I mean it from a cardiac point of view. That your heart should be strong and powerful and healthy. And that it should propel you for many years. But I also mean it from a spiritual point of view. That your heart should be kind and generous and good. And the only way I will know the answer is through your hand. The hand that will reach out to our synagogue, which is the heart of our people.

CHANUKA EVE ON DECEMBER 23

This year, our celebration of Chanuka will coincide with the Christian holidays. This coincidence of the calendar will cause some confusion in the Jewish community, especially in those circles where Chanuka is explained as the "Jewish Christmas."

Surely, we respect all religions. But we must emphasize the practice and meaning of our traditions.

I suggest we approach the season with positive Jewish reinforcement. By that, I mean we teach our children and grandchildren about the history of Chanuka, and the manner in which we recreate that history through prayers and blessings and the lighting of the menorah.

Every Jewish home should have an eight branch menorah (a ninth branch for the shamash) and a box of candles to last for the eight days of the holiday. Each member of the household should participate in the candle lighting ceremony each evening at dark, either by lighting one candle on the "house menorah," or, better yet, lighting his own menorah and reciting the blessings.

I know that it is very difficult to compete for the attention and interest of our children when the streets and shops and public schools are filled with reminders that we live in a Christian society, albeit an open-minded and understanding one, underscored by the Constitution's insistence on the separation of church and state and the equality under the law of all religions. We live in the finest country in the world; and at the end of the twentieth century, we can feel at ease and unafraid. No one is coming to put us behind barbed wire or to hang us from the nearest tree.

But if American society doesn't threaten us physically, it challenges us intellectually and spiritually. Free enterprise extends through the marketplace to people's minds. The bright lights and the seductive messages bombard us day and night and our youngsters are particularly vulnerable. Everything depends on how parents present and participate in our own Jewish traditions. So you decided to give out eight presents, one a night. But make sure that each night sees an increase in your Jewish repertoire. That may be the best present of all.

ROSH HASHANA: ENDING AND BEGINNING

I don't know if Bill Clinton will rank as one of the great Presidents, but in my eyes he and his wife, Hillary, rank as two of the best White House parents. Chelsea was allowed to grow up as a normal teenager, away from the prying eyes of the media (or as near normal as being the President's daughter, living at the most prestigious address in America, traveling surrounded by an army of body guards, and never worrying about over-charging her credit cards allows.) And when I saw the pictures of Bill and Hillary loading up the family car (actually, the fami-ly helicopter and the family Air Force One jet) and accompany-ing Chelsea out to the Stanford University campus, I thought back to the days my own children went off to college and began the transition to adulthood. Surely, we can all remember that moment as we let go of our little birds and they began to fly. We were excited and proud and apprehensive all at once.

King Solomon writes that for everything in the world, there is a time. A time to laugh and a time to cry, a time to keep and a time to cast off. For 18 years, our children share everyday with us. Everything they do is part of what we do. We are never sure where they end and we begin. Ideally, the family is a con-tinuum; a unit that moves and breathes and thinks together, resulting in a synergistic release of creative energy. And then one member of the unit breaks away and we are left to make up the energy loss by e-mail and AT&T; but it's never quite the same. The air is too quiet, the bathroom is too clean, the tele-phone bills are too low, and there is no one else to take out the trash!

For everything, there is a season, and every season must come to an end. But with every ending there comes a new begin-ning. Rosh Hashana ends the old year, but it also heralds the beginning of a new year, a time when everything is possible.

A clichéd advertisement proclaims "today is the first day of the rest of your life." Clichéd, yes, but true nonetheless. Imagine: to be a freshman on your first day of classes, with the entire world of knowledge stretched out at your feet. I am so excited for Chelsea and her parents, as I was excited when my own children took their places in the university classroom. Everything is possible.

Endings are sad, but beginnings are exciting and Rosh Hashana contains a bit of both. Who knows what the new year will bring? Who knows what nice surprises God has in store for us?

What a nice idea to contemplate as we daydream during the closing hour of the service.

THE SEFER TORAH

We have been repairing and inspecting our Torah scrolls, an expensive proposition. The Days of Awe are a time for return. The question is: to what? For an answer I offer an example given to us by the Rebbe of Strelisk, Reb Uri the Seraph. This is the way it unfolded:

Reb Uri once called a meeting of all of his hasidim during the days of S'lichot immediately prior to Rosh Hashana. Reb Uri began:

"Everyone knows that a Jew is supposed to write a Sefer Torah in the course of his lifetime. So the congregation commissions a sofer. He leaves the last letters open; just outlined. The letters are sold to each congregant and he has the opportunity to take the quill and write the letter. In this way, each person shares in the mitzvah. Each letter is accompanied by a donation and thus the Torah is paid for by the entire congregation. Since that is not always possible, a Jew is told to be like a Sefer Torah. What does it mean to be like a Sefer Torah?

"By tradition, a Sefer Torah has about 600,000 letters, representing the Household of Israel. If one of those letters is missing, the whole Torah is 'pasul,' invalid. The entire Torah is pasul, too, if one letter is touching another letter."

What this means is that every Jew is needed. Every Jew must return to the community. All of us together must search and find our Heavenly Parent, to reach out to God and be touched. It means that every Jew must stand with us. Every Jew is needed. We wait for every Jew to return. However, we are also individuals. Each of us has to stand on our own two feet. We can't lean on someone else. We can't ride on someone else's coattails. We have to be personally responsible for our actions.

SHOFAR

When I look out at this moment and see this vast crowd that is assembled here, I am deeply moved. Some Rabbis, for some reason, I don't know why, feel the need to chastise on this holy day. They use this time to berate their people and tell them their shortcomings. They complain to them that they have not come all during the year.

I don't do that. I feel the need not to chastise and not to berate, but to say to you: Welcome home, and thank you for coming!

The feelings in my heart at this moment are best expressed by a story that I once heard about Golda Meir. When she came to Russia as the Israeli Ambassador in 1948, no one knew how the Jews would react. There had been no legal Jewish education in Russia since 1917—perhaps they were gone as Jews. But when the word got out that she was coming to services on Rosh Hashana, more than a hundred thousand Jews came out to greet her. They lined up in front of the synagogue in order to see her, to touch her, to wave to her, to welcome her. They blew the Shofar to assemble.

She wrote in her autobiography afterwards that she was so moved that she could hardly speak. All she could say as she made her way through the crowd was one sentence: Thank you. Thank you, thank you, thank you for coming, thank you for being here, thank you for remaining Jews.

I say that to you today, too. Thank you for remaining Jews. It is not nearly as difficult, nearly as dangerous to remain a Jew here as it is in Russia, but there are plenty of temptations to take you away, plenty of other places you could be tonight, plenty of other gods you could be with tonight. Thank you for being here, thank you for being Jews.

And one thing more I say to you: Stay, don't disappear. Stay with us in all the year that now begins. Thank you for being here, thank you for being Jews!

B. THE SEASON
Getting Through the Year
6. World Affairs

THE PARTISANS

The European Jews during the Holocaust years were helpless victims under a death sentence. They were unable and unwilling to fight. They went to the gas chambers as lambs to the slaughter.

It is a lie. And once and for all we must destroy this lie. We do it with the truth about the Jewish resistance fighters. With the dedication of the Partisan Memorial, we honor the "gibborim," the fighting heroes of our people, who fought the Nazis with rifles and machine guns, grenades and bullets, rocks and sticks, bare hands, teeth, and sheer guts.

There were hundreds of Jewish partisan groups, and thousands of fighters. In every ghetto, in every region. With Tito in the mountains of Yugoslavia, with the Maquis in France, the ZOB, Zydovska Organizichia Boyova in Warsaw, led by Mordecai Anilevitch. The FPO, Farenikte Partisaner Organizatzye, in Vilna led by Abba Kovner, the Nau'mov brigade in Byelorussia and Ukraine, and the Bielski Brigade in western Byelorussia in the Naliboka forest. And sitting in our congregation are some of these very fighters.

Tuvia Bielski would greet his newest volunteers, people who barely escaped from the Lida ghetto with these words: "I don't promise you anything. We may all be killed while we try to live . . . . Life is difficult, we are in danger all the time, but if we die, we die like human beings."

And so it was. In the Warsaw ghetto, in the Vilna ghetto, in the Kovno ghetto, in a thousand other ghettos in Europe. Even in the concentration camps. Faced with certain death, the Jews resisted to the end:

October 7, 1944, Birkenau. The Jewish Sonderkommando, who were forced to help exterminate their own brothers and sisters, revolted. They set fire to the crematorium and attempted to blow it up. They killed the SS guards, cut through the barbed wire, and escaped. Most died in the attempt. But they died like men. I have a piece of German steel reinforcing rod. I took it out of crematorium V. Because whenever I hold it in my hand, I am reminded of Jewish bravery in the face of imminent death.

The Kovna Jews, all 30,000 of them, were taken out of the Slobotka Ghetto and murdered in the Ninth Fort. Kovna was one of the great Jewish cities. Rabbi Yitzchak Elchanan Spector was the Chief Rabbi before the turn of the century. My own yeshiva was named for him at Yeshiva University in New York. The Slobodka Yeshiva was one of the most progressive and famous yeshivas in Europe.

As soon as the Russians retreated and even before the Nazis came in, the Lithuanian fascists began killing the Jews. June 25, 1940, 2000 Kovna Jews were murdered in a pogrom by their neighbors. The Chief Rabbi Zalman Osovski was murdered as he studied the Gemara at home. His blood covered the page. A dying Jew, by the name of Akiva Pukerto, scrawled with his own blood on a wall, "Yidden Nekoma." And in the months and years that followed, Jewish people rose up to avenge their brothers and sisters.

In the Ninth Fort, the Jews knew that they were about to be murdered. By the dozens they would be stood up against the walls of the fort and machine gunned. The resistance began. Sixty-four prisoners planned an escape. Pinia Krakonovskis made primitive drills. They searched the dead bodies they were in charge of burying. They found pocket knives and used them to make drills. And one night, they cut through the bars and escaped. I heard the story in Kovna from one of the survivors. Most were shot, but they died like men.

And we honor them this evening. We dedicate this Partisan Wall to the memory of the Gibborim, who fought with a gun, and often died with the gun; who heard the cry "Yidden Nekoma";

and who avenged the Jews of Europe; and who took their place with Shaul and Yonatan and the gibborim of our history. As our Partisans monument reads:

How the mighty have fallen in the great war.

May God bless them and remember them: those who are with us this evening and those who lie under the rubble of Warsaw and the fields of Ponar. Yehi zichrom baruch.

OUR POLITICAL SON

When the biblical Patriarch Jacob gathered his sons for a few final words, it was a time of reckoning for the family. He registered his displeasure at his eldest sons' failures but he was wise enough to direct his anger at their shortcomings and not at them personally. No matter the embarrassment that Reuven caused him, Reuven was still his son. No matter what danger Shimon and Levi put him in, they were still his sons. Jacob never curses his sons, only their anger or their foolishness.

We all have high hopes for our sons, but no matter what a son does, he remains our son. You can curse his weakness or stubbornness, but he still remains your son. You can't disown him, you can't give him away. You have to accept him for what he is, help him and work with him for the better.

For our national family, it is now the time of reckoning. The Senate debates a trial for impeachment and possible removal of the President from office. All his fine accomplishments notwithstanding, what William Jefferson Clinton did was shameful, and about this most of us agree. He has been shamed in the eyes of the whole country and perhaps the entire world for the rest of his life. He may well have lost his exalted place in history. People will read his name and laugh, or cry as the case may be.

But now we must be concerned not so much with the man Bill Clinton but with President Clinton. We cannot shame or diminish the presidency; we cannot disown him. His is our political son duly elected by the will of the people and the legal constitutional process. And it may not be set aside because he acted immorally in his private life. Not even because he embarrassed every U.S. citizen.

In 1868, President Andrew Johnson was impeached by a partisan Congress. They were out to punish the South for the Civil War and President Johnson refused. He wished to bring the country together in accordance with the directive of President Lincoln. The vote in the Senate lost by one vote: Edmund G. Ross. With that one vote, he saved the Presidency, but destroyed his own political career. Years later he wrote:

"In a large sense the independence of the executive office as a coordinate branch of the government was on trial . . . . If the President must step down, a disgraced man and a political outcast upon insufficient proofs and from partisan considerations, the office of the President would be degraded . . ."

America faced the danger of "partisan rule and intolerance which so often characterizes the sway of great majorities and makes them dangerous."

The office of the President may not be degraded or demeaned, and a trial by the Senate on charges of immorality and lying to hide his immoral actions is not what high crimes and misdemeanors are all about. (And if it is, then "half" of the Senate and the Congress would have to go home.) This trial is about partisan politics and it must not happen. We must save the presidency if not the President.

William Clinton is the prodigal son, but whether we like it or not, he is our son, our political son. We elected him to serve out his term. He let us down, but we cannot let down the presidency.

As with Simon and Levi, we may curse his foolishness, and his "hubris," and his catch-me-if-you-can attitude, and his abuse of personal power. But we cannot curse him as president. We cannot disown the President; he is our president; we elected him. With all his glaring flaws, he should remain in office until we elect a new President.

STATE OF THE COUNTY 1999

Mayor Alex Penelas delivered his third annual State of the County Address at the Joesph Caleb Center Auditorium in Miami. For those of us "North Dadeans" who are not familiar with the address, the Caleb Center is in Liberty City. The selection of this site speaks as eloquently as the Mayor's words about his concerns and plans for the future. I was honored to offer the benediction prayer, and I was honored to be present at a significant moment in Miami's history.

In all my years in Miami, I never took the 62nd Street exit off I-95 and drove west. The people standing in tight groups on the street corners and sitting in old sofas on the sidewalk underscored the poor economic status of the neighborhood. But the possibilities for Liberty City were dramatically presented by an ensemble of gospel singers who opened the program. They sang with heart and soul, with unlimited energy, acting out every word and breathing electricity with every note. Multiplied by thousands, and tens of thousands, Liberty City, with visionary leadership and dedicated citizens could be on the verge of a renaissance, just as we turn the corner into a new millenium.

Mayor Penelas appears to be the leader who will take charge. In his remarks, he declares 1999 to be the year of the child. It is apparent that if we are to break out of the cycle of poverty, illiteracy, hopelessness, and tragedy, we must start with the new generation. A concerted effort will be made, supported by millions of dollars of the federal and state governments, to move the population of Liberty City up the economic ladder toward the realization of the American Dream. When half of the children live in poverty, and the basic necessities of life are missing all highfalutin programs are meaningless. We begin by filling stomachs and then we progress to filling minds. And eventually, the citizens of Liberty City will regain their self-confidence and self-esteem as they join the job market and compete successfully for a "piece of the pie."

I heard some fine leaders share with the audience their hopes and dreams for Liberty City: Congressman Carrie Meek,

Representative James Bush, and Commissioner Dr. Barbara Carey to name just a few. People are a community's greatest resource, and all it takes is the right cadre of leaders to light a fire under the people and get them moving. With the promised funding for the appropriate programs for increased day care, better schooling, more efficient job training, and just providing the essentials of proper food, clothing, and shelter, the innate dignity and diligence of the Liberty City citizens will rise to the fore. With Mayor Penelas' leadership and unwavering determination, the next time I drive across 62nd Street, I will see a neighborhood alive with positive energy and useful activity. A neighborhood taking its place as one of the economic showcases of Dade County. Perhaps Mayor Penelas will return to celebrate with the citizens from whatever position he may achieve in the upper echelons of our government.

TOWARD A JUST SOCIETY

New York can be dreary or glorious in May. We were privileged to have the best weather of the year as we sat out on the Columbia University quadrangle basking in the reflected glory of our daughter, Jordanna, as she had the degree of Master in Public Policy conferred upon her. (Bottom line: Do you have a job or don't you? And with all the tuition we have paid, why isn't our family name on one of the buildings? And I could have been retired already.)

But I digress even before I begin: The assembled faculty and graduates of Columbia University were addressed by the President, Dr. Rupp, and by the invited guest speaker, Rev. Jesse Jackson. In "black and white," they both presented essentially the same idea: America is becoming substantially wealthier but the gap between the rich and the poor is growing dramatically. They referred to this glaring disparity as a "moral gap." People who are poor tend to remain in the underclass, generation after generation, with the exception of the graduates of the university whose degree is a ticket to a better life for themselves and for their families.

America is spending inordinate amounts of money on bigger jails, more secure penal systems, drug interdiction, school police, and surveillance for (or is it, of) our citizens. "Big Brother" is watching you, protecting you and threatening your privacy all at once. In the United States, the richest country in the world, homeless people wander the streets searching in garbage cans for food. If they are lucky, they find a subway tunnel to sleep in or a packing crate to crawl into. Mentally unstable people are released from institutions to fend for themselves because the government does not deem their care a priority. Our working people can't afford to get sick because they have inadequate health care. A stay in the hospital can completely wipe out the finances of the average family. It is even too expensive to die in America.

It is apparent to all that education is one of the key elements in the equation. It allows our citizens to break the chains of poverty once and for all. It allows people to become contributing members of our society; it literally increases the tax base, thereby adding to our GNP. Of course, all is not measured in dollars and cents. A well-educated citizenry raises the level of the arts and sciences and gives real meaning to the term "civilized society."

It is time to redress the balance, to build a more equal society based on the principle of the Declaration of Independence that guarantees our citizens the right to life, liberty, and the pursuit of happiness. There is no pursuit of happiness for a seventh-grade dropout selling drugs on the corner or the Vietnam veteran sleeping under the Brooklyn Bridge pursued by the demons of the Mekong River.

It is so much cheaper to spend the dollars now for education, health insurance, and a living wage, than to spend a thousand times more, later, on police, jails, welfare, and rehabilitation systems, as we are forced to acknowledge our failures.

It may not be fashionable for sociologists who wrestle with these problems to quote the Bible, but Rabbis may certainly do so: We are commanded to try to maintain an equitable society. Whenever things become unbalanced, when the gap between the rich and poor grows exceedingly wide, the institution of the jubilee year (every fiftieth year) is instituted to redress the balance. Essentially wealth, which was measured in ancient Israel in real estate, is redistributed every 50th year. The original owners, who had to sell for whatever financial reasons, are given a chance to reclaim their property and start again. All are compensated fairly, and society becomes a "kinder and gentler place" once again.

One of the great medieval commentators on the Bible reminds us that we shouldn't wait for the fiftieth year. Whenever a brother falls on hard times, his fellows have the responsibility to help him out. Don't wait for him to collapse, prop him up now.

To illustrate: A porter struggling with a heavy load begins to collapse under his burden. One person can hold him up, but if he buckles under the load and falls to the ground, five people will have trouble getting him up.

We do not live in ancient Israel and unfortunately, the Bible rarely rules our lives. But our society is buckling at the knees. However, there is still time to come to the aid of the less fortunate and give them the opportunity to stand up straight and proud on their own two feet. If the underclass in our community collapses, it will take a superhuman effort to raise it up again.

What will it be? A great effort now, or an impossible situation in the future. If we call ourselves civilized people, then we know the answer and we know what is demanded of us.

ISLAMIC FANATICS AND FUNDAMENTALISTS

Afghanistan has long been a crossroads of trade between the Orient and Occident, and consequently of cultural exchange. Before Islam sallied forth from the east to conquer the world, the followers of Buddha had already crossed the Khyber Pass and penetrated into Kabul. The monumental statues at Bamiyan testify to the vitality of the oriental religions more than 1300 years ago in Afghanistan.

Last week, the Taliban leaders of the country, Islamic fanatics, decreed that the Buddhist statues constitute idol worship and must therefore be destroyed. Archaeologists, historians, cultural anthropologists, and responsible world leaders tried to stop this desecration of these world cultural monuments, but to no avail. A local video was sent around the world proving that the Bamiyan statues had been turned into rubble and dust, and the attempt to erase ancient history in Afghanistan was underway.

The people of Afghanistan are starving to death by the tens of thousands. The economy is in shambles, the central government does not function, and the only thing the Taliban seems interested in is measuring the length of women's veils, and executing all dissenters.

While women are abused, men are beaten for not having their beards at the appropriate length, and children freeze to death in the mountains. The western world is fairly quiet, turning away from the suffering and death. But the destruction of stone statues outraged the United Nations and provoked a huge concerted outcry. It was to no avail, but it underscores our skewed value system: stone statues yes, but human beings no. What really constitutes a cultural heritage, the people or their stones?

However, this is the nature of Islamic fundamentalism and we should sit up and take notice. Similar regimes are found throughout the Middle East and North Africa. And even when the government is a secular dictatorship, the Islamic fanatics wait in the wings to terrorize the government into submission. Islamic terrorism may be the biggest challenge to western oriented countries today. Their access to high tech weapons and their readiness to use them on any perceived enemy strikes fear in the hearts of western and pro-western governments. Nothing and no one is safe from these religious terrorists. There is nothing more dangerous than a fanatic.

The State of Israel is surrounded by secular Arab dictatorships on all sides: Syria, Lebanon, Egypt, and Jordan. Each country harbors a cadre of Islamic fundamentalists who are attempting to overthrow the regime and replace it with an Islamic state. Likewise, some engage in crossborder terrorism against the State of Israel, which deflects away from internal problems and keeps the terror cells occupied. When the Islamic fanatics become too powerful, they are quickly decimated without the slightest hesitation. They are tolerated as long as their targets are pro-western states, Israel being at the top of the list.

The Islamic targets in Afghanistan are beyond statues. They are the "infidels": any and all who disagree with their militant fundamentalist style or religious fanaticism. The Islamic targets around the world are all western oriented governments, all states that subscribe to the "corrupt" American influences, all states that support the democratic State of Israel, all non-Muslims, all "infidels." In short, consider yourself on the list.

We have been graphically forewarned; at Bamiyan, at the World Trade Center, at the U.S. Embassies in Kenya and Tanzania, in the Port of Yemen, in the U.S. Army barracks in Saudi Arabia, and in dozens of other places.

Fighting Islamic terrorism must be our number one concern in foreign policy.

FREEDOM—PASSOVER

The year is 1978 and the man's name is Yosef Mendelovich. The setting: a dank cell deep within the bowels of the Christopol prison in the Soviet Union. The date is April 12. On the Jewish calendar, it is 14 Nisan, one day before the start of Passover.

Yosef is a prisoner. He is a gaunt human shell, and he is about to light a candle. Made of hoarded bits of string, pitiful droplets of oil, and stray slivers of wax, this is a candle fashioned by Yosef's own hands. The candle is lit—the search of chametz begins.

Sometime earlier, Yosef had complained of back problems. The infirmary in hell provided him with mustard to serve as a therapeutic plaster. Unused then, this mustard would later reappear as maror—bitter herbs—at Yosef's seder table. A long-saved onion bulb in water has produced a humble bit of greenery. This would be karpas. And the wine? Raisins were left to soak in an old jelly jar, water occasionally added, and fermentation was prayed for. This was wine. The Haggadah, which Yosef transcribed into a small notebook before being imprisoned, had now been set to memory. The original was secretly passed on to another "dangerous" enemy of the State: Anatoly Sharansky.

Is Yosef free? He cannot do whatever he wants. He has been denied even the liberty to know when the sun shines and the stars twinkle. For Yosef, the world of free men doesn't even begin to exist.

Yet, Josef, perhaps, is more free even than his captors. Clearly self-aware, he knows exactly who he is, what he wants, and is prepared to pay any price to have it. Today, he walks the streets of Israel, studies Torah, and buys box after box of matza to serve at his Seder. He is a free man now, just as he was even behind those lifeless prison walls.

Self-awareness means that we are able to stand outside of ourselves; to look within and assess our goals, values, priorities, direction, and truthfulness. Unaware of these things, we remain mired in a dense fog of confusion and doubt. Can we ever be fully self-aware? Probably not. But aware enough to set ourselves free? Yes, and this is one of life's most pivotal challenges. Achievement and maintenance of freedom is available only though the ongoing struggle for self-awareness. This process of clarification, coupled with the conviction to follow wherever it may lead, is the only way to achieve a spiritually sensitive, value-driven life of liberty. Ironically, this freedom can land you in a prison where you are the captor, while your guards are the prisoners. Just ask Yosef Mendelovich—one of the freest people who ever walked the earth.

FREEDOM

Freedom means having the ability to use your free will to grow and develop. People think they are free when really they are "slaves" to the fads and fashion of their society. Slavery is nonthinking action, rote behavior, following the impulses and desires of the body. Our job on Pesach is to come out of slavery into freedom.

One of the freedoms to work on during Pesach is "freedom of the mouth." The sages view the mouth as the most dangerous part of the body. It is the only organ that can cause problems in both direction—what comes in (food and drink) and what goes out (speech). It is so dangerous, it is the only part of the body that has two coverings—hard teeth and soft lips. Most of us are slaves to the mouth, both in what we eat and what we speak.

On seder night we fix this. We have the mitzvah to speak about the Jewish people leaving Egypt to fix speech, and the matzah and Four Cups of wine to fix eating and drinking.

The structure of the Hebrew language hints at the goal of "freedom of the mouth." Pesach can be divided into two words: Peh Sach, which means "the mouth speaks"—We are commanded to tell the story of the Exodus the whole night. The Hebrew word, Paroh, (Pharaoh, the persecutor of the Jewish people in the Pesach story) can be divided into two words: Peh Rah, a "bad mouth." Our affliction of the slavery in Egypt was characterized as Perach, (difficult work) which can be read as two words: Peh Rach, "a loose mouth."

May we all merit on this Pesach to get free from the "bad mouth," and to overcome the "loose mouth" where too much of the wrong food and drink come in and too many inappropriate words slip out. Have a wonderful holiday!

KOSOVO AND THE HOLOCAUST

The long lines of refugees streaming out of Kosovo are all too familiar. With their tattered suitcases and terrified faces, we could be looking at Bosnia just a few years ago, or Nazi Germany five decades ago. As we watch the horror on our television screens, we cannot help but commiserate. Our hearts are touched and we empathize with the utter despair of these poor people who will probably never go home. They will spend a generation acclimating to a new country and a new culture. They will have to start all over again. Everything they worked for and built is gone to dust and ashes. Only vague memories will remain of smiling family members, neat little houses and prospering businesses. An album of fading photographs will be trotted out from time to time to remind the refugees of the life that once was, and the cruel turn of events that led to the collapse of their world. And maybe in the coming years they will be allowed back to visit the remains of those who were murdered and dumped into vast unmarked graves in the process of "ethnic cleansing" (a euphemism that seeks to disguise the process of beating, rape, eviction, and killing).

It has become journalistically fashionable to equate the horror in Kosovo with the Holocaust. Whatever is going on in Yugoslavia, and it is complicated beyond the ken of most of us, it is not the Holocaust. It is inhuman and unconscionable, and we are revolted and alarmed by it all, but it is not the Holocaust. The Holocaust was an attempt, that almost succeeded, to murder every living Jew in Europe. Yes, the Germans wished to make Europe "Judenrein" and they wished to steal all Jewish property and belongings. But mainly they wanted to reduce the entire Jewish population to burnt ashes. Six million missing Jews testify to the fact that the German murder machine was highly efficient.

This is not what is happening in Yugoslavia, as bad as it is. Yet, we are morally responsible to find a way to help, in spite of the record of the Yugoslavians during the Nazi era.

During World War II, the entire Jewish community of Macedonia, 7,147 people, was deported to the Treblinka death camp; not one returned. When the Germans invaded Kosovo in September 1943 and took over Pristina, the locals turned in their Jewish neighbors. The town's 300 Jews were taken to Bergen-Belsen. The Croats were quick to join the Nazis and they formed the fascist Ustashi, unlike the Serbs who, according to the Yugoslav Jews, did not join the Nazi persecutions. In all, 65,000 of Yugoslavia's 80,000 Jews were murdered. Yet, 200 Jews in Albania together with refugees from Serbia were hidden until liberation day (*Jerusalem Report*, April 26).

In those dark days, no one cared about the Jews, with a few bright exceptions. At least today, the world cares enough to try to do something, however questionably effective it might be, as evidenced by NATO's presence in the skies over Belgrade. Why we have selected the Milosovic Serbians be the recipients of our stealth-fighter-driven moral outrage and not the Hutu and

Tutzi slaughtering each other in Rwanda, or the Iraquis gassing the Kurds, or the Russians executing the Chechnyans, or a host of other possibilities is beyond my foreign policy comprehension. Maybe it has to do with the flying time between Aviano and Belgrade, or the need to exercise the Stealth Bomber now and again.

Unfortunately, no matter what happens, Yugoslavia will not escape from its history: Serbians will hate Kosovars, Bosnians will hate Croats, and Muslims will hate Eastern Orthodox. They will continue to murder each other at every opportunity, as they have done for hundreds of years, until populations will be exchanged, unwanted ethnic "foreign" groups "cleansed," and the borders redrawn. Only Tito, by force of his personality and his army, could hold that disparate hodgepodge of competing national interests together. He is long gone, and no amount of outside pressure and intimidation can accomplish the goal of uniting a country that doesn't want to be united, to force a people who hate each other to live in peace.

FIFTIETH ANNIVERSARY OF ANNE FRANK

You listen to Mep Gies, the 86-year-old woman who saved Anne Frank's diary and you marvel at the still echoing boldness of what she says were just small deeds. But 50 years ago, when nothing seemed possible, small deeds loomed powerfully heroic. All she did was seize the day and make it possible for the whole world to better remember its innocent dead. Carpe diem. Memento mori.

The stakes were high—death, arrest, the threat of torture—and she had only minutes in which to act, to scoop up scattered pages and save them from oblivion, remarkable pages of life-affirming testimony written in a secret attic where the dark-eyed Jewish girl hid from those who ultimately found her and killed her.

"I am not a hero," said Mrs. Gies. It is impolite to disagree, so the reporter just listened. "I just did what any decent person would have done." She is visiting from Amsterdam, and just before she joined Broadway actors in a reading from a new edition of the diary, sponsored by Steve Tannen's Free Theater Project, Mrs. Gies once again recalled what had happened on August 4, 1944, the day the Gestapo took Anne, her father, mother, and sister, and three family friends who had been with the Franks in hiding. "Every day I think about that day," she said.

When the war started, Mrs. Gies, recently married, was working as a secretary for Otto Frank in his food chemicals business. She was, she said, an ordinary woman. She had been born in Austria but was sent to Holland by her family in the hope that the Dutch climate would help strengthen her weak lungs. She remembered how, as a child, Anne would play on the office machines.

When the Franks and their friends went into hiding, she became one of the five people who knew they were in the secret apartment.

"One of my duties was to bring meat," she said. "I would go upstairs once a day, taking great care so no one would see. One time I went to the apartment and saw Anne writing. I knew it was a diary. She was arguing with her mother and she said she was going to write everything down. She smiled at me and said, "I am going to write about you, too."

For more than two years, Anne would write in tense confinement. Then on that August day, Mrs. Gies remembered a Dutch man in civilian dress came into the office and pointed a revolver at her face, ordering her to sit down. She could see and hear men in Gestapo uniform rush upstairs. The Jews were taken down and driven off. Then the leader of the Gestapo unit began interrogating the office workers, one by one. She recognized his accent to be Viennese. "I was the last one questioned. I said to him, 'We are both from the same city.' And he answered angrily, 'Yes, but you are hiding Jews, which can bring a great punishment.' Still, something must have touched him, because he told me I could stay and live in the office. But he also said he would come back and if he saw that I went anywhere else, he would take my husband away. I understood he meant I should not go upstairs to the hiding place."

Despite the threat, despite the fears, she went. "I saw the pages all over the floor. I picked them up. There were other things lying there, but I just gathered up the pages. Then from a hook in the bathroom I took Anne's cape. She wore it when she brushed in the morning so hairs would not fall on her blouse. I don't know why I took it. I still have it."

Almost as remarkable as Mrs. Gies's impulse to salvage the dairy was her decision not to burn it. "I can't fully explain it. But I can say that I never read the dairy then because I realized that if I would actually see the names she wrote, then yes, of course, I would burn everything."

Instead, she put the pages in an open drawer because "a locked place would call attention if we were inspected." When the war ended, she left the diary in the drawer, not even mentioning it to Mr. Frank when he returned from Auschwitz. Not until Anne's death in Bergen-Belsen had been documented by surviving inmates did Mrs. Gies tell Mr. Frank about the diary and give it to him. "You see, I was hoping she would still come back and that I would be able to give it to her. I wanted to see her smile at me."

On the fiftieth anniversary of Anne Frank's death, children and actors in New York read from a newly released diary that includes entries edited out by Anne Frank's father. Ceremonies were held at the Fifth Avenue First Presbyterian Church.

Today people are no longer sure if Anne Frank was Jewish. She is memorialized in a church. In another 50 years people will think Anne Frank stands for Christian suffering in the Holocaust. In 100 years, the Jewish component of the Shoah, the main component, will all but disappear—unless we continue to remind the world of the truth.

COLUMBINE HIGH SCHOOL

It has been about a month since the tragic shootings in Colorado. The shootings have shaken the people of America to our very soul. Why? We intuitively know that our children are our future and the future of humanity. Parents like to think that they are instilling good values in their children. When our children start blowing away their schoolmates with semi-automatic weapons, it makes us question the values and the role models we and our society are giving our children.

Judaism teaches that there is a lesson to be learned from whatever occurs in life. So what should our response be to Colorado? Is it really metal detectors that will solve the problem?

Perhaps we should ask ourselves why 50 years ago the top problems in America's public schools were talking out of turn, chewing gum, making noise, running in the halls, cutting in line, dress code infractions, and littering—and today the problems are drug and alcohol abuse, pregnancy, suicide, robbery, rape, and assault. Perhaps we should consider the overall effect of a society that teaches objectification of woman (via pornography), that teaches disloyalty (via adultery), that teaches lack of commitment (via divorce), that teaches rights over responsibility (via lawsuits), and that teaches the blind pursuit of every lustful whim (via the unregulated proliferation of violent video games, funereal rock music, comicbook fantasies, and apocalyptic films).

The solution is not armed guards at schools, weapons sweeps, or a ban against wearing long black coats (as Denver school authorities have imposed). Rather, it is getting adults to set examples for their children. The Hebrew word for parent comes from the root "teacher." And that is what we are, whether we like it or not.

So what point does it all boil down to? What one shift can society make to turn this ship around. At the risk of sounding like a fundamentalist preacher, I believe it's basically a spiritual issue. I spoke recently with a foremost forensic psychiatrist, specializing in children who commit multiple murders. This doctor examined the eight multiple murders committed by U.S. schoolchildren in the last three years. And he told me that the common denominator amongst these children is that they have no connection with God.

Newsweek reports that the Denver killers asked two female hostages a question: Do you believe in God? When they said yes, the gunmen shot them at point-blank range.

The Sages, too, teach that belief in God is the primary deterrent to murder. How so? The Ten Commandments are divided into two tablets. The first tablet (commandments 1–5) speaks about out relationship with God. The second tablet (commandments 6–10) speaks about out relationship with our fellow man. Furthermore, the two tablets are parallel: the first commandment—"Believe in God"—corresponds to the sixth commandment "Don't murder."

What's the connection? Every human being is created with a holy, divine soul. We are not meaningless hunks of meat hurtling on a rock through space and time. We may be uncomfortable with the primacy of man—because of the responsibility that entails. But the alternative is that by teaching our children that they are no better than animals, they will treat one another like animals.

But it goes deeper than this. The recognition that God encompasses everything teaches that in the spiritual dimension there are no conventional boundaries between entities. We're all one unit. When we appreciate this, then hurting the other guy—"paying him back"—is as ridiculous as hurting yourself. If you're slicing a carrot and accidentally cut your finger, do you take the knife and cut your other hand in revenge? Of course not. Why? Because your other hand is part of you, too.

Love of God is the most primary value to teach our children. Open a discussion of "Who is God" and how to build a relationship. Try family prayer at mealtime. Take a walk through nature and appreciate the genius of the Creator. Because when we love God, we love His children—created in the image of God.

Of course, love of God is erroneous if it doesn't translate into care for others. Belief in God does not give one the right to commit heinous crimes—like shooting abortion doctors, or burning infidels at the stake. True love of God brings greater humility, not indignant self-righteousness.

To teach kids to care for others, they need to experience the joy of giving. The Torah says that "the external awakens the internal." This means that even if you find it difficult to love others, you can still do actions that demonstrate love—with the understanding that this will ultimately affect your insides.

Here are a few practical suggestions: Volunteer to serve meals at a homeless shelter. Make an effort to spare others financial loss. Visit some patients at the local hospital. Don't embarrass anyone, especially in public. Don't gossip about others. Invite your friends to a Shabbat dinner. Show respect to the elderly. Find a poor person in your community and undertake to assist him.

Children are only a reflection of the adult world in which they live. What happened in Colorado should serve as a warning to each of us about the effect that society is having on our children. May we use this tragedy to strengthen ourselves and our children in the path of Torah, sincerely keeping its commandments and thereby setting shining examples for the next generation.

TRAGEDY IN AVENTURA

Dr. Bradley Silverman was murdered by a disgruntled patient and the entire City of Aventura was horrified, shocked, and frightened. A young man who dedicated his life to saving other people's lives had his own life brutally cut short. Some 2,000 people crowded into the Aventura-Turnberry Jewish Center–Beth Jacob Synagogue to join in their expression of sympathy with Dr. Ellen Lebow-Silverman and her family. Each of us felt that the bullets that hit Bradley were also aimed at us, and we looked to each other for support and encouragement.

We came to live in Aventura for its vaunted "quality of life," and suddenly the problems of the "outside world" graphically intruded. Our community was undergoing a trial by fire and we hoped to pass through the furnace unscathed, with our feelings of security and well being intact. And so it was that the citizens quietly filed into the synagogue and took their seats to give the last honors and respect to Dr. Bradley. Under the watchful eyes of the video news cameras assembled, we tried to draw some sense of hope in our despair; some feeling of warmth to thaw our numbed bodies and souls; some answers to the unanswerable questions.

In short order, our fine police force, under the guidance of Chief Ribel, found the murderer, and we all breathed a sigh of relief. But the questions that affect us deeply and viscerally remain.

It is time for us as citizens to demand an end to gun violence. A zero tolerance for guns could go a long way to improving the security of our society, and any law that restricts the purchase of guns is a step in the right direction. It should be apparent that Dr. Bradley would be alive today if the restrictions on gun purchases were tighter. How many more innocent people will have to die before we come to our senses?

However, we must never lose hope. We don't have the right to sink into a corner and wither away in our despair. Rather we must join together as a community of people and draw faith and energy from one another. We must take each other in hand and go forward together.

Dr. Bradley Silverman was a scientist, and as such he was certainly aware of the laws of physics: matter cannot be created or destroyed, but only transformed. Only the good Lord can create a human being, but once created, that human being had an innate energy that lives on. The body is transformed into energy. The soul lives on forever.

His colleagues and co-workers, from his surgery partners to his O.R. nurses and aides, came forward to remember Brad. Those who couldn't leave the operating room to come to the synagogue gathered a few days later at Aventura Hospital. Each one described Dr. Silverman as a genuine human being who really cared and was always ready to help and encourage. He appeared to have packed several lifetimes into his all too short years, and it remains to wonder what great things could have been accomplished given the full complement of time.

Yet, all our wonderful words cannot bring him back.

Bradley's body is gone, but his energy remains, and it is our responsibility to connect into his energy and continue his good work. What he was unable to finish, we will finish, and in doing so will honor his life beyond his years, and keep his memory alive forever.

TRUCKS, TRANSPORTATION, AND TRANSMISSIONS

I made the mistake of driving into the synagogue at school dismissal time. I was met by a column of trucks, each one larger than the first, coming directly at me; they weren't going to swerve out of the way. I pulled over to one side as they thundered by, Land Rovers, Range Rovers, Explorers, Expeditions, enough to outfit the entire NATO force going to Kosovo.

Each driver was a mommy with her little charges strapped into their seats; and every mommy drove with one hand on the wheel and the other hand on the cell phone stuck to her ear. They had just left the front door to the school; who were they already calling? What was so vitally important that a mobile phone call was necessary. The size of the truck, their ground clearance, and their engine size would allow them to climb right over me and anything in their path. That kind of power requires two hands on the wheel and total concentration. One hand on the cell phone and instructions to the housemaid to finish cleaning the guest bathroom certainly compromises the required concentration for driving one of those all terrain combat vehicles. I would rather not be anywhere near one of these "monster machines" when they come rumbling down the road with "cellular-mom" at the wheel.

Actually, it's not much better on Country Club Drive surrounded by cars with plates from New York, Michigan, and Illinois. It is apparent to us all that the traffic has increased tenfold in the last several years due to the proliferation of Mall America. One wonders what people did with their leisure time B.M. (Before Malls). A trip to the synagogue that should take twelve minutes now takes thirty minutes in February. And arriving at the morning minyan is no longer considered a mundane experience. The special prayer for escaping bodily harm (Hagomel) should be recited daily: the man who signaled left and turned right; the lady who pulled out to pass but failed to see me alongside; the silver-haired driver of the Rolls who can't seem to get his vehicle moving faster than 18 MPH in a 30 MPH zone causing every car within the cloud of his muffler exhaust to roundly curse the snowbirds from Chicago; the matron coming out of Lord and Taylor so excited with her new dress that she fails to understand that STOP refers to the brake pedal in the car, not the charge card. In fact, driving in Aventura is an adventure in survival of the automotive fittest.

But it doesn't have to be this way. A proper public transportation system would go a long way to relieve congestion and reduce the daily fender bender accidents. So many people have stopped driving at night because of failing eyesight and reduced reaction times. They attend services at the synagogue only during daylight hours, and even then, they drive reluctantly. They have to shop for food, and visit the doctor, and go to the pharmacy, and do all the necessary daily chores, and the only way to get there is by car. Without the car they are lost, their sense of independence is obliterated, and their world shrinks to the area between the pool and the condo lobby. The only alternative is a bus system that is so effective, so convenient and so comfortable that every citizen would look forward to using it.

Of course, it would help to ban the use of hand-held cell phones by drivers in moving cars as they have done in Israel and other European countries. Likewise, it would be nice to limit the new SUVs to the truck lane where they won't frighten us lesser mortals. There they can admire the eighteen wheelers and dream of even larger vehicles in which to go shopping and attend the gym and do all those things that only a big, four wheel drive, chrome bumpered, halogen lamplit truck can do.

In the meantime as they "keep on truckin'," we better stay off Country Club Drive until the last car transport rolls away headed north, and until school is out for the summer.

THE BIBLE AND THE *NEW YORK TIMES*

One of my congregants commented that when he comes to the synagogue he wants to hear what the Bible says, not what the *New York Times* or the *Miami Herald* says. After all, the news media is filled with stories of violence, sex, adultery, robbery, and a host of other disconcerting subjects upsetting to already frazzled nerves.

So I began turning the pages of the Bible to find a suitably calming and inspiring story that would set nervous minds at ease. Here is what I found: Cain murders his brother Abel in the opening pages of Genesis. Abraham makes an arrangement for his wife Sarah to live in the harem of the Egyptian Pharaoh. Sarah sends her son Ishmael out into the desert to die. Jacob steals the birthright from his brother Esau. Dina, Jacob's daughter, is raped by Shechem; her brothers murder the entire tribe in revenge. Judah carries on an incestuous relationship with his daughter-in-law, Tamar. Joseph is almost seduced by his bosses' wife. All this before the first book, Genesis, is even completed.

Obviously, the pages of the newspapers are tame compared to the Bible. But the biblical stories are not written to titillate a jaded society; rather they are supposed to teach a lesson of morality. We develop our value system based on the lives of our ancestors. We learn right from wrong in clear, unequivocal terms. Good is rewarded, evil is punished.

Furthermore, the newspaper reports everything going on in our society, just the way the Bible reported everything going on in ancient society; and the Rabbis, from time immemorial, tried to show how the biblical principles are relevant to our daily lives. No one can hide from real life; it goes on around us and is dutifully reported by the media. However, it is our job to interpret these events and demonstrate how our tradition views them, for our edification and behavior modification. If we compartmentalize the Bible, then it has no relevance to our daily lives, and if it has no relevance, then we reduce it to beautiful poetry, myth, and historical account, but not binding divine legislation. It will never regulate our lives unless we see its relevance to the 90s.

We need to understand the Bible as a sophisticated, divinely inspired legal document that must be studied over a lifetime and allowed to govern our daily lives. It takes a great deal of intellectual effort and physical commitment to incorporate those biblical ideas into our lifestyles.

I happened to be flipping the TV channels one Sunday morning looking for my favorite news program and I came across a "televangelical" preacher, in a huge glass church dressed in a beautiful blue velvet-trimmed robe addressing a large audience of a thousand people or more. He promised his congregation that he would deliver to them a message of help and happiness. He began with a quote from the Bible saying, "This is the day the Lord hath made, let us rejoice on it." Then he exclaimed "Wow"; and told his spellbound audience that he would suggest to the publishers of the Bible that they add the word "wow." This was the great message for the day to more than a thousand people who sat in the glass church and were busily contributing many dollars into the plate that was passed around. A thousand people being fed intellectual pablum masquerading as the divine word; "wow" presented to the congregation as God's exclamation. A thousand people who must have cerebrums the consistency of mush. And this passes for biblical scholarship, and this is presented as "God's word."

The *New York Times* reflects exactly what is happening in our world. The Bible offers the key to decipher those daily experiences. The Rabbi turns the key and reveals the meaning through relevant interpretation. That is what happens on any given Shabbat in the synagogue; perhaps you would like to come and listen.

A DISCUSSION WITH PRESIDENT CLINTON

My invitation was hand written from the White House and it summoned me to join a prominent group of clergymen in the Lincoln Room on November 20. We would have the opportunity to discuss with President Clinton his "Initiative on Race Relations."

According to the liaison to the Jewish community at the White House, we were selected as "respected religious leaders who command an important constituency and who could forcefully and persuasively bring the President's ideas to the American community across the country."

Represented were clergymen from a broad spectrum of religious life in America: Greek and Russian Orthodox, Sikh, Muslim, Jewish, Baptist, Protestant, Roman Catholic, and many others, including men and women, black and white.

At the outset, the President took the opportunity to make a statement on the Iraq crisis to the assembled press and media. Then the reporters and cameras were dismissed, the doors were closed, and we proceeded with the business at hand.

The President expressed his concern for an America that is becoming more diverse and more contentious as we approach the twenty-first century. Shortly, there will no longer be an ethnic majority of any kind in the United States, emphatically not the historical majority of whites of European descent. To illustrate his thesis, he noted that a public school in nearby Fairfax County has more than 100 distinct ethnic groups composing the school student body, speaking 100 languages and dialects, English being their second language. A way needs to be found to bring the disparate elements in our society closer together in an atmosphere of tolerance and mutual respect.

Furthermore, divisiveness and mistrust need not be the common ground of competing ethnic groups. The President referred to the recent slaughter between Hutu and Tutsi tribesmen in Africa. As recent as a month before the horrible outburst of violence, these same tribesmen were neighbors, breaking bread together. And in Bosnia, Radovan Karadzic has lived all his adult life in a high-rise occupied by Bosnians, Croats, Serbs, Muslims and Christians, prior to the eruption of "ethnic cleansing."

So the familiar violence that seems to be sparked when ethnic groups bump up against one another is not automatic in history and may be prevented by appropriate educational and cultural programs.

The ensuing two hour discussion brought a myriad of ideas. All of us offered our suggestions, including Vice President Gore and the several cabinet ministers who were sitting with us.

I offered my colleagues an idea from the South Florida Jewish community: Several years ago we wrestled with the Holocaust and its lack of impact on our citizenry. We wished to sensitize the greater community, to raise consciousness and to combat lies and misinformation that were being passed off as scholarship. With the leadership of the Holocaust Documentation Center in Miami, a Holocaust curriculum was written for public schools. Then, our representatives were persuaded to pass legislation mandating the teaching of the Holocaust in all Florida public schools. The program has been a resounding success, coupled with a program to bring survivors to speak to the students concerning their experiences during the Nazi era.

In the same manner, a curriculum on tolerance and understanding could be written for the public school system that would include information on various ethnic and religious populations in America as it enters the twenty-first century. Spokespeople from the various groups could form a cadre of speakers. They would then stress what we have in common as American citizens, and the beauty and vitality of a heterogeneous population. "American" would be redefined for the new century and the concept of citizenship would be rewritten to reckon with the new demographic reality.

At the conclusion of our formal meeting, the President remained to continue "one on one" conversations. I took the opportunity to bless him with our traditional beracha mandated by the Talmud upon meeting a king or prince (or president as the case may be): "Blessed are you Lord our God who has shared his glory with mortal men."

President William Jefferson Clinton is a highly intelligent and charming man who can switch from "down home" Arkansas kibbitzing to the vocabulary and seriousness of Oxford and Yale in the blink of an eye. I was honored to be chosen to join an august body of clergy to speak with the leader of the free world. I have been honored to speak with presidents and prime ministers of Israel, and I have always felt blessed to be with them. They represent almost 6 million Jews in Israel, and perhaps 12 or 13 million Jews around the world.

But President Clinton leads 260 million citizens of the greatest country in the free world—and he was seeking my advice.

I thought of my grandfather (A.H.) who fought in the Russo-Japanese War and emigrated to America in the 1920s. His grandson is invited to speak with the President of the United States. What a country of opportunity.

A DAY FOR ISRAEL IN WASHINGTON

At 5 A.M. in the Fort Lauderdale air terminal, no less than three "minyanim" were participating in the morning prayers. Wrapped in tallis and tephillin, the people gave graphic evidence that the leaders of the march on Washington in solidarity with the people of Israel and against Arab terrorism were predominately from the modern Orthodox community. One of their compatriots, Gita Galbut had personally put her money down to charter the plane that was to carry us to D.C. Once at the capital steps, it was again clear that the modern Orthodox movement had reacted and organized at warp speed compared to their counterparts in the rest of the Jewish world. That is not to say that the other segments of the North American Jewish community were not present. Almost a quarter of a million people came to Washington to "stand with Israel" in a moment of crisis. Just that the Orthodox community seemed to move more quickly and precisely, perhaps because they are unequivocally united in their support of the State of Israel, the people of Israel, and the duly elected government of Israel. The rest of the Jewish community, argues, debates, discusses, equivocates, and hesitates. It takes a long time to form a consensus of opinion and to move forward. A Merkava tank moves more quickly and appears to be more effective.

However, with just a few days notice, close to a quarter of a million people stood shoulder to shoulder on the lawn of the Capitol building on Monday, April 15, 2002. It was an unseasonably hot day and people were fainting from the heat. But none were faint of heart. They thundered their applause for Benjamin Netanyahu, Elie Wiesel, and Anatoly Sharansky, among others who eloquently and emotionally addressed the crowd. It was Sharansky who addressed us at the last major Jewish rally in Washington, back in 1987. When Gorbachev came to speak to Reagan, a quarter of a million Jews came, and within a year, "let my people go" became a reality for the Jews of the Soviet Union. Now the issue wasn't freedom for the Jews; it was the very existence of our Jewish State. The right to live in security and in peace for its citizens. The right to walk the streets, sit in the cafes, and shop in the market, and ride the buses unafraid. The right to be protected from homicide bombers, deranged terrorists, and assorted barbarians who come in the name of Palestinian "leadership."

The Washington metro could not accommodate the tens of thousands pouring into the station at RFK Stadium, where the buses had parked. Aileen and I were swept into the subway cars, clutching our "Miami Stands with Israel" sign. The people erupted in spontaneous applause, marveling at the fact we came all the way from Miami. People came all the way from Toronto and Texas and California and Michigan and all across America. We came because we knew instinctively that it was the place to be and the moment to be there. It was a watershed moment in modern Jewish history.

Together we expressed Jewish power, Jewish concern, and Jewish solidarity. Our voices resounded through the Senate and the Congress and across America. There was no doubt what we wanted and expected from our political leadership. We were one powerful direct voice, proclaiming "Am Yisrael Chai" (the nation of Israel lives), and that we expected people of good will everywhere to ensure the safety and the viability of the only democratic state in the Middle East, the only state that proclaims the value of human life and seeks to live in peace with its neighbors, but will protect itself at all costs.

It was a long tiring day but an uplifting and satisfying one. The walk back to the buses was fatiguing. It was Chabad volunteers who handed out cups of water to the thirsty. But it wasn't free: you had to put on tephillin or swear that you had, women excused, of course. One good turn deserves another, or one mitzvah prompts another, as the Talmud says.

C. MR. OCTOBER
Sermons for the High Holy Days

A VIOLENT CULTURE

Columbine High School in Colorado will forever be remembered as a place of horror. The place where two teenagers murdered 12 of their classmates and a teacher. To this day ,we are horrified when we think back to those events of last spring.

Two youngsters spent a year building 35-pound pipe bombs in their rooms. Two youngsters spent a year planning how to murder their classmates. They collected sawed off shotguns, pistols, and other guns. And one day in April, they calmly and methodically eliminated the people who annoyed them at school.

And it was not the first incident of its kind. Across the country, in little towns and big cities, youngsters murder their school mates to the horror of the community.

Just one month ago, a man walked into the Granada Hills Jewish Center and shot five people including three little children. Little children. He was quoted as saying he "wanted to encourage people to kill Jews." For a minute, I thought I was hearing about a Nazi commandant picking up little Jewish babies and dashing them against the wall at the Auschwitz train station.

Surely you have asked yourself how this can happen? Why does this happen? Is there a mass movement toward violence in our society? Is the younger generation totally depraved and degenerate? Have we completely failed to transmit the value of the sacredness of life, that every person is created "be'tzelem elokim," in the image of God? Is our society so violence prone that it completely pervades our culture fostering a contempt for human life. Are we looking at a monstrous tendency within our society that can't be controlled much less eliminated?

If these two youngsters Harris and Klebold were such monsters shouldn't it have been obvious to everyone, long before they opened fire? The telltale signs should have been there for all to see. It should have been written all over them: We are killers; try and stop us.

But it wasn't. Nobody really noticed until it was too late. Because nobody was looking. Nobody was paying attention. Nobody cared. Not parents, not teachers, not political leaders, not anyone in a position of authority. The signs were there all along, but we haven't been reading them properly. Our whole culture is out of whack and we think it is normal and proper. Our values are completely twisted.

Or maybe they are missing all together. Our children's lives are molded by the popular culture. Instead of being taught by teachers, they are taught by Hollywood stars. Instead of learning in class, they learn on the street. Instead of parents as authority figures, they have sports stars. Instead of the value system of our tradition, they have the value system of the corner gang.

The result can't be anything else but tragedy.

This problem is not new. It is as old as our history. Consider the very people about whom we read today in the Torah: Abraham, Sarah, Ishmael, and Isaac. Parents and children.

Isaac and Ishmael were born to Abraham. But something went wrong with Ishmael. So wrong that Sarah noticed it. She realized that Ishmael was becoming a violent monster. He might destroy Isaac. So she got rid of Ishmael. She sent him away with his mother, Hagar, into the wilderness.

What did she notice? What did she see developing in Ishmael? Nothing huge. Nothing so obvious. Midrash says (Raba) she saw Ishmael catch little locusts and then crush them as a sacrifice. As a little child, he was already cruel to living things. He enjoyed their blood. He enjoyed destroying them. Soon he was taking Isaac into the field to practice shooting a bow and arrow. Only he was using Isaac as the target. There was something wrong with the kid.

So before it grew any worse, Sarah got rid of him. A terrible influence, a future monster and murderer.

It should sound familiar. Youngsters setting cats on fire or drowning dogs. Exhibiting behavior that if left unchecked can lead to more terrible things.

Little things you say, not such a big deal. But it is these little flaws that soon widen into cracked personalities. The kind that explode pipe bombs in a school. The kind that have no qualms about murdering their fellow classmates.

The Midrash comments on Ishmael's social behavior. Very matter of factly, it says that he terrorized the young women in the neighborhood. He attacked them, with no regard for law or morality or even common decency.

And his father didn't notice. Or maybe he looked the other way. Or maybe he was busy making money. But his mother noticed and she was horrified. And she didn't want this young hoodlum influencing Isaac. So she sent him out of the household, before a major disaster occurred.

So we come back to Columbine High School and the murder of young people by young people. And, of course, Colorado wasn't the first place. It's been going on for years. In the ghettos, in the suburbs, by white children, black children, by poor children, by wealthy children. It is time for decisive, drastic action. Sarah saved her son Isaac, by eliminating entirely the bad seed.

Rather drastic action. But we are all parents and grandparents. We have grandchildren that go to those same schools. We had better be concerned. More than concerned. We had better learn from it. We had better devise a plan of action.

Many ideas have been put forward. Of course we need a major reconsideration of our gun laws. Thousands of people in America are killed by guns every year. In England nine people were killed last year. In Germany, two people. They have strict gun laws. You have to have a very good reason to own a gun. Something is wrong with America.

But the problem is much deeper. It has to do with the degeneration of our entire culture.

When you went to school, did you ever see a gun? Would anyone dare even to think of bringing one. What were the big problems in school? Talking out of turn, chewing gum, running in the halls, throwing paper on the floor, wearing pants instead of a dress. When I went to school, maybe someone was caught with a switchblade. And they were just showing off for the girls. But when our children went to school things were already changing. Now the problems are major: drug use, alcohol abuse, pregnancy, suicide, robbery, rape, and assault. What happened?

What happened is the total degeneration of our culture. Life imitating art, if we can call it art.
Who teaches our children? Hollywood teaches our children. The Internet teaches our children; the rock stars teach our children; the super sports stars teach our children; and what do they learn?

That women are objects to be used at will. This they learn from pornographic film material. They also learn from video games, rock music, and movies that you settle differences through violence. You have a problem with someone, you blow him away, just like Bruce Lee does or Sylvester Stallone or a dozen other violent stars. And you learn to use your body to get what you want just like Madonna does or Sharon Stone does or a dozen others.
How do we fight against this? The answer is not more armed guards at school, or more sophisticated metal detectors, or turning schools into prisons, or banning long black trench coats. Although, this will help. The final answer is you and me. The parents and grandparents. The answer lies in getting adults to set proper examples for their children. To become responsible for their children. To teach a value system and demonstrate it by example.
The word parents in Hebrew is *horim*. It means literally, teachers. We are the primary teachers, whether we like it or not. We can't pass the buck. Not to the principal. Not to the teachers, not to the Rabbi, not to the policeman. We the

parents are all these things in one. The Horim. The ones who show the way, the correct way.

There is a custom that the father of the Bar Mitzvah boy recites a blessing after his son reads from the Torah. The blessing goes something like this: "Blessed be He who has relieved me of the responsibility for this child's transgressions."

However, the custom is not to mention God's name in reciting this blessing. Why not? Because perhaps the blessing is not fully accurate. Because even though the child is now technically an adult, the parent may still be responsible for the child's future transgressions (either directly or indirectly). Because perhaps the parents taught the child the improper behavior through bad example, or perhaps the parents did not try to correct the negative behavior.

So what point does it all boil down to? What one shift can society make to turn this ship around?

At the risk of sounding like a fundamentalist preacher, I believe it's a basic spiritual issue. I spoke recently with a foremost forensic psychiatrist, specializing in children who commit multiple murders. This doctor examined the eight multiple murders committed by U.S. schoolchildren in the last tree years. And he told me that the common denominator amongst these children is that they have no connection with God. God = laws = responsibility.

Newsweek reports that the Denver killers asked two female hostages a question: Do you believe in God? When they said yes, the gunmen shot them at point-blank range. The Sages, too, teach that belief in God is the primary deterrent to murder. How so?

The Ten Commandments are divided into two tablets. The first tablet (commandments 1–5) speaks about our relationship with God. The second tablet (commandments 6–10) speaks about our relationship with our fellow man. Furthermore, the two tablets are parallel: the first commandment—"believe in God"—corresponds to the sixth commandment—"don't murder."

What's the connection?

Every human being is created with a holy, divine soul. We

are not meaningless hunks of meat hurtling on a rock through space and time. We may be uncomfortable with the primacy of man—because of the responsibility that entails. But the alternative is that by teaching our children that they are no better than animals, they will treat one another as animals.

But it goes deeper than this. The recognition that God encompasses everything teaches that in the spiritual dimension, there are no conventional boundaries between entities. We're all one unit. When we appreciate this, then hurting the other guy, "paying him back," is as ridiculous as hurting yourself. If you're slicing a carrot and accidentally cut your finger, do you take the knife and cut the other hand in revenge? Of course not. Why? Because your other hand is part of you, too.

The belief in God is the primary value that we must teach our children. What I mean by the belief in God is the realization that our existence depends on accepting the rule of God's law; that law means responsibility. That a civilized person is responsible for his neighbor. That we are all sacred beings, all created with the same rights, one deserving of respect and consideration.

In the end, children are a reflection of the adult world. Students are a mirror image of their parents. What happened in Colorado is one more warning to us.

AN ACT OF WHOSE GOD

Rosh Hashana is the anniversary of the creation of the world. But which world? Our sages indicate that God created worlds and destroyed them. He seemed to be experimenting. Finally, he got it right.

Then comes Adam and Eve, Cain and Abel; and God regrets his work. He destroys the world one more time, one last time. Except for Noah, and this is the section of the bible we should read today on Rosh Hashana. The section that reminds us of the world's vulnerability. The section that speaks of the great flood in the time of Noah.

In Noah's generation, a great flood inundated Mesopotamia, the land between the rivers, the Tigris and Euphrates. The rivers brought life to the desert. Advanced irrigation techniques created the great empires of the Sumerians, the Babylonians, the Chaldeans, and the Assyrians. The great northern powers that rivaled Egypt in the south for control of the world.

But every now and again something went wrong. A great flood swept through the valley of the Tigris Euphrates and destroyed everything. With all their technology, scientific understanding, and careful planning, nothing could stop the unleashed force of nature. The flood in Noah's time must have been so catastrophic that it was even recorded in the Bible.

The story was handed down for generations until Moses wrote it down in the Torah. This oral tradition was so powerful that all the ancient peoples had the same story in their own cultures. The same story in the Bible appears almost word for word in the Babylonian epic, the Gilgamesh cycle. Only the names are changed.

A warning is issued by God. Prepare for a force-5 hurricane. It will be the worst in memory. Evacuate your family. Build a boat and sail away while you can. Warn your neighbors and fellow citizens to do the same.

They, of course, laughed at Noah. They refused to prepare. They were not living in Mesopotamia long enough to remember the last great storm and flood.

The rest of the story you know. Noah's family survives. The water recedes. Life starts again. Only this time, the rainbow. God promises never to destroy the whole world again. He says nothing about only destroying Dade County, or Hawaii, or Guam, or Bangladesh. He doesn't say anything about not destroying my house or your house. He doesn't say anything about ruining the food in your refrigerator or the furniture in your living room. He doesn't say anything about making thousands homeless, about ruining hundreds of lives, about killing dozens of people. He only talks about not destroying the earth, all of it. Not destroying mankind? All of them? But what about you and me?

Noah had a guarantee from God. He would survive. His family would survive. He could rebuild the world. What guarantee do we have? Who said we would survive? Who promised that we would survive to rebuild our worlds? No promise, no guarantee.

Where is God when we need him? How can he allow such destruction, death, and devastation? "A mentsh tracht und Gott lacht." Is this really true? Is God just playing with us, laughing at the futility of our attempts at living?

Tuesday after the hurricane I visited Lincoln Road and Collins after checking the synagogue and Torahs. Lights are out, windows are smashed. I meet Jesse Zabelinsky. He is already taking off the boards from the windows and cleaning up. He sees me coming and the first words out of his mouth are: "an act of God, not my God, not the Jewish God." "My God doesn't do such things."

What he said was precisely what I had been thinking. For our own peace of mind, let us not blame God. The hurricane was not an act of God. It was an act of nature. If I thought for one minute that God was out to destroy me, I would run away from Him. I would try to hide. I certainly wouldn't be praying to Him or asking for His help. He certainly wouldn't be the source of our hope and faith. God is the source of our intelligence, of our understanding, our strength, and our courage. If we understand what God is saying to us, then we can make our lives better. God is not a destructive force. On the contrary God, is a positive force in our lives.

But nature is a different story. Nature works according to its own internal laws. God created nature in that fashion; since then he doesn't tinker with nature or change its laws. And nature has two faces. It can be the very source of our lives or it can be the instrument of our deaths.

Every year the farmers in the Redlands west of Homestead planted their crops. The best tomatoes and corn in the whole country could be bought on the side of the road in Homestead. The winter vegetable crop was exported to every state. Homestead fed the entire country. In Publix, I could never buy a good tomato. But in Homestead, all the tomatoes were wonderful. Because in Homestead, nature smiled on the people. Rain in its season. Just enough rain to nourish the seedlings. Not too much rain to wash them away. Just enough fresh water, not too much salt content in the rich soil. And sunshine. The radiance of the Florida sun to bring out the natural sweetness and juiciness of the fruit. And the chill of winter never came. Homestead was a natural paradise. The farmers worked hard and prospered on the land. Migrant workers came from Texas and California and from Mexico to find work that would feed and clothe their families. All this because nature smiled on South Dade.

Until this year. Until last month. And suddenly we saw an entirely different face of nature. An angry one, a cruel one, a destructive one. After Hurricane Andrew passed, everything was destroyed. All plants and trees so laboriously tended by the farmers were uprooted. Not one plant survived. The soil was covered in ocean salt. Houses were reduced to splinters in a matter of minutes. People crouched in terror in the ruins. Then they wandered in shock. No water, no food, no shelter. Where to go? How to get help? Bathing in the polluted canals. Drinking the same polluted water.

And this is also nature. Vicious, relentless, destructive, catastrophic.

Talmud indicates that each person has two sides: good and evil. Yetzer hara and Yetzer hatov. God created man, but God is not responsible for man's choices. We have free will to make our own choices. Man is a part of nature, and nature also exhibits the same duality, the same two sides, the same two forces. A force for good and a force for bad. A constructive face and a destructive face. And we surely have seen them both.

But one important point. The terms good and bad are only meaningful for us; in our lives. If we have food to eat, it's good. If we starve, it's bad. If we live in a nice house it's good. If our house is destroyed in a hurricane, its bad. For us. But there is no good or bad in nature. It only appears that way to us, in our lives. Nature just is. The world has existed for billions of years. How many hurricanes has it endured? How many earthquakes and typhoons and tsunamis and forest fires? How many trees have been destroyed, how many mountains have moved, how many deserts have been formed? And yet the earth remains. The water recedes, the trees grow again, life always returns, even stronger and more resilient then before. Nature never will destroy the world. It is an internal principle of nature. It is what God promised to Noah. Never again will the earth be destroyed.

But what about us? What about my little world, my house, my life. The world will go on. But what about my little world?

How do we deal with nature? What does God want from us?

What are we expected to do? Vos vilt Er fun meine leben?

First, God wants us to understand the nature of the world. According to a famous law of physics, which is a law of nature, matter cannot be created of destroyed, only transformed. We are the ones who are supposed to do the transforming.

During our lifetimes, we are supposed to be working to transform the world. For the good, to transform human society for the better.

The directive to Adam from God is conquer the earth. It means subdue the forces of nature. Learn the secrets of nature. You have the intelligence. Harness the forces of nature for the good of all men. You have brains to do it. You can transform the matter of the universe. Use your head. The God given spirit of man can achieve anything.

If earthquakes destroy cities it is because we still haven't learned enough to control them. If hurricanes and volcanoes devastate communities, it is because we still haven't learned the secrets of nature. If disease kills people by the tens of thousands, it is because our understanding of medicine is still primitive. With all the fantastic advances of modern medicine, we still have a long way to go. If famine kills thousands, it is because we still don't know enough about agriculture and agronomy. With all our wonderful new farming technologies, we are still scratching the surface, literally.

We were told through Adam, at the very beginning of history, that nature is difficult; it has to be conquered and dominated, ve-kivshu'ha. The forces of nature have to be harnessed for the benefit of all of us. Otherwise nature will destroy us. Otherwise the flood will come again. And we can't blame God. Only ourselves.

Sign on bus stop: "South Florida: We will rebuild." What does it mean? It means that we will continue to struggle until we harness those terrible natural forces. We will use our sechel to outsmart nature. To understand how to build safer houses, stronger houses. We will use our sechel to discover how to negate the force of a hurricane. How to weaken it. How to interfere with the process that allows a hurricane to form altogether. It is not farfetched; we can do it. God created us with the potential, and he expects us to use it.

A news commentator was reporting on all the people involved in helping, all the wonderful effort on the part of the volunteers to help the hurricane victims. It apparently seemed like such an overwhelming task. To provide enough food, water, and shelter. Just to take care of the basic elements that sustain life. He finished by saying "an act of God is a hard act to follow."

He didn't have it right. The act of God *is* the act that follows. The hurricane was the act of nature. What we do to help is the act of God. What we do to overcome the tragedy, what we do to try to prevent future tragedies is exactly what God calls us to do. It is our response to God.

Come. Join us. Get up from your lethargy. There is work to be done. The world will be a better place. We can do it. We will do it. With God's help, we will conquer nature. Amen.

JONAH FOR THE TWENTIETH CENTURY—ROSH HASHANA 5753

Forget about the whale. Save it for *Moby Dick*.

Nineveh—capital of Assyria; the world's strongest empire at the time. The empire that destroyed the northern kingdom of Samaria in 722 B.C.E. and almost destroyed Jerusalem some 15 years later.

Could it really be that Jonah is asked to go to the capital of Assyria and preach to them? Like Daniel entering the lions den. Would you go? I wouldn't go. I could also be tempted to run away. Just like Jonah did.

He went to Jaffa to take a boat for Tarshish. The ancient remains of the port can still be seen. Tarshish is either Tartesus in southwestern Spain or Tarsus on the southern coast of Turkey. From the Phoenicians, the Israelites learned to sail. Sailors hugged the coast and went all around the Mediterranean. A voyage was a frightening thing in those days, no compass or radar. But Jonah was more disturbed about going to Nineveh than risking his life on a dangerous sea voyage. Why?

Jonah runs away not because he can't do the job. He is most qualified. A great speaker, teacher, a Rabbi. Rather, he runs away because he fears he will be too effective; they, the people of Nineveh, will actually listen to him and repent. He wants them all dead. He wants them to pay for their sins. He wants them to pay for their attacks on Israel.

In this, he is quite normal. What would you do about captured PLO terrorists who murdered innocent women, men, and children in Ma'alot, Jericho, Ben Yehuda, and the shuk? Lets talk to them. Lets see if they are sorry. Lets get them to do teshuva. And then we'll let them go to become fine upstanding citizens of Israel. Of course, we wouldn't.

What would you have done if you were with the Israeli agents who captured Adolf Eichmann in Argentina? Let's rehabilitate him. We should have sent him to a minimum security prison where we could teach him to be a good person. Then, we should have released him to go on with his life. If given a pistol and the opportunity, any one of us would have put a bullet in Eichmann's demented brain. The man who boasted that he would jump into his grave laughing about the millions of Jews he murdered.

Why should the enemies of Israel go free? Why should the persecutors of our people not be persecuted themselves? Where is justice? An eye for an eye?

And yet God sends Jonah to do this impossibly difficult thing. And amazingly it works. And that bothers Jonah even more. The least he expects is nekama. He expects God to avenge his people. Sometimes when we are hurt, when we are injured, the only thing that makes us feel a bit better is nekama.

But Jonah is denied. It is not to be. The walls of Nineveh will not come crashing down. No screams of agony from dying Assyrians will be heard.

Instead, the sound of prayer. Penitence. Teshuva. The people of Nineveh, led by their king himself, repent and are saved.

You see, Jonah wants an end to the people. He wants to see every last one of those murderers dead. But God wants to see an end to the evil. He wants to see evil dead, not the people.

God says to Jonah that revenge may be sweet, perhaps it will make you feel better, but you need to attack the heart of the problem. You have to work to change peoples' attitudes, their value system. Otherwise you are going to be very busy in the revenge business. To the very end Jonah fights this idea. He finally does his job, and does it well, but he is never satisfied. The people of Nineveh repent. But he is never avenged.

Jonah's job is our job. To bring the idea of God to the world. We did a wonderful job. To teach God's absolute value system to the world. Usually, through our own actions. And again, we have done a wonderful job. If there is any justice or morality or ethics in the world, it is because of us, the Jewish people, because of our Torah.

Many times the world resented what we were trying to do, and we paid a terrible price. Anti-Semitism is the attempt to shut the Jews up. The attempt to reject the concepts of justice and morality.

Hitler saw the Jews as a challenge to his message of atheist moral nihilism. His mission in life, in his own words, was to "destroy the tyrannical God of the Jews and his life-denying Ten Commandments."

The cost to us was horrible, almost unbearable. Six million Jews murdered.

In the old Soviet Union tens of thousands of Jews died. But hundreds of thousands of Jews stopped being Jews under threats from the state. The communist regime couldn't have people walking around preaching the ideas of the dignity of man, the rights of the individual, the belief in God as the highest authority. Again, the cost to us was terribly high. Jews starving to death in the Gulag. Jews tortured to death by the KGB. Jews reduced to non-citizens, to invisible people.

But the Jews refused to disappear. In the basements and in the attics, in the middle of the night, in absolute secrecy, the Torah was studied. The word of God was repeated, letter-by-letter, sentence-by-sentence. And eventually, it penetrated even the iron curtain.

Our job description in this world remains the same. It hasn't changed since the time of Jonah. But every once in a while we get tired. The cost to our people is too great. Everyone once in a while we also want to run away, to get lost, to lose our identity as Jews. But we can't. God will find us. The world will find us out. We can't runaway.

Consider this idea from a literary point of view in the text of the book:

God says to Jonah: "Arise, go to Nineveh." Jonah instead goes down to Jaffa, down to the ship, down into the hold, down into the sea. The word *yarad* is repeated over and over and over. In Jonah's journey, as long as he is running from God, he is going down, sinking as long as he is running from his identity. As a Jew, he is sinking. As long as he is running from his responsibilities, he is going straight down. There is no escape from God.

The high point of the book comes in the middle of Jonah's voyage. A storm comes up. The sea rages. The sailors can't control the boat against such strong winds. They are being blown out of sight of land. They lose their bearings. They are deathly afraid. They begin to look for a reason. Something to blame. And they remember Jonah, the stranger, the outsider. He's sleeping in the hold while everyone else is praying for his life.

In order to find out who is responsible, who the gods are against, they cast lots. Jonah draws the lot. It must be his fault. The sailors demand to know who he is and what he has done to anger God and put the ship in jeopardy.

There is nowhere for Jonah to run, nowhere to hide. And in the most important verse of the book he stands up straight and declares, *Ivri Anochi*, "I am a Hebrew." He tells them the whole story about how he tried to run away from God, how he tried to shirk his responsibilities, how he tried to hide his identity. But no more . . . . He suggests they throw him into the sea to calm the storm. He knows God is after him. But the sailors refuse to do such a horrible thing. They try to row toward shore. Finally, they desperately throw him into the sea and the storm subsides.

But Jonah is saved by the whale. God isn't letting him off the hook. His mission will be accomplished. Why did Jonah deserve to be saved? Why not get someone else for the job? Forget about Jonah. Jonah is still God's elected because he redeemed himself with two words: *Ivri Anochi*. I am a Hebrew. Jewish pride. His test: to hide his identity or expose it.

So many Jewish people seem totally lost. We think there is no hope. Nothing will ever bring them back. They are ignorant of Jewish life and traditions, of Jewish history and culture, of the Torah and the Talmud. They assimilate in huge numbers. Then, every now and again, we hear *Ivri Anochi* where we never expected to hear it. Those same Russian Jews who seemed lost, almost 3 million. Suddenly, we began to hear *Ivri Anochi*. Secret classes were formed.

Hebrew books were smuggled in. The Torah was studied. People demonstrated in Moscow and defied the KGB. They chanted in front of the Moscow synagogue: Nye byusa niko-vo, krome Boga odnavo. I fear no one, except God the only one." That is *Ivri Anochi* in Russian words. And with those words, they were redeemed. They began the journey back.

My neighbor spent the first 30 years of her life as an Israeli rock star. She moved in a fast crowd of easy living, alcohol, drugs, and easy sex. Israel, Europe, America. One husband, two husbands, a third husband. Then a car accident almost killed her. She had a lot of time to think lying in the hospital for a few months. Don't think that because she was an Israeli, a sabra, that she was Jewish in any meaningful way. But one day, lying on her back in the hospital she declared *Ivri Anochi*: I am a Jew. And she was determined to change her life. To go through the process of teshuva. To live a meaningful Jewish life. And now, I see her two boys get off the bus from the yeshiva every day. She and her husband live a life devoted to Yiddishkeit, quietly and humbly. She is a devoted friend to us, a wonderful human being. With those two words, *Ivri Anochi*, she took the road back to her people.

In an open society, in a pluralistic society, it becomes so much harder to remain Jewish. Because it is so much easier to disappear. We have no color to change. And anyone can have a nose fixed. And anyone can change from Cohen to Kane, or from Cohen to O'Coon. It was easier to remain Jewish in Cuba. The community was a small closed society. There was no choice, nowhere else to go. Few Jews were ready to mix with the Gallegos or Mestizos or the Negroes. And I mean it only in a social-religious sense. Few people were ready to consider marriage outside the Jewish community.

Now conditions are completely different. And the rates of assimilation are astronomical. But every now and again, someone gets up and declares *Ivri Anochi*. A family suddenly makes a decision to make their house kosher. A family decides to send their child to the Jewish day school. A family decides to come to shul every Shabbat. A family decides to live by the law of the

Torah. A family decides that being Jewish is not a burden, but a privilege.

My friends, these ten days between Rosh Hashana and Yom Kippur are given to each of us to declare *Ivri Anochi*. Stand up and be proud of your identity as a Jew. And let your lives in the coming year reflect that pride.

THE GAP

Michelangelo is undoubtedly one of the greatest artists that ever lived. When I am in Italy, his works are the highlight of my trip. His *David* in Florence and his *Moses* in Rome are my personal favorite works of art, and I never grow tired of looking at them. Michelangelo was also a painter. He is known throughout the world as the creator of the dome mural that adorns the Sistine Chapel. (Recently cleaned amid great controversy, its bright colors emerged.)

I shall never forget the first time I gazed up at this magnificent work. One had to practically lie on the floor to appreciate the full splendor of the work. Directly at the center of the mural is depicted the moment of creation. There is Adam reaching forth his hand to God. And God extends his hand toward Adam. The spark of life is transferred from heaven to earth and mankind comes alive. It is a fantastic sight. You can almost feel the divine spark as it jumps across the universe to lodge in Adam's soul.

And yet there is a strange thing about that painting. God stretches his hand towards Adam and Adam stretches his hand toward God. But their fingers never meet. There remains a gap. A gap between man and God, between heaven and earth that can never be bridged.

This is essentially a basic Jewish idea. As the Midrash relates: Moses never went up on high and the glory of God never descended below. The verse continues with God saying to Moses, "I will call you from the summit of the mountain and you will ascend."

Evidently the first part of this Midrash proclaims denial of Christian doctrine: "and Moses never went up on high." No son of man ever went up bodily into heaven. We may orbit this physical planet of ours; we may take trips to the moon; and eventually to all the planets and stars. But we are still bound within the physical universe. No man of flesh and blood can enter into the world of Godhood.

"And the glory of God never descended below." God does not become flesh and blood. God does not leave the world of the spirit to enter into the world of the physical.

From this first part of the Midrash, we are left with a very clear impression. God cannot be man, and man can never be God.

But the last part of the Midrash has another idea. "I shall call you from the summit and you will ascend." There is a way for man to reach God. There is the possibility of a union between mortal and immortal.

Let me explain this bridging of the gap between man and God with an illustration. There were once two cities on opposite sides of a turbulent river. A great engineer was hired to design a huge bridge that would join the two communities. After months of planning and design, the work was begun. From each bank of the river the project began to take shape. A lofty structure rose majestically from each shore to almost meet high in the air in midstream. Then it was time to lower the central span into place to complete the bridge. But somehow it didn't fit. It fell short by four inches and no degree of precision or ingenuity could bridge that gap. Four inches out of three or four miles, but because of those four inches, the bridge could not function.

The construction crew was extremely frustrated. They immediately called the designer of the bridge to ask him what to do. When the reply came, it left everyone mystified. All he said was "wait till tomorrow noon."

The next day came but the great engineer did not arrive, nor did he send any further instructions. However, the construction team began to witness a near miracle. As the sun rose in the sky, it heated the metal girders and expanded the steel so that the sections began to unite. The gap soon disappeared and the span fitted precisely. The separate sections were riveted together and the bridge was at last completed.

In our lives, we notice so many uncompleted bridges. So many people live isolated lives. They are lonely. They are bored. They are frustrated. They live within the span of the next man's life; just a few inches away. Comfort is almost within reach, but not quite. People fall short by inches of reaching out to their fellow man. Comfort, companionship, and common achievement are missed by inches.

The relationships within a family are supposed to be the most beautiful that are afforded us. The members of the family—mother, father, sons, daughters—they are able to create a wonderful unit. And, yet, I know so many fathers who are strangers to their sons. So many children who feel like foreigners in their homes. They live together, they eat together, they sit together. They pass within inches of each other. Yet, they remain strangers. A hand is never extended in true friendship. A hand is never taken in response. The gap is never bridged.

It is possible for two people to live together a whole lifetime and remain strangers. They can share every aspect of life and yet, they never share each other. They can come close to each other and yet remain so far apart.

This kind of situation in a marriage is not hopeless. It doesn't have to be. Those few inches that separate can be bridged. A kind word. An extended hand. A warm embrace. (Hardest words to say are, I love you) A thoughtful deed. It is so easy. Yet it is so hard for so many unfortunate people.

We think that the gap between us and eternal death is the widest and most fearful. How false that is. The widest gap is between us and the living. (Very often as we sit in shul during Rosh Hashana we remember those who are no longer with us) We can all remember how many things we should have done that we didn't do. Little things. A visit; a phone call; a letter. All the little things we could have done more often that we didn't do. All the little joys that we could have shared with them. They were right near us then. The gap between us was just a few inches. Yet, we failed to bridge it. Now, the gap is impossible to bridge. And we regret all the times we had the opportunity to bridge it and didn't.

But we must concern ourselves with the living, We must learn to bridge the gaps in our lives.

The two halves of that bridge were joined by the warmth of the midday sun. We can join with our brothers and sisters through the warmth of our love. Just the slightest additional evidence of our love and concern can bridge the distances within our families. Just another little step towards God and our faith will jump the gap. By the slightest additional effort of charity, our hand reaches the poor.

I was listening to one of our UJA volunteers make a call one evening. You would be amazed at the difficulty involved in getting our Jews to contribute. Can you imagine a Jew unwilling to support the State of Israel. Even with five dollars? And, yet, I listened as our volunteer did his darndest to convince this person of his obligation. In the end, all he was able to elicit was a few dollars in pledge. But the gap had been bridged. This man never gave anything before. But now he did. The first connection with the State of Israel had been made. From now on, it would be easier. Next year, he will be in the habit. The responsibility has been accepted. Just a few dollars, but those few dollars formed the bridge over which a whole new attitude will roll.

God said to Moses, "I shall call you from the summit and you will ascend." We have only to attune our ears to hear God's call and we can lift ourselves to divinity.

We can make our world a divine sanctuary if we reach out to our fellow man. This is the lesson of our faith and its challenge. We try to bridge the past when we recite the Kaddish and Yiskor service. Let us remember that it is perhaps more important to make bridges to the present. To unite ourselves with the living. If we can build bridges to the present, then we shall have indeed honored our past. If we can build bridges to the living, then we shall have honored those who are no longer with us. Then will their memories always be an inspiration to all of us.

At this holy moment, look at your families. Resolve not to waste a minute with them. Love them with all your heart and with all your might. Show them your love. And may the Ribbono shel olam God) love us all. Amen

WHAT IF:
THE FIFTIETH ANNIVERSARY OF THE
UPRISING IN THE WARSAW GHETTO

Today, we dedicate to Israel and its support through the purchase of Israel bonds.

Events of the last few weeks are breathtaking. It is too early to tell if they will lead to peace or further war. Is it a step toward coexistence or merely a step toward the destruction of Israel? We hope it will be for peace. But we prepare for any eventuality. We are too close to recent events to evaluate them properly. Therefore I look to the past to determine what path we must take in the future.

FIFTIETH ANNIVERSARY OF WARSAW UPRISING

When World War II began, there were almost 400,000 Jews living in Warsaw, a third of the city's population. They were eventually crowded into an area of 850 acres, 18 blocks by 6 blocks. I know because I walked along every street and counted them. Eventually the Jews in the Warsaw ghetto numbered more than 500,000. 13 people to a room, thousands homeless, everyone starving slowly to death.

By the time the Jewish resistance got organized, there were about 65,000 Jews left. The rest had become ashes in Auschwitz or had died of hunger or disease in the ghetto.

As I said, I walked the streets from Umschlagplatz, where Jews were rounded up for deportation, to Mila 18. Mila 18 was headquarters for the ZOB, led by the famous Mordechai Anielewicz (Yad Mordecai): Zydowska Organizacja Bojowa: the Jewish fighting organization. Not since Bar Kochba led his armies against the Romans some 2,000 years before had there been a Jewish fighting organization under Jewish command.

Mila 18 is a mound marked with a plaque. Somewhere under the mound are the bones of Anielewicz and some 100 of his comrades. Buried in their bunker under the tons of debris as the buildings came down on them. The plaque is in Polish and Yiddish. The word Jew does not appear.

As far as the Poles are concerned, only Polish partisans fought the Nazis. Only Poles formed the resistance. Only Poles died in the Jewish ghetto.

And speaking of the Jewish ghetto, nothing is left. Not a brick, not a stone. What survived was all bulldozed after the war. Mila 18 is hidden between rows of apartment blocks built by the communists. Every apartment house is built on the remains of Jewish bodies. This entire section of Warsaw is a Jewish cemetery. Only there are no headstones, no markers, no monuments, no inscriptions, no memory—no Jews. Their bodies are crushed to dust, their memories are erased, Poland is practically Judenrein.

All of you know what happened there on Passover 1943, 50 years ago: A German force equipped with tanks and artillery moved into the ghetto to round up the remaining able-bodied Jews to ship them to the camps. They were met by a determined resistance. Molotov cocktails, pistols, some rifles and grenades, even rocks—against steel-helmeted Nazis with machine guns. Against tanks. Lo and behold, the Nazis retreated. But they returned, and in the street fighting, they still couldn't dislodge the determined Jews.

Finally, they began to systematically burn down each house. From April 19 to May 8 the Jews refused to give up. Then ZOB headquarters, Mila 18, fell. It was the end. On May 16, the German General Stroop reported to his superiors the complete liquidation of the Warsaw ghetto. Es gibt keinen Juedischen Wohnbezirk in Warschau mehr. As a token of his "victory," he blew up the great synagogue on Tlomacka Street.

I visited Warsaw in 1976. I stood in front of the statue of Mordecai Anielewicz and his comrades in the middle of the old ghetto area. My mind drifted back to those terrible days in

1943. And I had a vision of paratroopers dropping silently down into the ghetto. Each one held an Uzi machine gun. Each one had the letters "tzadi-hey-lamed" imprinted on his uniform. Tzahal. "Tevah Haganah LeYisrael." The Israel Defense Forces. Overhead circled a flight of Hercules transports with the markings of the Israeli Air Force, a blue Magen David.

> But I was just dreaming, confusing the story. My dream was born in Uganda, at the Entebbe airport, in 1975. That's where the Hercules landed with a troop of Israeli paratroopers. That's where Jewish soldiers flew 4,000 kilometers from Israel to Uganda to rescue our people held hostage and threatened with death by Palestinian terrorists. July 4, 1975. One minute after midnight, the IDF dropped out of the sky, in a lightening attack called Operation Thunderbolt. They eliminated the terrorists, swept up the frightened hostages into the safety of the big bird, and off they flew to Israel, and to safety, to the amazement and joy of the entire free world.
>
> When the commandos broke into the building where the hostages were being held, the order went out to drop on the floor. Those who remained standing, the terrorists, were shot down. As the people dropped to the floor they began shouting to each other one word: "mishelanu": they are ours. Israelis coming to rescue Israelis, Jews coming to rescue Jews—mishelanu: Our own people are taking care of us.
>
> 50 years ago, if only that word could have been heard in the Warsaw ghetto, how different the story would have been. If only there had been an independent State of Israel. If only there had been an Israeli army. If only . . .

When Mordecai Anielewicz threw that first petrol bomb down onto a German tank, a new chapter in modern Jewish history began. When his comrades began shooting with pistols at the Nazi Wehrmacht troops armed with machine guns, a new kind of Jew was born. A Jew who served notice to the world that we would defend ourselves to the death if need be. That Jewish blood would no longer come cheap.

When the defenders of the Warsaw ghetto were reduced to throwing rocks at Nazi armored cars, they buried the myth of the Jews going like lambs to the slaughter forever. When the smoke cleared over the ghetto and it became apparent that a handful of brave Jewish fighters had bloodied the troops of the invincible Third Reich, the world reacted with amazement and admiration. For us, it was a turning point in our history. We regained some of our dignity. We lost some of our fear. We put aside some of our sense of inferiority, born of centuries of degradation and persecution in Europe. And the Warsaw ghetto was only the beginning of the story.

The rest of the story began unfolding in 1948, in the Galil, in 1956, in the Sinai, in 1967, in Jerusalem, and in 1973, at the Suez. A Jewish army, fighting to protect a Jewish homeland.

When my grandfather made his first trip to Israel, he wrote back in Yiddish about meeting a general in Tzahal: "a Yiddisher general." He was so amazed by the fact that the Jewish people had their own army and their own generals. My grandfather fought for Russia in the Russo-Japanese War and in World War. I against Germany. He often told me the stories of getting up early in the barracks to put on tephillin before everyone woke up. I realized how much courage and determination it took to stand up to anti-Semitic Russian officers. And when he saw an Israeli General, a "Yiddisher general," he cried with joy. For him, the messiah was clearly on the way. Jews could defend themselves.

But the story that began in the Warsaw ghetto reaches its most exciting chapter in 1976. When Israeli commandos in Israeli planes flew into Entebbe, Uganda; when Jews went to rescue their brothers and sisters, when they crossed deserts and seas and dropped down out of the skies to pluck Jews literally from the jaws of death. Since then, there have been many rescue missions: to Ethiopia, to Russia, to Bosnia. But nothing excited us like Entebbe.

Our enemies fear us. They can run, but they can't hide. Anyone who raises a hand against a Jew will have it cut off.

The old Nazis are found and brought to justice, one by one. The Arab terrorists are hunted down, cell by cell. The Palestinian murderers are eliminated, one by one. The murderers responsible for the massacre of Israeli athletes in the Munich Olympics have been hunted down by the Mossad: They are all dead. Irony of ironies, we are now negotiating with their leaders, the people who trained them, sent them, and protected them.

Every Rosh Hashana I stand quietly during the Amida and recite the prayer—dear God, strike fear into the hearts of our enemies. Fifty years ago, who feared the Jews? Who was afraid of an unarmed, unprotected, disenfranchised people? We had to beg for the right to exist. We were happy just to be left alone. Even in the worst slums of Europe's cities. Places we called ghettos. And when the drunken mobs came looting and burning and raping and murdering, we packed up what was left and moved on. To another ghetto, where the process would eventually be repeated—over and over, ad nauseum.

The state of Israel is a pledge to the Jewish people that it will never happen again. No more ghettos. We have a home to go to. We have the power to protect ourselves. And we intend to use it.

Strike fear into the hearts of our enemies: the world prefers to feel sorry for Jews. They are always ready to shed tears over us. To put up monuments over our graves. Well we don't want their sympathy. We don't want their tears. We don't need their love. What we demand is their respect. And when they fear us, they learn to respect us.

Lord, grant respect to your people.

Those days of frightened Jews standing against the wall with their arms raised in terror in the face of Schmeisers and Mausers are over. Those days of naked corpses and charred bodies are gone forever. Those days when Jewish history was one unending parade of pogroms, persecutions, and pitiful existence are done. We have the respect of the world because the power of Israel is fearful.

We feel proud. We feel secure. More secure than we have felt for 2,000 years. It is a new feeling. Just 45 years old. We will never go back to those days of fear, uncertainty, and horror. This year, for the first time in the 45 years of Israel's modern statehood, we dare to hope that peace may be coming. It is too premature for celebrations; but it is never premature for hope. In the next months and years, agreements on paper will be tested in the laboratory of human relations. It takes strength to make peace, it takes power to force a peaceful resolution to strife, and it takes strength to enforce the peace. And Israel's strength depends on us. All of us. Every Jew who takes pride in Israel. With God's help, and the help of every one of us, we will insure the future of our homeland.

Yechi Medinat Yisrael. Long live the State of Israel.

MAZAL OR LUCK

Mazal tov. You made it to another year. Thank God. Baruch Hashem.

The two best known Hebrew or Yiddish words are mazal tov. Even non-Jews know these words.

A congregant came in to see me about a marriage. She wore a Chai, a Magen David, an eye, a "chamsa," and a horseshoe, all in gold, of course. I asked why. She needed a lot of luck. It was her second marriage.

At the end of the wedding, after the glass is broken, mazal tov. During the wedding party, when the waiter drops the load of dishes, mazal tov. When the father of the bride signs the check, the caterer says mazal tov. Maybe after it clears the bank, he says it again.

It means good luck. But mazal tov, in reality, is an astrological sign. Aries or Gemini or Aquarius. The "mazalot."

First time I met Dr. Baron, he guessed my sign. Then he proceeded to tell me all about myself, everything positive, of course. I was very impressed and flattered, then I realized that he does that with everyone he meets.

Synagogues are not supposed to have figures or statues. Yet many ancient synagogues of Israel have the astrological signs on the mosaic floor as a design. Tiberias and Bet Alpha. Clearly, our ancient ancestors believed in the mazalot, the astrological signs. What we call the daily horoscope.

To this day many Jews believe in various good luck signs: Safaradim wear "chamsa" or hands. It is the hand of Fatima and comes from the Arabic culture. Or the eye against the Evil Eye. In Brazil, the Figa, and in Cuba, the Asabache. Ashkenazim wear the Chai or Magen David or Mezuza.

Rain. For the whole world it is disturbing on a wedding day. The new dresses get wet. For Jews, it's good luck. Mazaldik. A sign of fertility, growth, life.

Step in dog droppings. My grandmother says its good luck. It doesn't smell like good luck.

Jews have a special optimism. We turn bad to good. We invest things with a new, positive, revised meaning. We have faith in God, in ourselves, and our history.

We move, or write contracts, or make a deal, or get married on Tuesday. "Tov" twice in the Bible.

Friday is also good, when God created people. Tov is also written twice and it says Tov Me'od. Very good. Tuesday is the lucky day. Mazaldik.

But do we really believe in luck, in Mazal?

Bereshit (15:5) God tells Abraham to go outside at night and look at the stars. God promises that his descendants will be as numerous as the stars. Rashi says: Your horoscope is written in the stars (mazalot). It indicates you won't have a child. I will change your name to Abraham and your mazal will change. You will have a son.

Change your name and your luck changes. Take a new identity and new opportunities will present themselves.

When a person is deathly sick, the custom is to change his name. Actually, to add a name. So that his mazal will change. So that the Angel of Death, the Malach Hamavet, won't be able to identify him.

When you sustain a loss as a mourner, you come back to the synagogue after shiva, you are supposed to sit in a dif-

ferent seat. The Talmud says: Change your place and you
change your mazal.

And, yet, the most famous line about mazal in the
Talmud is:

Literally Ein mazal leYisrael it means there is no Mazal
for Israel. I think it means that we don't believe in blind
luck. We don't believe in astrology. We don't regulate our
lives by the daily horoscope.

And, yet, we keep hoping for a little mazal in our lives.
As the Yiddish saying goes: "Vo nimt man a bissel mazal"
where do we find a bit of Mazal?

We can arrange everything. We can put everything in
order. We can see to every detail. We can do everything in
our power. But success always depends on a bissel mazal.

How many times have I sat and discussed the future of
the next generation with parents. You send them to the best
schools. You give them every material advantage. You teach
them right from wrong. You show them by example. You
hope and pray that they turn out all right. But in the end
you need one more ingredient—a bissel mazal."

Exactly what is this mazal? Is it just blind luck?

I was standing at the kiddush one Shabbat and I wished one
of our congregants mazal tov. Maybe it was an anniversary or
birthday. He said, "Do you know what mazal really is?" It
stands for Makom, Z'man, Limud. Which means, place, time,
and knowledge. Luck comes to a person who is in the right
place, at the right time and who is smart enough to capitalize
on the situation.

Now, that's a good working definition of Mazal, one that we
can all accept.

Michael Jordan. Even if you aren't a basketball fan, you
know who he is or who he was. I saw him win a championship game for the Chicago Bulls with three seconds to go.
He let fly a three pointer from the top of the key, and swish.
There he was at exactly the right time. Three seconds to go
and the opposing team would never have time to take anoth-

er shot. Exactly the right place: Scottie Pippin had set up a block for him—"he set a pick" as we say in basketball lingo and he had a clear, unobstructed shot. And swish. He made it. What a lucky shot. No; not luck. Skill. Michael Jordan had prepared every day of his career for that shot. He worked and sweated for that shot. He was in perfect physical condition for that shot and he had been studying the game for years. He knew the percentages of every shot. He knew the strategy that would free him for a shot. He had mastered the play like a chess master. Everything came together. The right time, the right place, the intelligence to capitalize, and swish, the shot went in. The Chicago Bulls won the championship.

Michael Jordan got his face on the Wheaties box. Michael Jordan became a millionaire from his endorsements. Michael Jordan, what a lucky guy they said. But they were wrong. They should have said Michael Jordan, what mazal. He was in the right place, at the right time, and he was smart enough and prepared enough to seize the moment.

You never heard of Roy Plunkett. He died last spring, but I'm sure you heard of what he discovered. Teflon. Every time I try to fry eggs and the eggs slide easily off the pan I am thankful for Teflon. I remember the days when I would fry eggs and a black mess would remain in the pan. I hated the job of cleaning that disgusting frying pan. Along came Roy Plunkett: He was a scientist for Dupont Laboratories in New Jersey conducting experiments for a new refrigerant. The experiment didn't seem to go right. He wound up with a glob of a white waxy substance at the bottom of his test tube. At first, he thought his experiment was a failure. But then his scientific curiosity got the better of him. He began to test the material for other properties. He found out that the new substance had a very low surface friction. That meant nothing would stick to it. Voila! Teflon. The trade name for tetrafluroethylene resin. The new household name in pots and pans. Three quarters of all pots and pans sold in the United States are coated with Teflon, thank God.

Dr. Roy Plunkett was in the right place at the right time. In a high-tech laboratory putting the right chemicals together, and what luck. Out came Teflon. Not luck. Mazal. He had the intelligence to realize the application for this new strange substance. Had I been in that Dupont laboratory, I probably would have taken one look at that waxy stuff and I probably would have thrown it right into the garbage can.

You all heard of Bernard Baruch. Economic Advisor to the President. Unfortunately he wasn't a very strong Zionist. He argued against a Jewish state in Israel. He suggested Uganda instead. But that's another story.

At the time of a stock market crash, he had invested heavily in copper futures.

The bottom of the market fell out and copper futures started plummeting. Baruch's brokers called him frantically to sell immediately before things got worse. But Baruch had positioned himself perfectly. He had carefully studied the market and he was aware of the impending economic changes. He left word with his brokers to buy more copper. Everyone else sold and the price went down. The end of the story was that copper futures went back up a few days later, and Bernard Baruch became a multimillionaire on that one deal. And they all said "what a lucky guy." No. Not luck. Mazal. He was at the right time and in the right place and he was smart enough to capitalize. And one more thing. His brokers couldn't reach him. It was Yom Kippur. He was in shul, and he left word with his office that he was not to be disturbed. He couldn't have sold if he wanted to. By the time he got back to his office, after Kol Nidre, after Neila, copper futures were on the way up. What Mazal.

So maybe God has a little something to do with mazal also, but don't leave mazal only to God. I believe you have to make your own mazal. God help's those who help themselves. The world belongs to those who are well prepared. One of our congregants told me about his grandson's first job out of law school. $75,000 starting salary with one of New York's most prestigious firms. What mazal. Then he went on to tell that his grandson graduated from Columbia Law magna cum laude. He was editor of the law review. He was second in his class. He spent summers working in the firm. His grandfather was friends with the senior partner—What luck! No, mazal. This young man was well prepared, he worked hard. He made his own mazal, and God smiled on him.

The sign for the month of Tishrey is the scales. Because we are being weighed in judgment by God. Mazal can tip the balance for us in the coming year. There is no blind luck.

We have to work hard to achieve our goals. We have to position ourselves to be in the right place at the right time, and we have to use our intelligence. We have to do our homework, and with God's help, we will succeed.

Look around you my friends. Look at our beautiful synagogue, and I don't mean just the material surface. The beautiful architecture, the choice materials, the beautiful ark and bima. The artistry that suffuses every object and every item. The Jerusalem stone, the fine woods, the marble, the Meisler sculptures. Look beyond all this. To the most beautiful aspect of our synagogue. You all. The people. The members of our community. You who feel the holy obligation to be an official part of our congregation. You have come to Aventura-Turnberry from all over the country and, indeed, from all over the world. From Chicago, Washington, Columbus, Detroit, Pittsburgh, New York, Lima, Caracas, Montreal, Toronto, Tel Aviv, and Jerusalem, and all points in between. You have been members and leaders of every major synagogue in the country. You could have said, enough, I'm retired. I did my share, let someone else do it, but you didn't step back, you came forward and said *hineni*—I am here, I am ready to help again. I am ready to be part of one of the finest synagogues in South Florida.

And the people of Florida look at us and they say what a lucky community. Exactly in the right place at the right time. Here we are in the fastest growing neighborhood of Dade county. Here we are in the only Jewish neighborhood that is still expanding. Here we are surrounded by new residential construction, thanks to Soffer enterprises, and may you have a great success, and may we benefit from growth in the Jewish population.

Here we are in this wonderful synagogue led by one of the most capable, creative, and progressive leadership teams ever assembled in any Jewish community at any time. Poised to establish ourselves as a leading force for the Jewish tradition in the entire country. And they say, what a lucky group. No, not luck, mazal.

More than a dozen (18) years of hard work by dedicated and determined people brought us to this moment. This beautiful Jewish community did not spring out from thin air. It is the accumulated working hours of hundreds of people. It is the accumulated vision of dozens of wonderful leaders. And they call it lucky. Not at all. It is mazal. It came from hard determined work. We positioned ourselves, we prepared ourselves, so when the time came we would be in the right place at the right time. We looked for people with intelligence and the vision to capitalize on this extraordinary confluence of events, the right people who could make it happen. We made our own mazal. And God saw fit to help us along. And now we have it, the right place, the right time. The right people.

So let's go. This is our year. This is our decade. Join with us as we focus ourselves on the twenty-first century. Become an integral working part of our great institution.

And, oh yes, one more thing: mazal tov!

FRIENDSHIP

At the start of every new month, we recite special prayers. Birkat Hachodesh. We ask God for the important things: Chaim-Life. A long life, a peaceful life, a healthy life, a life of wealth and honor, a life of commitment to the Torah and the traditions of our people. (This prayer is not said before Tishrey because all the Rosh Hashana prayers are devoted to these themes as a new year begins).

Then we ask God to redeem all the Jewish people and gather us from the four corners of the world to our homeland, the land of Israel. The prayer finishes with chaverim kol yisrael. A statement that all Israel are chaverim, friends.

Is it true? Is every Jew the friend of every other Jew? Would you call yourself a friend of Ethiopian Jews who just came from Addis Ababa? Are you the personal friends of the Soviet Jews who came yesterday from Leningrad? You don't even know their names. Did you ever have a friend whose name you didn't know? Do you know their address, or how many children they have? Do you know anything about these Jews except that they came to Israel? So how do we have the chutzpah to call these people our friends, chaverim kol yisrael. Kinship, but not friendship.

Chaverim: What does it really mean, chaver, friend. Lechaver: Means to be tied together, to be so closely associated with another person, as if the two of you were one. A special relationship where you can anticipate each other's thoughts and needs. Where your greatest pleasure comes from fulfilling your friend's needs and wishes. You can't pick your family, but you can pick your friends.

Gerer Rabbi: How is Moshe Chaim, your chaver. "I don't know." You study with him, you sing and dance with him and you dare to tell me you don't know how he is. Friends always know and always care.

If we make one or two true friends in our lifetime, then we are lucky.

We need friends.

That is the nature of real friendship. And how do we find a real friend? Because without a real friend life is a lot harder to endure. How do we find a true chaver, one who will be totally committed to us? Who will be ready to give us the shirt off his back if we need it? [Ads in the personal column, people are lonely].

Talmud:
Buy a friend. Kinyan is a business term.
Acquire a friend. You have to pay for friendship? You have to earn it by first being a good friend. If you want to have a friend then be a friend. Make the first move. Extend

your hand. Extend yourself. "Man who stood in a corner and called our people unfriendly in Shul." No one is dispensable. Sara Haut—No one puts out his hands, "no one calls to see why we are missing."

Moishele Mein Freint—Reminisce with friends. You have shared a lifetime of experience. When you sit together, you get a good feeling.

Two of our best friends live in Connecticut. We see them perhaps twice a year. But when we get together it is as if no time has passed.

Chavrusa: Term used to denote two people studying Talmud. In Yeshiva, you are required to study with someone else, not by yourself. Because one plus one equals more than two. One brain and one brain equals more than the brain-power of two people. Synergism.

How to tell a good friend from a bad friend. There is no greater disappointment than to realize that you have been betrayed by a supposed friend. It always happens in a crisis. The test of the friendship is always in a crisis, when you need a friend, when you need a favor.

How to be a good friend: Have a good eye. A good eye is a sign of real friendship. One who is kind and considerate. One who does not cast upon you an Ayin harah, an evil eye. One who doesn't fa'gin you. A good friend is happy for your success, rejoices in your simcha as if it were his. Doesn't envy you.

A good friend doesn't become angry with you, or at least if he becomes angry he quickly gets over it and forgives you. Don't become a chaver with a person who is quick to anger. An unstable person.

Psychologists call it a toxic relationship. Toxic relationships versus supportive relationships.

Toxic relationship—A person who poisons your self-esteem, your confidence. Who always criticizes you, who doesn't let you forget your faults, who always knocks you. Seek out friends who will support you, boost your confidence, and give you spiritual and moral strength. People you can let your hair down with, where you don't have to watch every word you say and keep up your guard.

"My wife is my best friend." Our most important friend should be our wife or husband.

A friend is really interested in how you are and if he can help you. Your acquaintances ask you "how are you," but they really don't want to know. If you tell them, they get bored. If you insist once too often, they will run away from you when they see you.

I visit a member. I ask him how he is, he spends the next 45 minutes telling me all his problems. Every time I come. He never gets around to asking me how I am. Only a good friend is sincerely interested in you and your problems.

Israel and the United States enjoy a special relationship. It would be very difficult for Israel without American foeign aid, loan guarantees, and political support.

And it would be difficult for America without one absolutely reliable ally in the Middle East.

"Nations don't have friends, only interests"—Kissinger via Clausewitz. But Israel and America are true friends; they share more than mutual interests. We share the vision of a better world, a world of peace. Our friendship is not based on oil interests, or only on realpolitik, or only military agreements. It is based primarily on our mutual understanding of morality. Our friendship is firmly established on the spiritual plane, all other interests flow from there.

Just after midnight on May 15, 1948, David Ben-Gurion proclaimed the birth of the State of Israel.

Eleven minutes later, President Harry Truman recognized Ben-Gurion's government as "the defacto authority of the new State of Israel." The United States thus became the first nation to recognize Israel's existence. It was not a decision arrived at easily.

Many of the President's advisors, including Secretary of State George Marshall, had cautioned against immediate recognition.

Some doubted Israel's ability to survive the invasion being threatened by its Arab neighbors. Others worried about jeopardizing American interests in the region's oil fields. Almost all advised the President to move slowly.

But Truman was not deterred by their arguments. As he told one advisor, "I don't care about the oil, I want to do what's right.

Moved by historical heritage, the memory of the Holocaust, and the plight of hundreds of thousands of Jewish refugees, the President saw Israel's cause as just. And he believed a strong democracy in the Middle East would inevitably help promote those values that are cherished between the two countries.

In the 46 years since, America and Israel have been united in the cause that President Truman saw so clearly—the cause of peace and democracy in the Middle East.

As the ancient prophet said: Israel is Or lagoyim, a light unto the nations. We provide the moral direction for the world. When the world runs amok, when nations are bent on destroying one another, when the world seems about to self destruct, we remind everyone that there is a better way, a rational way, a peaceful way. The way of shalom.

So we all need friends, nations as well as people. We need a chaver to share our life's experiences. The good times and the bad times. The simchas and the tzuris. That's what friends are for. (Latin wedding: the whole family in the procession). Imagine making a chasana and having no one to invite to the simcha? Imagine a person sitting shiva with no one to visit him. Imagine your daughter being accepted to Harvard and no one to tell it to. That's what friends are for.

Who do you talk to when you're having trouble with your parents, grief from your mother-in-law, pressure from your creditors, threats from your loan officer. You talk to your friends. Who do you go to when you need some mezuman. You look for help from your chaverim. That's what friends are for.

Do you know the song "That's What Friends Are For"?

Close your eyes and know these words are coming from my heart, and if you can remember, Keep smiling, keep shining, knowing that you can always count on me for sharing. That's what friends are for. For good times and bad times. I'll be on your side for evermore. That's what friends are for.

May you learn to be a good friend. May the New Year bring you friends and friendship.

ARMAGEDDON

Excavating at Megiddo, digging in the garbage and dirt. Good garbage and dirt, because it belonged to our ancestors. The Israelites who lived some 3000 years ago. Up at 4:30 A.M. Pick and shovel work until 1:00 P.M. Lunch. Work again. Lecture. Fall down and go to sleep.

Dogs barking, kibbutzniks barbecuing and shouting to one another. South Americans on ulpan learning Hebrew for aliya. World Cup has them screaming in the night. No sleep.

No food. Shomer Hatzair founded in 1948. No kosher food to eat. Can't even make good salads. An embarrassment to all Israelis.

On the way to work, carrying the picks or shovels or the water cans, I would pass the kibbutz cemetery. One day I walked in. Kibbutz founded by Holocaust survivors from Poland, and I could see all the Polish-sounding names. I always look at ages, especially in Israel, where you are dealing with the war dead. One grave read 17 years old. I asked. He came off the boat and was given a rifle and sent to the battle for Latrun. He probably didn't even know how to load a Mauser or move the bolt. He survived the Holocaust to die in Israel, or for Israel. I don't know if he had parents alive— If they were alive, do you think they were overjoyed to find out that their son had to go to war? Do you think they were happy to see him with a gun on his shoulder marching off to face Arab gunfire? Were they enthusiastic about sacrificing their son for the State of Israel? No. On all accounts no. No normal parent wants to send a son into harms way. They wanted peace. They wanted life. They had enough after the Holocaust. But they let him go. They realized that the State of Israel came with a price tag, a very high price tag. The blood of young Jews. The alternative was back to the gas chambers. There was no alternative. Ein Breira.

44 years later I am standing in front of his grave thinking at 4:30 in the morning. The sun is still below the horizon. A dim light marks the gravestone (matzeva). It is mostly dark. It fits my mood. A 17 year old dead before he could even live. His parents wanted him alive. I wished him alive. He would have been riding the tractor in those fields on the edge of the Emek. Maybe he would have been working in the kitchen (maybe we would have gotten better food). Maybe. His parents wanted peace—I wanted peace for him. For all the Israeli people.

Who in his right mind wouldn't want peace? Do you think Yitzchak Rabin doesn't want peace? Do you think Yitzchak Shamir doesn't want peace? Could there possibly be any Jew who doesn't want peace?

The question is not do we want peace. The question is what is the best way to achieve peace. A lasting peace. So that we never have to see the grave of a 17 year old killed in war again.

And my question is what do the Israelis say? What is their solution? I am not referring to the political leadership. We read their statements every day in the paper. What do the cab drivers and the garbage collectors and the supermarket check-out girls think? The common people, Amcha? What do the professors and students at the university think? The intelligentsia. I listen to them all. Carefully. Here is what I heard.

The excavations at Megiddo were supervised by several professors from Tel Aviv University led by the chairman of the department of Archaeology, Yisrael Finkelstein. A man named Yisrael has to come from a family of strong Zionists. And the leadership of the kibbutz were already part of the International Zionist Movement before the war. No one could question their Zionist credentials. All these people had one thing in common. They were affiliated with the labor movement. They were always socialist oriented. They were all anti-religious. Exactly my landsman. Daniel in the lion's den. No, actually we couldn't be further apart, in the political spectrum. (I grew up in the Bnei Akiva movement). This was good for me. To hear the other side. To debate, to argue, to sharpen my point of view. Maybe to be convinced. Maybe to change my point of view—or at least to modify my point of view.

Every morning at 4:30 I found myself walking to the dig with Professor Yisrael Finkelstein. We became friends but intellectual adversaries. Our debates would continue even as we began to swing the picks and shovel the dirt, and, of course, I was down in the hole covered with dirt and he was up on top grinning. The entire work crew joined in this debate. They looked forward to the daily battle of wits between the American Rabbi and the Tel Aviv professor.

One morning we stood on the tel. The sun was just rising over the Carmel mountain range. In my mind's eye, I could see the chariots of Ahab or the armies of Josiah wheeling into place to face the mighty Egyptians, or the Canaanites.

The great earthshaking battles of the ancient world took place here at Megiddo, for control of the entire Middle East. The great southern Egyptian empire, against the great Assyrian northern empire. With Israel in the middle, as usual. Therefore, the place is called Armageddon, the place of the last great battle, according to the Christian Book of Revelations. Actually, Armageddon is a combination of the two Hebrew words, Har Meggido. Even the prophet Zechariah refers to the end of days, and the great battle at Mediggo. The great destruction to be followed by a new beginning for the people of Israel. Perhaps a prophetic vision of a Holocaust followed by a rebirth.

But the chariots were long gone, and I stood listening to a young man who represented the State of Israel in 1994. This is what he said standing on the very spot where the kings of Israel stood 2500 years ago and watched their armies collapse and disintegrate under a more powerful force. Where the results of the wrong political choices, and the wrong strategies brought destruction on the people of Israel. The veritable Armageddon.

The country is divided into two schools of thought: Those who believe that our right to the land of Israel comes from the Bible, from the weight of history. And our connection to the land is rooted in our religious experience. For these people, the strongest attachment is for Jerusalem and Hebron and Shomron. These places where our forefathers lived and died. Where Jewish history and Judaism was born and developed. Where the earth and the stones take on a life of their own. Where the mere recitation of the place names evokes a strong emotional and intellectual reaction. For these people the mention of Jerusalem recalls 3000 years of prayers and 27 years of pride and joy and excitement since reunification. Prayers for Jerusalem, not Tel Aviv.

And the second category of citizens are those who believe that the land of Israel comes to us through the Balfour Declaration, the League of Nations, and the United Nations. The Bible is ancient history; it does not apply to this century. War on the battlefields and war in the political arena created the State of Israel. For these people, Israel is Tel Aviv and Haifa and Netanya. These are the places where Jews live and develop a modern country, where commerce and industry thrive. The stones of Hebron and Shomron and even Jerusalem are only stones.

Mute. Pieces of material. Devoid of any real historical connection. To be honest, there is some nostalgic connection. But if realpolitik demands that we retreat from some of these places then so be it. For peace, it is worth it. And these people consider the religious elements as fanatics, holding back the peace process for a pile of stones and earth in the West Bank.

At the beginning of July, 100,000 people demonstrated in the heart of Jerusalem demanding that Jerusalem remain the united capital of the State of Israel, and that Arafat's claims on the city be rejected. We made it a point to be there, to add our presence and our voices! The next morning at Megiddo my friend the professor says to me: We have to break the backs of these religious fanatics. They are holding back the peace process.

Imagine. Up until last year, for more that 25 years, these same people were considered the pioneers, the modem Zionists, the latest heroes of the country. They disregarded hardships and danger. They moved into the newly liberated territories of Yehuda and Shomron. The government asked them to go create Jewish facts on the ground. To outflank and outnumber the Arabs in the strategic Judean hills and in the Jordan River Valley. Many of them were religious people. Religious people tend to be idealists. The people with the kippot are fired by a sense of history and destiny. They are strong, they are brave, they don't pack up and run away at the slightest sign of trouble. They are ready to live their lives as Zionists. That quaint concept that has been abandoned by so many people in the new generation.

And my friend the professor talks about breaking the backs of the religious people. Tell me, what kind of state should we have in Israel? Should it have some connection with the Bible, with Jewish history, with Jewish culture, with the Jewish religion? Do Jews live in Israel or do Canaanites live there? Does Israel strive to be the Jewish homeland or a New Zealand on the Mediterranean coast? New Zealand is a wonderful country. Many Israelis visit. Many stay. They are attracted by its beauty, its good people, its political climate, and mainly its peaceful nature. But it isn't Israel. As Uganda wasn't Israel and as Brooklyn isn't Israel.

I resent the demonization of the religious elements in the West Bank. Now, understand me clearly. I am not in favor of imposing a theocratic biblical system on all the people of Israel. In a democracy, each is free to choose his life style. But I am insisting on respect for one another. Every Jew in Israel is important. Every Jew has something to contribute. Every Jewish life is dear.

Yes, I wince when I see more people at the beach on Rosh Hashana than in the synagogue in Tel Aviv. Maybe that's the fault of the Israeli Rabbinate. Maybe a more progressive and creative Israeli Rabbinate will eventually be able to influence more people. Maybe a complete overhaul of the educational system will bring a heightened respect for and knowledge of tradition. Religion cannot be legislated; it must be taught. In the meantime, it is a free country. But I don't want to hear an academic leader in Israel talk about breaking the back of any Jews.

And I certainly don't want to see Jews throwing rocks at fellow Jews in an attempt to literally break their backs. Frank Meisler told me that while I was excavating in Megiddo, archaeologists in Jaffa, just a block from his studio, uncovered bones. In one hour, the dig was surrounded by rock-throwing Chassidim. For the sake of old bones, they were ready to break living Jewish heads. Incidentally, Meisler tells me the bones were determined to have been from a Christian cemetery. Then the Chassidim melted away.

For me, the answer is in the time-honored rabbinic fashion: you're right and you're right. Israel is Tel Aviv and Haifa, but it is also Jerusalem and Hebron. By that, I mean that Israel belongs both to the religious people and the secularists, and they are going to have to learn to get along. At least, to respect one another. Internal peace is at least as important as peace with our Arab neighbors. Maybe more important.

And speaking of Arab neighbors, the pace of the peace process has been breathtaking. Arafat sends shana tova. Who would ever have dreamed just 15 months ago that the border between Israel and Jordan would come down? It is the Middle East equivalent of the Berlin Wall coming down. And who would ever have imagined King Hussein speaking to the Israeli leadership from his own jet flying over Israeli airspace? A week before, he would have been shot down by Israeli F-16s. And Hussein is a capable pilot.

To my mind, the Jordanian connection has the most far-reaching implications for the future: One of our greatest concerns has been the status of Jerusalem. By reaffirming

King Hussein's traditional role as the guardian of the Muslim holy places, the PLO is effectively removed from the picture. And Arafat understands this, and that is why he reacted so angrily. Israel and Jordan have effectively pulled the political rug out from under the PLO in Jerusalem.

Furthermore, in another brilliant maneuver Prime Minister Rabin has made the extension of PLO autonomy contingent on containing the terrorist violence that continues. He is saying to Arafat, live up to your part of the bargain, then we will talk again.

Even more important is the fact that if Hussein is officially recognized as representing the Arab presence in Jerusalem then the question of Jerusalem as an Arab capital evaporates. Amman is the capital of Jordan. King Hussein has no other political ambition in Jerusalem. Furthermore, if the Arab population of the West Bank wishes to express itself politically, then they can vote in Amman. Essentially, the Arab population of the West bank become confederated citizens of Jordan, if they choose. If not, they continue to live in their own autonomous region within Israel. Once again, we hear Jordan is Palestine. I hope this is the way it ends.

This was the amazing proposal out of the mouths of my new friends at Megiddo. And when I asked them what about the Jewish settlers, they said, as long as they do not set out to intentionally provoke the Arab population, let them stay. Maybe not in downtown Hebron, and certainly not in Nablus. But why not in Ariel and Karnei Shomron and the Jordan River Valley?

The process moves forward toward self-empowerment, toward autonomy, maybe toward a state. Most of the Israeli population seems to have adopted a cautious optimism. They are quick to tell me that no one really trusts the PLO. But if the peace negotiations can buy 20 years of peace, if at least one generation of young Israelis won't have to go to war, if the next group of 18 year olds doesn't have to enter the filthy and dangerous alley ways of Gaza, then it will be worth it. Who really knows if the Arabs really mean to have peace or are merely taking Israel a piece at a time? But most Israelis are resigned to giving it a chance. The most committed leftists will tell you they don't want to see the Arabs anymore. Let them live in peace in their own areas. But not in Tel Aviv.

And if it fails. If after the Palestinian Arabs establish their own autonomous region. And they control all aspects of their lives. And they prosper. But they are unable to control their radical elements. And the West Bank becomes a launching pad for terrorist raids into Tel Aviv and Haifa and Jerusalem. What then?

Then, in the words of my friend the professor, Armageddon. "We will go to war and we will destroy them," he said. But at least I will be able to look at my son and say, "we tried." We tried to give you a better life. We tried to bring you peace.

On the last day of work, we struck bones in the dirt. They were quickly revealed to be human. By the beautiful bowls and cups surrounding it, we determined that it was a Philistine burial, 3000 years old. From the Philistines, came the term Palestinian. Jews in Palestine until 1948 had Palestinian stamped in their passports. Now, only the Arabs are called Palestinians. Actually, there is no connection between the ancient Philistines and the modern Arabs. It comes from the name given to Israel by the Romans, Philistia. It was an attempt to remove all Jewish traces from the map.

Here was a Philistine buried in the ground of an Israelite city, probably from the time of King Solomon. What was he doing there, so far from his capital city of Gaza down on the coast? My first reaction was to deny the evidence. I think I could have removed the bones and thrown them into the dump if no one was watching. This was ancient Israelite territory. One of Solomon's great chariot cities. No place for Philistines.

But archaeology deals with facts, not emotion. Archaeologists are not in the business of revising history. They leave that to the politicians. A Philistine lived or at least died in Megiddo. I would have preferred not to find him there in Israeli territory. But he was there nonetheless.

I would have preferred not to find Palestinian Arabs living in Jerusalem and Hebron and Shiloh and Shomron. But there they are. They have been buried in the soil of the West Bank for hundreds of years. As much as I want to, I can't deny this fact. It was not their land, it wasn't their cities. But here they are. And as much as I would like to throw them away into the historical dump, I can't. I will have to live with it. We Jews are not in the business of ethnic cleansing.

Let us go forward with a cautious optimism. Let us continue to maintain Israel's strength, for Israel's strength is our strength. Let us pray that the bloodshed will finally end; but let us resolve that all the Jewish blood spilled for the State of Israel will not have been spilled in vain. Whatever the new year will bring, we will face it with courage, and with faith in the future of the people of Israel.

WORDS MATTER

Sticks and stones will break my bones, but names will never hurt me.

When I was a kid in public school, in third grade I think, an Irish boy started picking on me. I remember him well. He was a head taller than me, at least 20 pounds heavier, and he had a crew cut. Somehow he found out that I was Jewish. From that day on, it was "Jew Boy." Whenever he saw me, he would yell "Jew Boy." He was looking for a fight, a fight that he knew he could win.

I knew what Jew was; I knew what boy was. Nothing wrong with those words. But somehow I knew by the tone of his voice and the sneer on his face that he wasn't offering me a compliment. He followed it with a few other chosen words, one starting with a K and ending with an E. Rhymes with like. And just for good measure, he ended with Christ killer. That really baffled me. I didn't know anyone by that name. And the only thing I ever killed was a fish.

I told my mother. She answered: "Sticks and stones will break my bones but names will never hurt me."

The next time that tough Irish kid called me a "Jew Boy", I started reciting "Sticks and stone. . ." He said, "Oh yeah, watch this." And he grabbed me by the front of my shirt and knocked me down on the ground, and almost broke my arm.

Names do hurt. Words matter. The Talmud reminds us.

Life and death are in the power of the tongue. Words lead directly to violence.

The single most violent episode in the history of the United States took place last April. A bomb exploded in the Murrah Federal Building in Oklahoma City.

169 people were killed including little children in a day care center, and even babies.

We were horrified. We thought this only happens somewhere else. In Tel Aviv, in Jerusalem, in London, in the Paris subway, in the Tokyo subway. Somehow we forgot about New York and the World Trade Center. We quickly dismissed it from our minds.

An aberration; an exception. It wouldn't happen again. The FBI will protect us. The CIA will keep *them* out of the country. "Them" were the Muslim fanatics. Terrorists who murder innocent people.

Then we were horrified a second time when we learned that the terrorists were some of us. Americans. Mid-Westerners with a Midwest twang. Good neighbors. Nice people. So they said. But they had a nasty habit. They played with guns and with explosives. In their twisted minds, the enemy was the federal government. Was this 1995 or was this 1865 in the middle of the Civil War? To this moment, I am still struggling to understand how this happened.

Now, we know all about militias. Thousands of people across the country who spend weekends dressed in combat boots and camouflage; prowling through the woods, machine guns in hand; firing at the unseen enemy. Besides the caliber of their bullets, they have a few other things in common: They hate. They hate blacks, Jews, Hispanics, Orientals, Chicanos, Puerto Ricans, Cubans, Chinese, Japanese, Vietnamese. They hate everyone and anyone who is different. And they blame the government for all their troubles. The government is a threat. The federal government wants to limit their rights, take away their guns, force them to abide by the laws of the land. They refuse. They have been secretly preparing for war. Oklahoma City was the first major battlefield. The casualties were very high. Almost 200 dead. The concussion waves are still being felt.

But again I ask. How did this happen? It began with words: Angry violent words that lead to violence.

A few weeks after the bombing, a group of Nobel Laureates in literature gathered in Atlanta. The bombing was very much on their minds. Here is the way they put it: "The bombing in Oklahoma City was a result of a society grown inarticulate and unused to expressing itself with language."

Translated into more direct terms it means: A man comes home from a mean and frustrating day at work. He is tired and angry. He doesn't know how to express himself to his wife in order to vent his anger. So he curses at her in the most vile language. And then to punctuate his point he uses his fists. Her bloody nose and broken jaw mean he hates his boss.

The television is filled with talk shows. What they all have in common is the crude and primitive people they parade in front of the camera to discuss everything crude and primitive about their lives. Are they the new role models for the 21st century?

I noticed they have another thing in common: They lack the ability to convince logically and articulately. And when their comments are not accepted positively, they raise their voices. They begin to shout. As if the louder they speak the more convincing they will be. Eventually, they appear to be on the verge of punching one another. One actually shot another off stage.

It reminds me of my first visit to France. I had studied a few years of French in school. I figured I could make myself understood. I tried to explain to an old lady in a bakery shop that I wanted that size baguette. She wasn't understanding me. So I began to speak louder, throwing in English words for good measure. Suddenly, she grabbed her broom and threatened me. I beat a hasty retreat. I guess by the loud tone of my voice she thought I was threatening her.

New York has one of the highest crime rates in the country. I discovered one of the main reasons.

A big headline in the *New York Times* read: "Welcome to New York, the curse capital of the country." A five year old in a day care center in Manhattan was asked to sit down. She opened a mouth at the teacher using more four letter words than I ever knew. Where did she learn them? From her family. Why do her parents use such language in their casual conversation?

Because life in New York is so difficult, so stressful. That's the excuse given in the article.

Do you know the most violent address in new York? Madison Square Garden during a New York Ranger Game. Last May, Stephanie Glazer, 25, was kicked out of Madison Square Garden for yelling obscenities at one of the Ranger Players. The men around her were also yelling obscenities. But they only threw her out. The rule book states that "unfeminine" behavior is reason for ejection. She's suing for discrimination. But the bottom line is that the Rangers' player she was cursing at started climbing over the glass to attack her. A huge fist fight broke out in the stands. And you think that words don't lead to violence?

When my grandparents came to New York, life for them was just as stressful. More stressful. No body helped them. There was no low-income housing. There were no food stamps. There was no monthly welfare check. And there was no cursing. I never heard my grandfather use a bad word. They believed in Shmirat halashon. Careful speech. It gave a person dignity and mentchlechkeit. Language was holy. Not just the language of the Bible. But the language of communication that linked one person to another. And if any of the grandchildren became so Americanized that a curse word was heard in our house, then we were marched straight to the sink. Soap in the mouth has a way of improving the vocabulary.

Not that there were no curses in Jewish. But they were so much more sophisticated, actually witty and even poetic: "You should have a toothache and the dentist should remove every single tooth except one, and that tooth should be the one giving you the toothache." Or: "Your mother-in-law should be a shrew like your wife and the two should live together with you in the same house with only one room." Or my favorite: "You should be a like a chandelier: Hang by day and burn by night."

Very different were the Italians next door who would often start cursing at each other. The next thing we knew would be the sound of a beating. Someone would come flying out of the house with a bloody face. We considered such behavior low class, not fit for Jews.

We understood that angry words, dirty words lead to violence.

When I was in high school, we were off on Friday, Erev Shabbat. All the day school kids had to go to school on Sunday instead. We met on Fridays at the local park to play basketball. We occasionally got into arguments about a call. Maybe we shoved each other in the heat of the game. But in all those years I never saw a violent confrontation.

A few years ago, in that same park, in the Bronx, a basketball game ended when one kid took out a gun and shot another. He didn't like the call. His fellow player had called him a name. Made some disparaging remark about his mother. A bullet ended the argument.

You get the picture. *Hachaim ve'hamavet beyad halashon.* How we speak to one another really is a life and death matter.

Oklahoma City begins with Skokie, Chicago.

Nazis march spewing their anti-Jewish and anti-black hatred. The government protects them. Right in the middle of a Jewish neighborhood. Right in front of hundreds of survivors of the Shoah, with the numbers visible on their arms. If the government protects the rights of Nazis, then what does the public conclude. That it's okay to attack Jews verbally. And it will logically follow that it's okay to attack them physically.

The paranoid ravings of talk show hosts leads to Oklahoma. On the Michigan radio, we hear "Death to the new world order." G. Gordon Liddy advises his listeners how to kill federal agents. "Shoot twice to the head and groin."

Anti-abortion fanatics preach that every abortion is murder. Just talk you say? Meaningless ravings? A doctor was executed by an anti-abortion lunatic. The words of a fanatic preacher are directly responsible.

Rush Limbaugh calls the people who disagree with him, "feminazis." Pat Robertson, leader of the Christian Coalition, tells his followers that a Satanic conspiracy started centuries ago by European bankers (with Jewish names, of course) trying to destroy America under a new world order. Newt Gingrich calls Democrats "the enemy of normal Americans." Jesse Helms tells President Clinton "not to come to his state without a bodybag."

Do you think these words have no effect?

A crazed Viennese house painter named Shicklgruber was arrested in a Munich Beer Hall. He wrote a book called *Mein Kampf*. "Just words," said the Western European leaders. By 1945, they realized just what words can do. Hitler and the Nazis taught us a lesson that we will never forget.

What about the word "Jihad"? Yassir Arafat makes the rounds of the Gaza mosques calling for a Jihad to liberate Jerusalem from the infidel Jews. When word gets out to the Israeli press, he claims it's only words, words for the benefit of his audience who expect these words from him. Nothing to be alarmed about. Only words.

Jihad. Only a word? I could recite the list by heart of all the times in the modern history of the State of Israel that the call for Jihad led to the massacre of Israeli citizens.

The word Jihad led to four major wars. Jihad led to bus bombings, supermarket explosions, knifings, brutal axe murders, gasoline bomb incinerations. 140 murdered in the last two years.

Everything brutal and horrifying in Israeli life has been the result of that one word: Jihad. In 1929, in Hebron, dozens of Yeshiva students were dragged out by their beards and hacked to death by the local Arabs. Jihad.

In 1948, the Etzion bloc of kibbutzim on the Bethlehem-Hebron road was overrun. The kibbutznicks were massacred. Jihad.

In 1973, the Israeli emplacement on the Hermon in the Golan Heights was overrun by the Syrians. The next day, when the Israelis retook the position, they found a dozen men dead in the snow. Their arms were tied behind them, they were surrounded by blood. The Israeli army doctor verified that they had been horribly mutilated and left to bleed to death. No one wishes to speak of it in Israel. Such barbarism. Such horrible deaths for 18 and 19 year olds. Why? One word! Jihad.

If there is ever to be peace in Israel, and the government is trying with all its might to achieve it, then the word Jihad has to be erased from the Arab vocabulary. And in its place, we need to put the word Salaam—Shalom.

One last bad word, a violent word. Right from the headlines. The word that Detective Mark Fuhrman used to describe Black men. A variation of the word Negro; but a way of referring to Blacks with contempt, with venom.

Do you think it's just a word? How many times did a white mob come for a Black man shouting that word? And that Black man choked to death at the end of a rope. That word meant that Black people weren't human, that they were field animals that it is okay to murder them. All this in America, just six decades ago. Words kill.

And this word devastated the reputation of Mark Fuhrman, and this word devastated the reputation of the Los Angeles police force.

Do you realize what it will now take to win back the confidence of the people of Los Angeles?

So the Talmud was right. *Hachaim ve'hamavet beyad halashon.* The words we speak are indeed a life and death matter. Words can kill, like bullets, like bombs. The wrong words lead to mavet, destruction.

On the other hand, the right words, good words, lead to chaim to life. They can change our world for the better. Words of friendship, words of love, words of poetry, words of peace.

Now, I realize this is all easier said than done. It's very hard to train ourselves to watch our words more carefully. And words are like arrows. Once they are out they are on the way to their target. You can't take them back. Once you say it, you have to live with the consequences. Once you fire away, your target is going to be wounded.

So I suggest to you a slogan, as a reminder. I saw it printed on a card in the office of a prominent CEO: "Make sure brain is engaged before mouth is put in gear."

And the last words I wish to share with you this morning are the nicest words I know for this day:

May God bless us in the new year with health, happiness, and peace, and the good sense to speak politely, logically, and softly like mentchen, and to cultivate the habit of saying the right thing at the right time.

THE LIVING DEAD

Rosh Hashana—time for family gathering. Also a time when we are reminded of those who are missing. It culminates in athe Yom Kippur Yizkor, when we recite the names of the dead, we honor their memory, and pledge to remain true to their ideals.

Those who left us—our grandparents, our parents, our loved ones—are not really gone. If we open our hearts, we can feel their presence. Whenever we reach out to them, they are there. They continue to inspire us and guide us. In a sense, they continue to live in our midst.

On the other hand, I know people who are walking around but are as good as dead. They breathe, they function, they are healthy, their bad cholesterol is low, their good cholesterol is high, their blood pressure is moderate, but they are dead. They are dead to the community, because they refuse to be part of us. They isolate themselves from Jewish life. They have hearts, but they don't feel. They have eyes, but they don't see. They have ears, but they don't hear.

These are the living dead. Bodies with out souls without a Yiddishe neshama.

The Talmud actually describes four categories of the living dead. Way before Hollywood showed us Bela Lugosi and Lon Chaney (Talmud Nedarim 64b).

The poor, the leper, the blind, and one who is without children.

Poor—does not mean one who has no money or material possessions. It means someone who can't part with a dollar. A person whom it hurts terribly to put his hand in his pocket. The Talmud defines rich not in terms of what you own, but what owns you. Do you own your money or does it own you? The important question is, what do you do with it?

One of the greatest Rabbis of the Talmud was Hillel. So great that to this day everyone recognizes his name, and most of us can even tell you something he said. (Love thy neighbor as thyself).

Yet, he was so poor that if he was living today, he would be using food stamps and might be living in a cardboard box under the I-95. His colleagues had a saying: If a man claims he can't come to the synagogue and study Torah because he is too poor, and he has to use all his time earning a living, he should be asked, are you poorer than Hillel? (Yoma 35b)

But Hillel was rich. He had a richness of character, of personality, of intelligence and understanding. He enriched the entire Jewish people, every person who ever opened a page of the Talmud down to this very day.

So you don't have to be wealthy in dollars to be rich in spirit. Yet, our leaders always understood the value of material wealth. A famous Chassidic Rabbi came to a rich man for a contribution. He came every year. Finally, the exasperated rich man asked the Rabbi, why are you so concerned with money, money, money? Money is nothing, it is *bloto*, a swamp. To which the Rabbi replied: I would like to get into such blotte. Clearly, money can be a great source of good if used properly. When used improperly, money is, indeed, blotte, a swamp, a worthless weight around your neck that drags you down until you suffocate.

Remember Sophie Tucker? What did she say? "I have been rich and I have been poor, but, believe me, rich is better."

So when the Rabbis of the Talmud talked about the poor as one of the living dead, they meant people who have tens of thousands of dollars, a million dollars, but they have nothing to give. A wealthy person who can't share some of his wealth for good causes is a poor man indeed.

Afternoon Yizkor Service. Our service to the Aventura-Turnberry community. I doubt that anyone is so poor that he or she can't afford to be a member (even at a discount).

I know a very wealthy man who comes yearly for his yahrzeit. He makes no contribution. He comes to shul for the holy days. He comes to listen to our guest lecturers, and he makes no contribution. He could afford to be a member. He could afford to buy a classroom in our new school building.

They say he's a very wealthy man. But I don't think so. He's a poor man. He is a taker. He takes from every one of our pockets, because we have to give for him. He uses the synagogue that we built and we continue to build.

Newspaper story. A recluse lived on welfare in a one-room apartment in the middle of a slum. When he died, they found a half a million dollars under his mattress. The newspaper called him a rich man. They were wrong. He had a lot of money, but he was a very poor man. He lived by collecting charity. He was a taker. He never gave anything to improve the community. For the community, he was always a dead man no matter how many dollars he had under his mattress.

Last month another story appeared: Down in Hattiesburg Mississippi, Oseola McCarty turned 87 years old. For almost 75 years, she took in bundles of dirty clothing. She washed them and pressed them for a few dollars and change. She managed to save $150,000.

Last month, she made a donation. She gave $150,000 to the University of Southern Mississippi. "It's more than I could use, " she said, "I wanted to share my wealth with the children. I couldn't go to school, but now they will." So she decided to finance scholarships for deserving Black students.

Imagine her: Wrinkled black skin, white hair, bent over a scrub board day after day. A poor little woman. No. A rich woman. A rich spirit. A great inspiration. She'll be remembered by the dozens of students who benefit from her great heart. She may be Black, but she had a Yiddishe heart.

The second category of the living dead are the blind. Now God forbid that the Rabbis should call a blind man a dead man. It doesn't mean the physically blind. As a matter of fact the Talmud has a beautiful name for a blind person. Sagi N'hor, one who sees perfectly. They knew that people without sight often possess a great deal of insight. As the poet and philosopher Ibn Gabirol once wrote: "Not the eye, but the heart is blind."

Rabbi Sheshet of the Talmud was blind. Yet, he taught thousands of students and colleagues. He opened other eyes to Jewish values. He molded Jewish personalities.

When I was a student at Yeshiva University, an upper classman named Yossi was in charge of the Bais Medrash. In the Bais Medrash, we were expected to prepare for our daily class in Talmud. Whenever anyone had a problem, with a difficult line in the text, or an esoteric Rashi, we would ask Yossi. Yossi was brilliant. He knew every page and every word, and he could explain it simply and beautifully. Yossi was blind. He knew it by heart. Every line in the Talmud was in his memory. He had incredible insight into

Jewish law. He made me see more clearly than most of my professors.

On the other hand, people whose eyes are perfectly normal, who have 20/20 vision, are often blind. Because they refuse to see the truth. They refuse to open their eyes to the realities of life.

In the early 1940s, President Roosevelt was shown graphic proof of the murder of thousands of Jews in Auschwitz and other camps. He refused to listen. He and the entire State Department chose to close their eyes. So thousands of murdered Jews became six million murdered Jews.

Most of the world chose to look away. The leaders of the Western world refused to see that was happening. Even members of the Jewish community closed their eyes. No one wanted to be pained by the horrors of the Shoah. These people shut their eyes to the truth. They might as well have been dead.

When we close our eyes to the problems of the world, we are the living dead.

I turn on the TV and see with my own eyes Serbs and Croats taking turns raping and murdering each other's populations. I don't want to watch it. I turn the channel. I see Hutu tribesman hacking to pieces their Tutzi neighbors in Ruwanda. How disgusting. Barbaric. I don't want to see anymore. I turn off the television.

The next day I turn on CNN just in time to see color film of a bus in Tel Aviv that was exploded by an Arab terrorist.

The camera zooms in close so I won't miss the bloody bodies and the pieces of hands and feet and heads that blew across the street and into the trees. The Chevra Kadisha are trying to gather up the body parts and the blood for proper burial. I can't take it anymore. I turn off the TV.

But I can't turn away. We can't just turn away. We have to open our eyes. We have to open our hearts. We have to feel. And we have to do something. I refuse to sit by helplessly while my Jewish brothers and sisters quake with fear every time they have to board a bus or go to the supermarket.

And it doesn't matter what our political orientations might be. Whether we believe that peace will be assured when the

West Bank and East Jerusalem will become a Judenrein Palestinian state or we believe that peace will come only when the Jewish people have total control over their security in the historical borders of Israel. Either way we must continue and strengthen our support for them. We must never turn away. We must never close our eyes.

The third category of the living dead are the lepers. In ancient times, a leper had to live "michutz lamachane," outside the camp. Quarantined, so he couldn't spread the disease.

The Talmud however, speaks of a spiritual leper. What is a spiritual leper? I never found such a term in a medical book. It's a person who isolates himself from the community. A self imposed Jewish quarantine.

They might be perfectly decent people, but we never see them in the synagogue, we rarely see their names on a check to a Jewish charity, they never get involved, they never help. They hideout on the 23rd floor of their high rise. They go from the card table, to the golf course, to the restaurant. They never take a little detour to the synagogue. When they travel they cruise the world, to Majorca, to Venice, to Istanbul to Hong Kong. Never a detour to Haifa. *Al tifrosh min hatzibbur.* We are warned, do not separate yourself from the community. The richest most meaningful experience comes from working together with others for the common good. Ask our synagogue volunteers, ask those who volunteer in the hospitals. It gives them a reason to get up in the morning.

It gives them a feeling of being useful, of accomplishing something with their lives. By yourself you are overcome by loneliness and uselessness. You become part of the living dead.

The last category of the spiritually dead are childless. Once again, the Talmud meant this only figuratively. Biology and genetic codes determine if we can have children or if we can't. Enzymes and hormones dictate fertility. And, in this day and age medicine, can work miracles in the new science of fertility. Couples that 20 years ago could only adopt if they wanted children now have many biological options.

The Talmud was talking about spiritual children, the mitzvas that a person does during a lifetime. The effect of the good deeds that remains long after we are gone. The ma'asim tovim.

So imagine a person who dies and leaves nothing important behind. I would call his life a waste, even a crime.

Detectives speak of the perfect crime, when no trace of the perpetrator can be detected. No fingerprints are left to identify someone. Indeed it is the perfect crime when a person walks this earth some 120 years and doesn't leave a single footprint in the sands of time.

No sign of his presence, no trace of good deeds, no positive influence on anyone.

Methuselah is a name from the Bible that everyone knows. The name even crept into our language. We use it to denote a person who lives a very long life. According to the Bible, Methuselah lived to be 969 years; and he died. Period. Nothing else is said about him. He lived. And he died. I think he is a tragic figure. With all the time he had on earth, he did nothing important. Not a single thing worth mentioning. He just took up time and space. He left no spiritual children. No legacy.

Moses had a much shorter life. 120 years. Yet, look what he left us. He led the Jewish people out of Egypt and to freedom. He gave us the Torah, the law.

He was so pervasively influential in our history that we still speak of him with awe and great respect. We are all his spiritual children. He influenced every Jew who ever lived, to this very day.

One of my friends was a founder of a wonderful vocational school in Israel for disadvantaged children. He saw a need for it on one of his first visits to Israel. He put his body and soul into that school. He worked for it day and night. He never stopped talking about it. He never stopped badgering his friends to contribute to it. It became a great source of strength and blessing in the city of Jerusalem.

One day he was giving me an update about the school. And in the course of conversation he referred to it as "my baby." "That's my baby." He spoke about the school as if it were his child; as if he and his wife had given birth to it. And indeed, they did. It was their spiritual child.

When we associate ourselves with a great institution, whether it be a synagogue, or a school, or a community center, or a hospital, when we give our energy and our material wealth to nurture and build for the benefit of our people, then we give birth to spiritual children.

When I was a youngster we loved to go to horror films. And I still remember *The Night of the Living Dead.* It gave me nightmares for months. At the really scary parts we would cover our eyes and try to hide under the seats.

But we are not kids anymore. We can't just close our eyes and try to hide under the seat. We have to stand up and accept our responsibilities. We have to open our eyes and face reality.

We have to open our eyes and open our hearts. We have to involve ourselves in the needs of our people, and our community. We have to leave a trail of good deeds as we pass this earth. And if we do our jobs properly, then we won't need a stone monument to mark our passage. Our good names will live forever.

WHAT IS RELIGIOUS?

I drive down Biscayne Boulevard every evening and make a turn on Miami Gardens Drive on the way home. Staring down at me from a huge billboard is a man with a long white beard, a black hat, and a black coat. The coat is called a kaputa, and if the hat were of fur, it would be called a shtreimel. And the style of dress is of eighteenth century Poland. The Lubavitcher Rebbe smiles down at me, enigmatically, a Jewish version of the *Mona Lisa* (lehavdil, of course). The time of your redemption has come. I don't wish to discuss the word Moshiach printed in huge letters under his picture. What I want to know is this: What does religious

mean in our day and age? Does a big black hat and curled
"payes" around the ear and a long black coat signify religious? And can the rest of us who don't look like that call
ourselves religious?

At the daily minyan, we put on tefillin as commanded in the
Bible. Tefillin come in different sizes, depending on what
you wish to spend. One man has a huge pair of tefillin,
almost as big as his head. Is he a better Jew than the rest of
us who wear smaller tefillin? Incidentally, a young lady
came to our minyan last year for several months and she
wore tefillin. They weren't pink; they were the requisite
black; and our minyan men still haven't recovered. But she
wore a pink tallis. Is she more religious than I am with a
black and white tallis?

As I was writing this, a family stopped in to see me
about joining the synagogue. In the course of the conversation, they explained that they would prefer to join a conser-
vative congregation because they weren't that religious.
They light candles and say the blessings on Friday night.
They come to synagogue occasionally and observe some of
the holy days, but they are not religious. So, I asked them,
what is religious? They really couldn't answer. This morning
we are going to look for an answer.

First, let me tell you about Aaron Feuerstein: Perhaps you
read about him in the newspaper last December. Several weeks
before the winter holidays, his factory burnt down in a mysterious fire. Malden Mills is a textile company in Massachusetts. It
was started by Aaron Feuerstein's grandfather to manufacture
sweaters. Most of the mills of Massachusetts moved first to the
south and then to Asia, looking for cheap labor. Unemployment
became a serious concern in the old mill towns across New
England. But the Feuersteins remained. Leon's answer was not
to abandon the community but to look for new products to manufacture. In 1981, the mill filed for bankruptcy. But the company persevered. They put their money into research and devel-
opment. The result was a new product called Polartec. You may

not recognize it because it is used to make lightweight shirts and fleeces that keep you warm but dry even when you perspire from exercise. I have been buying Polartec for many years, but suddenly I find out that the owner of the company is Jewish. Not only Jewish, but Orthodox, and a member of a prominent Orthodox synagogue in Brookline.

So Aaron Feuerstein was faced with a disaster. His 90-year-old family business went up in flames. The popular thinking around town was that Aaron Feuerstein would collect the insurance money and retire to Aventura-Turnberry. That would put 2,500 people out of work and devastate the town, because Malden Mills was the largest employer. The first thing Feuerstein decided to do was not to cry. And then he got up in front of his employees and made the most incredible promise. He would continue paying every one of them until the factory could reopen. That amounted to $1.5 million dollars a week. And he intended to pay them for at least 90 days.

Well, you can imagine the reaction at the factory and throughout the town. The workers could hardly believe what they heard. In this day and age of downsizing and cutbacks, who ever heard of a boss with a heart? President Clinton himself was amazed, and so impressed that he invited Aaron Feuerstein to come to his State of Tthe Union Address and to sit next to Mrs. Clinton and be acknowledged.

When I read about him, I was so impressed that I sent him a letter. And I invited him to come to our synagogue the next time he came to Florida. A few weeks later, he sent me a letter of thanks. And he wrote as follows: "I did only what I thought was right. I believe in the words of the prophet Micah, "act justly and with lovingkindness and walk humbly with God."

Now that is as good a definition of religious as I have ever heard. Aaron Feuerstein is a religious man. One of the most religious people I have ever heard of. He doesn't wear a black hat. He doesn't even have a beard. But he is a religious man. Because his religion taught him to take care of people. And he did. His religion taught him to be kind and compassionate. And he is. And his religion taught him that a person will ultimately be judged by his deeds. And Aaron Feuerstein performed a mitzva for his workers that shook the very gates of heaven.

I mentioned that Aaron Feuerstein doesn't go to shul every Shabbat. How do I know? Because a few months ago, he called my office and said that he was taking me up on my invitation. He was going to the Turnberry Hotel for a weekend and would like to come to shul. I was thrilled. I immediately arranged for an aliya. I explained to the gabbaim to be on the lookout for a tall, distinguished visitor and to bring him to me as soon as he came in. 9:30 comes and no Feuerstein. 10:00, 10:30, 11:00. He doesn't come. Not even for kiddush. Several days later, his secretary calls to offer regrets. He was in the Hotel but he couldn't make it. He would come another time.

Maybe Aaron Feuerstein slept late. Maybe he was so exhausted he needed to rest. Maybe he felt embarrassed walking in late. Maybe he wanted to play a round of golf and he could only get a tee time in the morning. No matter. Because the definition of religious is not limited to synagogue attendance and prayers. If Aaron Feuerstein never sets foot in shul again, he will still be one of the most religious men I have ever met.

Now a second case:

In the Flatbush section of Brooklyn, everyone knows the Schick Bakery. Strictly shomer Shabbos, scrupulous observers of the Sabbath, and all the minutia, of Jewish law. The family was always generous to the needy. They established a fund for poor brides. "Hachnasat calah." They produced scholars and teachers for the Yeshiva. Then came David Schick, 36 years old, attorney and successful real estate investor. Because of his reputation as a religious young man, from a religious family, wealthy Jews from the Orthodox world came to invest their money with him. A man who prayed 3 times a day, who could be

seen every Shabbat in the front of the synagogue could be trusted. The man who arranged a meeting for his Yeshiva support-
ers with President Clinton himself had connections. Orthodox
Jews around the world entrusted him with millions of their dollars, and they felt comfortable with this young man who had
letters of recommendation from great Rabbis in the community.

Last spring, an investor called him about $1.7 million dol-
lars that David Schick was supposed to be holding in an
escrow account. David Schick answered: "I took it. I'm sorry,
I'm a wicked person". According to the Manhattan and
Brooklyn district attorney, Schick defrauded investors of
more than $200 million dollars. David Schick, son of a
famous Orthodox family, pious and righteous, observer of
every jot and tittle of Jewish ritual, turned out to be a
swindler, a crook. The man who was thought to be a paragon
of virtue, strictly ethical in accordance with Jewish law,
turns out to be a criminal, betraying the trust of more than
1,000 people. The scandal spreads from New York to London
to Geneva. More than $100 million dollars is already
involved and the number grows.

I would like to be able to ask David Schick a few questions when they bring him before a judge: Aren't you
ashamed to call yourself religious, much less Orthodox?
Weren't you paying attention when your parents and teachers were talking to you? Did you think that a big yarmulka
can hide a scheming brain? Did you think that a large tallis
can hide an evil heart?

All of us would like to be more religious. To add more of a spiritual dimension to our lives. You don't need a big black hat or
a fancy sheitel. You don't have to go out and buy a bigger pair
of tefillin. You don't even have to come to shul more often. No,
strike that. It would help to come more often. What you really need to do is take the advice of Aaron Feuerstein who took
the advice of Micah the prophet. Always do the right thing.
Always act with kindness. And always maintain a sense of
humility.

The word religious comes from the Latin meaning to rebind. To connect once again, with our history, our culture, our tradition, our people. To me, religious means to live by a Jewish value system. The same values that we read about in our Torah. The values adopted by Abraham and Sarah and Moses and King David. None of them were perfect people. And the Torah always makes a point to point out their mistakes. It is not easy to live by a value system. It is much easier to forget about principles when it is convenient or profitable to do so. But we are expected to do the very best that we can.

Our rituals help us to do the best we can. They serve as reminders of Jewish values. And we need reminders. Everyday. We live in a dangerous environment, in a violent culture that worships power, aggression, and winning at all costs. It is very hard to maintain our Jewish principles, to do the right thing, to act with kindness and to maintain a sense of humility.

The latest buzzword in the Jewish community is spirituality. Last year, it was continuity; this year, it is spirituality. What does it mean? Nobody really knows. No one can really give a good definition. People vaguely speak of feeling connected with God, being visited by an overpowering sense of the spirit, of being inspired, being uplifted.

Do you want to know how to feel more spiritual? I'll tell you how to feel more spiritual. Go sit with your friend who is suffering and take his hand. A friend dying of a terminal disease. A friend distraught over the loss of her husband. A friend in anguish over his children's bad decisions. A friend who just lost his job. Give of yourself. Let part of your humanity and empathy jump across from your fingertips to hers or his. Let your feelings of sympathy enter into your friend's heart. Help another human being to get through his day, and, I assure you, you will feel a sense of spirituality.

And this is what it really means to be religious. It's not some vague notion that derives from a mystical Eastern religion. It is down to earth—very here and now. All people are God's creation, and when they suffer, God cries. And He waits for us to alleviate the suffering, at least some if it, even a tiny bit of it, in the world.

We all are presented with the opportunity to do it. Some of us turn away. And some of us seize the opportunity. Those of us who take the opportunity are doing the greatest mitzva. Those of us who go out and help the sufferers are truly religious.

Aaron Feuerstein is religious because when the opportunity presented itself to help hundreds of distraught workers, he didn't hesitate; what he did is called a Kiddush "Hashem", the sanctification of God's name in public. If we in the Jewish community could bestow sainthood, I would nominate Aaron Feuerstein.

So, this morning I salute Aaron Feuerstein, a Jewish factory owner who never forgot where he came from. Who embodies that which is most noble and exemplary in the Jewish tradition. Whose life is the definition of what it means to be religious. And if at this Yizkor moment, you are searching for a way to honor your parents and grandparents; if you are looking for a way to connect with their holy spirit, and thus to become more spiritual yourself, now you know exactly what to do.

AFRAID

Are you afraid of something?

I know that everyone is afraid of something. I have a friend who is afraid of flying. She would rather take the train for 26 hours from New York to Miami instead of flying for three hours. She was promoted to a new position. But it required that she fly out to Los Angeles every three months. She almost refused the job. Instead she found out about these little blue pills. She convinced her doctor to give her a prescription. She takes two a half hour before take-off. Upon boarding, she tells the stewardess not to bother her about anything and to wake her up 15 minutes before landing.

Many people are deathly afraid of getting up in front of a room full of people and giving a speech. They have no trouble at home lecturing their wife or husband or children, but the prospect of addressing strangers starts their heart pounding and raises the sweat on their forehead. It's not a good thing for Rabbis on Rosh Hashana. I had a friend in college who was a superb musician. He played the violin well enough to warrant an audition with a major orchestra. I so admired his mastery of the music. How he intuitively understood what the composer wanted to express. And his technical mastery of the instrument was incredible.

One day our maestro asked him to lecture to our class about the life of Pablo de Sarasate, one of the greatest of all violinists and the composer of a piece we were studying. He couldn't put two words together without stuttering. He was deathly afraid of speaking in public. Musical notes he was fluent in. But English words frightened him.

We all have our fears. And we deal with them by avoiding them. We don't want to talk about it. We don't want to admit it. We don't know how to handle it.

I also have fears, and I have always considered fear as a weakness. Intellectually, I know that a certain amount of fear is good for you. It keeps you healthy. When you are afraid of speeding in the car at 100 miles per hour, it keeps you alive. Or at least it keeps you out of jail. But when your fear begins to take over your life, then you can't function. There are people who are afraid to go out of their house. They are deathly afraid of other people. It is called agoraphobia.

I have been bothered by a certain fear all my life. And this year I decided to do something about it. I began by having a little discussion with one of our congregants who is a veteran of the World War II invasion of Normandy. He landed on Omaha beach, some 52 years ago. I asked him how was he able to overcome the fear of dying right there on the beach. He told me in graphic terms what it was like. Scrambling down the rope ladders into the landing craft. Waves tossing the boats around. Trying not to get crushed in the process. Soldiers falling into the water and drowning under 50 pound packs. Crouching in the landing craft as machine gun bullets flew all over. And then that awful moment when the door drops open and you have to run up on the beach straight into enemy fire. (Do you want to live forever?). "Weren't you afraid," I asked. "How did you do it? How did you get yourself moving forward?"

He thought for a few moments and said: I had no alternative. Where could I hide? I had nowhere to hide, boys in front of me and boys in back of me. I could only go forward. And you don't know how many times I said the Shema. I prayed constantly. I had faith in God. And I had confidence and faith in myself. The army trained me well in boot camp. That was the gist of it. That was his answer to fear: Prepare yourself well and have confidence in your ability. Pray to God and have faith. And place yourself in a position where there is no alternative but to go forward. And then you will overcome.

Now, as I said, I have a fear that I have been trying to overcome. It is not a life and death matter, but it has been nagging me over the years, bothering me, haunting me. Its called acrophobia, a fear of heights. It's not out of control, but it's there. And I figure that if I can learn to control a minor fear perhaps I can deal with some of life's major fears: aging, sickness, and death itself.

I remember the World Trade Center years ago and standing on the top floor. It's all surrounded by glass and you can see all the way down more than 100 stories below. I walked up to the glass, took one look, and shrank back horrified.

Now to make matters worse I enjoy hiking in the mountains, and there are certain hikes that I avoid because I don't want to choke up, to freeze out on a ledge high up on a mountain. And I thought that if I can learn to overcome this irrational fear of heights, then I could also learn to overcome other fears, even more difficult fears.

So I set off this summer on a 15 mile hike which took me along the edge of a mountain 3,000 feet above the valley floor. I was aware in advance that I would be walking on a trail no more than three feet wide, and any lapse in total concentration could be disastrous. And, in three places where the trail narrowed even more I would have to hold on to a fixed cable for security and support. And once I was out on the trail, there would be no way to get off except to continue to the end.

The end of the story is that I made it. I was very pleased with myself. I took the advice of my World War II veteran. I put myself in a position where I had no alternative. I had to go forward. No excuses. Just do it, as they say; and I was well prepared. I had confidence in my ability to do this. And I prayed. Boy did I daven. For 15 miles, I had an ongoing conversation with the good Lord.

Before I started out, I had a flashback. A picture flashed into my mind of the Great Synagogue in Jerusalem. I always sit in the same row when I am there. And once in a while, when my attention wanders from the Siddur, I read the beautiful stain glass window next to the Holy Ark. *Al tira avdi Yaakov* it reads. "Jacob, do not be afraid." My name is Yaakov, Jacob in Hebrew, and I always feel that the Good Lord is speaking directly to me. Don't ever be afraid. Don't ever be paralyzed by fear. Prepare yourself and go forward.

Actually, those words were first spoken to the first Jacob. He needed the encouragement. He needed it badly. Jacob started his life afraid of everyone and everything. He had no backbone. He was afraid of his mother. She told him what to do. She insisted that he fool his blind father into granting him the birthright. He was afraid of his powerful brother Esau. He had to run for his life when Esau threatened to kill him after being tricked out of the birthright.

He was afraid of Laban his father-in-law. He allowed Laban to trick him with Leah instead of Rachel. He worked for free for 14 years. And he hardly opened his mouth to protest.

And he was probably afraid of his wife, who was the only one who dared to stand up against Laban.

But Jacob finally realized, he can't spend his life running away from his fears. He decides to turn around, go home, and face his most terrifying fear, his brother Esau. At that moment Jacob began to win the battle against his demons.

The angel he wrestled with that night was the incarnation of his own fear. And when he subdued his demon he was a new man. With the sunrise, he was calm and collected and confident. He was now Yisrael. The fighter. The old Jacob, the man dominated by fear was gone. And he turned to face the fury of his brother with confidence in himself and faith in God.

We don't know what was in Esau's mind. He probably thought he would wave his sword and Jacob would run, but when Jacob stood before him confident and unafraid, ready to do battle if necessary, Esau the demon melted away. And he quickly came forward and embraced his brother. His hatred may not have turned to love, but it certainly turned to respect.

We all battle with our demons. Every day we get up, the demons are there. We are afraid of so many things. How are we going to pay the bills? Will we have a job next month? What if the market crashes and I am wiped out? What is the doctor going to tell me after the CAT scan? Who will take care of my family after I'm gone? But if we don't stand up to the demons, if we don't chase them into the corner, then they will dominate our lives. Our fears will paralyze us.

I don't have all the answers for you. But I know that the only way to deal with fear is to look it in the eye. Face it and stare it down. Don't turn your back and run away. It will only chase after you.

God made us strong. Strong enough to face anything that life has to throw at us. We have the necessary strength and the necessary resilience to overcome. We just have to reach down and find it.

A few weeks ago, I listened to Cardinal Bernadin of Chicago. I feel just a tad uncomfortable mentioning him on Rosh Hashana. But I was very impressed and moved by what he said. He was diagnosed with a terrible disease. He had less than a year to live. But he seemed totally composed, even at peace. He was facing the most terrifying fear a man can face. He was looking directly into the jaws of death. And he said: "If you see death as an enemy, then you will be afraid. And you will go into denial as you try unsuccessfully to cope. But I see death as a friend," he said. "I have faith in God, who is escorting me to life everlasting."

The Cardinal is a very unusual man. He believes that God gave us the strength to overcome our most terrible fears. And our strength can only come from an unshakable, absolute faith that God holds us by the hand, he will never let us go. He is our friend.

Rabbi Nachman of Bratslav and Uman. Hasidim gather at his grave on Rosh Hashana from around the world. What draws them? He had the secret: *Ha'ikar lo lefached clal*. The basic principle is do not be afraid. Have faith. Because if you have faith, God is with you.

So reads the prayer for the month of Elul: *Hashem ori. Mimi efchad*. God is my light. Who will I fear?

And so we turn to face the New Year. Let us face it with hope and with confidence, with courage and faith. It is not easy to fight our fears, but fight we must. And with God's help, we will survive and we will prosper.

Shana Tova.

YERUSHALAYIM—CITY OF STORIES

This is the year we complete the celebration of the three thousandth anniversary of the founding of Jerusalem by King David. Around the world, in English, French, Russian, Hebrew, Italian—in whatever language they use to speak to their people—Rabbis are speaking about Jerusalem and what it means to us.

How do you convey a three-thousand year love affair in one talk? How do you capture the miracle, the mystery and the majesty of this City, when all you have to work with is the instrument of words? Whatever you say about Yerushalayim is an understatement.

Let me give you a little recognized example of what Yerushalayim means to the Western world. Almost every state we know has a town of Salem in it. Do you know why? Because Salem is an abbreviation of Jerusalem. The people who built the cities felt the need the express the connection between their city and Zion, and so the name Salem. This is what Yerushalayim means in Western civilization.

What does Yerushalayim mean in the Jewish civilization? An example from daily life is this one from Hassidic tradition. The text of the invitation that Reb Levi Yitzchak of Berditchev sent out for his daughter's wedding reads: "The wedding will take place at 8:00 P.M., the twentieth of Cheshvan, in the holy city of Yerushalayim. But, if God forbid, the Moshiach doesn't come by then, then the wedding will take place here in the city of Berditchev."

Or a second example: in Reb Levi Yitzchak's living room were two clocks. One showed the time in Berditchev, and the other the time in Yerushalayim. At any moment, he could look up at the clocks and think what time it was in Yerushalayim. The Jew who lived in that room lived in two worlds. One part of him lived in Berditchev and another part of his was in Yerushalayim. That is how Reb Levi Yitzchak of Berditchev marked the time. (Jonathan in Jerusalem). I called when he was asleep, so I set a Jerusalem clock. Still keeps Jerusalem time.

Today, Jerusalem is a short distance away—less than 1 hour from Tel Aviv by car (Sephardic taxi driver), 5 hours from London by jet. You can get there in 14 hours from Miami. But it was not always that way. "In 1840, a man set out from Poland to Jerusalem to see the holy city before he died. He left just after Sukkot, he arrived in Palestine—spent, sick, and exhausted—just in time for Pesach, eight months later. He had crossed mountains and rivers, and fought off robbers and diseases in order to get there. There were many such pilgrims in the nineteenth century.

Yerushalayim—still a place of mystery and magic. It is still a place where you turn a corner and wonder if you will bump into a prophet, a madman, or a memory. It is a place where you feel the presence of King David, King Solomon, Rabbi Akiva, Rabbi Yehuda Halevi, David Ben-Gurion and Chaim Weizmann. It is a city in which all the people of Western civilization have a share. Yet, it is uniquely, in a very special sense, our city, a Jewish city, *the* Jewish city. It is ours. We are the only people I know of on earth who pray for her, three times a day. The only people I know of who thank God for her in grace after meals. The only people I know of who mention her at the end of every wedding and every funeral. We are the only people I know of who face Yerushalayim when we pray. For others, Jerusalem may be a place to visit, a place to tour, a place to fight over, or a place to play politics. For us, it is the City of David—the city of our past, our present, and our future.

Jerusalem has some amazing stories to tell:

> Do you remember Alfred Dreyfus? He was the man with whom modern Zionism began. He was an officer in the French army who was falsely accused and convicted of selling state secrets to the Germans in 1894. During and after the trial, there was such an outpouring of anti-Semitism that it shocked the young journalist from Austria who was covering the trial, making him realize how deep and widespread anti-Semitism really was. That journalist was Theodor Herzl. (Der Judenstaat). That moment in history led to the creation of modern Zionism.
>
> Here is the almost poetic ending to this story. Dreyfus came out of Devil's Island a broken man and died in obscurity. He had one son who died in the Second World War. That son left behind one daughter—who settled in Yerushalayim a few years ago! She now lives on Rechov Herzl in Yerushalayim! With her homecoming to Yerushalayim the story comes 'round full circle. Who would have believed it— that this assimilated French army officer would end up with a grandchild who lives on a Yerushalayim street named for the very journalist whose life he changed!

The second story: Rav Levin, the late Chief Rabbi of Moscow, never said a word about Israel all his days. He kept his lips tightly sealed. His duty was to be silent so that the Moscow synagogue could stay open. He refused, no matter how much pressure was put on him, to sign petitions that condemned Israel. Still, he was unable to utter one syllable in favor of Israel either.

Some years ago, Rav Levin died. Soon after, his daughter, with her children, got out of Russia and came to live in Yerushalayim. When interviewed by the Israeli newspapers, they asked, "Why did you come?" She said, "It was my father's deathbed wish." He never got to Yerushalayim. He had never spoken a word about Israel in public, but he succeeded in planting this dream within his daughter's heart. Now that he is gone, she lives in Israel for him. Rav Levin's body is buried in Moscow but his heart beats in Jerusalem.

Third story: Do you remember the name of Bruno Kreisky? He was himself a meshumad—a convert from Judaism to Christianity. He was the Austrian prime minister who, in response to acts of terrorism by the Arabs, shut down the refugee camp aiding Soviet Jews on the way to Israel. Do you remember how angry we all were at him? Golda Meir went to Vienna to try to reason with him—just before the Yom Kippur War—to no avail.

Bruno Kreisky, the meshumad, came to Israel a few years later. He came, together with a delegation of socialists leaders from different countries in Europe, as part of a tour of the Middle East. They met with the Israeli cabinet and urged Israel to withdraw from all the territories; a gesture they believed would lead to peace.

The newspapers covered the tour and wrote about the delegation's meeting with Israeli cabinet. What they did not mention was that Bruno Kreisky took off from the rest of the group one afternoon while they were in Yerushalayim. He went to see his brother in Meah Shearim—whom he had not seen for more than 35 years! It was an attempt to come home.

One of my favorite spots in Yerushalayim is in Ramat Eshkol. They put up new housing there on what was once the border. There, at Givat Hatachmoshet, stands a monument for the young Israeli soldiers who died in the Six-Day War. Next to it is a sign in memory of the Jordanian soldiers who died at that spot. It says: *Gam heym lachamu k'arayot*—they, too, fought like lions." At first, I was troubled, but now I find that inscription very impressive, another true story of literary magnitude. Only a Jewish state, only Jews, could be that magnanimous in victory.

A story from the Midrash, and a few from my own experiences in Jerusalem.

Where was the Holy Temple built? Legend has it that, even though it was his father's deathbed wish, King Solomon put off building the Temple month after month because he did not know where to build it. If he built it in the rich part of town, the poor would find it unapproachable. If he built it in the poor part of town, the rich would feel uncomfortable going there. So he waited for some sign from heaven.

One night, Solomon heard a voice: Solomon! Solomon! He woke with a start but no one was there. He took it as a sign, and quickly dressed and went outside. He walked around the streets of Yerushalayim but saw nothing. Then, just as he was about to turn back, he heard some movement. Quickly, he hid behind a tree to see what was happening.

There were two other people in Yerushalayim who couldn't sleep that night. They were two brothers. One was rich and had many children; the other was poor and had no children. The first brother lay awake thinking to himself: How can I enjoy all the food that I have when my brother is so poor? But he won't take any charity from me—he is too proud. So he got the idea to take some of his grain and put it in his brother's barn without his brother knowing. At the same time, his poor brother was lying awake, thinking: How can I enjoy what I have when my brother has so many children to provide for and so needs more than I do? So he got the idea to take some of his meager harvest and put it into his brother's barn.

The two brothers passed each other in the dark night. No one saw them. No one that is, except King Solomon. The next morning he called the two brothers to the royal court, told each what the other had done, and said: Now, I know where to build the Holy Temple. The holiest place on earth is the place where two brothers try to help each other. He bought the land between their two farms and that is where he built the Temple.

1973, Solomon's Palace, City of David excavations: Shabbat was a day to take a long nap after synagogue. In the late afternoon, a walk through the shuk to Karain or the Via Dolorosa near the Lions' Gate. My son starts back ahead of me and never reaches home. I find him sitting with a Muslim merchant outside his store, sipping a Coke, while the storekeeper keeps telling him don't worry, your abba will be back soon to find you. I had nightmarish visions as I pushed aside everyone in the shuk as I ran. But everything was fine. That Arab merchant was also a father, and his paternal instincts outweighed the politics of the day.

I am very zealous of my city. It belongs to me and every Jew, as it belonged to our ancestors for 3,000 years since King David. But that day I sensed a glimmer of hope. That maybe peaceful coexistence might be possible.

Then came the Intifada and relations between Jews and Arabs continued to degenerate and those relatively quiet days in Jerusalem were lost in my memory. But now I bring them forward. Occasionally, I go looking for that Arab storekeeper, to thank him again and to remind myself that human kindness is stronger than national politics, and, perhaps, peace is not as elusive as it occasionally seems.

Ehud Olmert, mayor of Jerusalem, likes to remind me that twice in the year we pray Leshana haba beYerushalayim, at the end of the Seder and at the end of Yom Kippur. But he never makes a connection, only a statement. He asked me to make the connection.

The Yamim Noraim represents the center of our religious life. When we gather 2,000 strong to express our spiritual selves, to reconnect with our Jewish souls, the very last word we say, on the last page of the Machzor is Yerushalayim. Jerusalem is the heart of our religious life. Without Jerusalem, our religious energy is without focus. It is scattered, it is weak. With Jerusalem, all the spiritual energy of the Jewish people comes together in one focused beam. And that beam is refracted through the holy place of Jerusalem, the Makom Kadosh and it disperses to illuminate the entire world. Which is the way I understand Ki meTzion tatzay Torah. Out of Zion shall go forth the Torah.

The Seder of Passover represents the center of our national life, the moment we threw off the chains of slavery and became a free people. The moment we turned our back on the degradation of Egypt and took our first steps toward Jerusalem. When our people reached the Promised Land, then they became a nation. And from the day King David made Jerusalem his capital, Jerusalem became our national center. We may live in Miami or New York, or Paris or Rome, or any corner of the world, but we are all citizens of Jerusalem—"Ani Yerushalmi." Whenever we choose, we can go up to the holy city, and Jerusalem will welcome us with open arms. Every Jew has a reserved place waiting for him or her in Jerusalem. (Of course, you have to pay the rent or the mortgage but that's a minor matter!)

My grandfather, Zaide Shmulke (Shmuel), first visited Palestine in 1929. He sailed from New York to Southhampton. When he reached England, he received a cable to stay put because the Arabs were rioting and killing Jews all over the country. He arrived in Israel in time to attend the funeral of the Yeshiva students massacred in Hebron. He wrote to the family about the urgent need for an independent Jewish state, safe and secure. God was good to him. He lived to see a proud independent state proclaimed with Jerusalem as the capital.

He traveled back and forth many times. Eventually, he grew older and weaker. But he had one more task. Against the warnings of his doctor, he boarded an El-Al plane with a one-way ticket. And when he left, he said, "if you want to see me—visit me in Jerusalem. I have been saying "Leshana haba beYerushalayim all my life," he said. "Now it is going to come true. For Good." When I was a student in Israel, I often spent Shabbat with him. When I left the country, he escorted me to the central bus stop in Jerusalem and no further. He wasn't leaving the holy city. And I knew I wouldn't see him wave to me again. The next time I came to Jerusalem I visited his grave at Har Hamenuchot, opposite Nebi Samwil, the grave of the prophet, Samuel.

And I said to him, Zaide, I'm back. I haven't forgotten you. I haven't forgotten our Jerusalem.

And as long as we have the strength, we shall return. And then as I turned to leave, I whispered to the wind:

Leshana haba beYerushalayim.

Rosh Hashana 5758

A PLACE OF REFUGE

I still expect to see Diana, Princess of Wales, get out of a Rolls-Royce on the Champs Elysees or Fifth Avenue. I am waiting to see the beautiful gown she will be wearing or the elegant suit topped by those stunning hats. How I admired those hats. Aileen admired them even more; so I wrote to her to find out the name of her hat maker. Through her secretary, she sent me the name and address, but when I received the price list, I decided that maybe Lord and Taylor was a better idea.

But the Princess is gone, hats and all. We will never again see that dazzling smile, that coquettish glance that charmed a whole world of admirers. She breathed vibrancy and excitement into the fusty, musty British royal family. Prince Charles frowned and Diana smiled. Queen Elizabeth frowned and Diana smiled. The British people loved her and they couldn't get enough of her. They enveloped her, they engulfed her, they ingested everything about her. And eventually their insatiable appetite for all things Diana killed her.

What really killed Diana was not a motorcycle paparazzo, or even a drunken chauffeur. They were only contributing factors. What destroyed Diana was the realization that there was nowhere in the world where she could hide. Nowhere to be alone with her boys, nowhere to be alone with the people of her choice. Nowhere to be alone with herself. To hear herself think. To contemplate in solitude.

No jet plane or helicopter or chauffeured limousine could take her to such a place. Because for Diana, it didn't exist. The long lens of the intruders would always find her in any city, on every continent. No matter how fast she ran away, it wasn't fast enough.

At first it seems like such a glamorous life: admired and recognized and applauded by the whole world. Important, famous, wealthy, pursued, and idolized. More famous than prime ministers and kings. But fame is a monster that continues to grow and can't be contained. Eventually the monster consumes you. Diana was swallowed by the monster. And we will never see that dazzling smile again. And two young boys will grow to manhood without the love of a mother. How sad.

Mind you, I never saw Diana as a paragon of virtue, as the world's perfect mother. I was never ready to sign a petition to the Vatican to have her proclaimed Saint Diana. When it comes to being a moral role model, she certainly doesn't make the list. But neither do most people in the public eye. I just felt sorry for her. The exquisite moth flying too close to the flame and finally being consumed by the fire. I feel sorry for the fact that she never had a private moment, or a private place. Not on vacation, not in the gym, not on a boat, not on a plane. Always somebody bothering her. Always the photographer's lens, or the TV camera. She lived in a palace surrounded by high walls, but she might just as well have been living in a glass house.

The Torah speaks of a place of refuge. A place where no one can find you. A place where you are safe from harm.

Ir Miklat. Cities of refuge. Six cities were set aside in ancient Israel, three on each side of the Jordan River. A person accused of a murder could go there and be safe from an avenging family. Eventually the court would decide guilt or innocence. Eventually it would be determined if it was premeditated or an accidental killing. In the meantime, there was a place of sanctuary or refuge. Ir Miklat.

I once heard my teacher, Rabbi Joseph Solevetchik, A.H. explain that everyone needs his own place of refuge, an ir miklat. Everyone needs some time for himself. Everyone needs his own space. Not because we are running away from the world. Not because we want to avoid our responsibilities, but because we need to be rejuvenated once in a while.

High in the Italian Alps are a chain of huts for mountain climbers. The weather in the high mountains can change without warning. What starts out as a sunny, quiet morning can suddenly turn into a fierce, life-threatening storm. So the Italian Alpine Club built little huts where, in case of emergency conditions, you can take refuge from the storm. The huts are called *refugio*, refuge in Italian. Out of the roar of the wind and out of the freezing cold, a climber can warm up a bit, collect his thoughts, calm down, wait for the storm to pass and plan his next move.

That's what I need once in a while. That's what you need once in a while. We need a "refugio," or as the Bible calls it, a miklat.

Incidentally, in Israel the word miklat is used to designate an emergency air raid shelter. In every kibbutz, in every town neighborhood, you see small mounds. In the middle of a park, in the back of a garden. With the sign on the door miklat. For emergency use. In the kibbutzim on the Lebanese border, emergency means incoming Katyusha rockets. Russian-made rockets that can wipe out an entire family in one explosion.

Emergency in Tel Aviv means incoming Scud missiles from Iraq that can explode an entire neighborhood. Chinese- or North Korean-made missiles that can reach most any town in Israel. They need a place to take refuge, to be protected from the storm, a miklat. To gather their wits, to calm their children, to calm themselves, and to wait for the all clear signal.

I need such a place. And so do you. Sometimes we are bombarded in our daily lives. We feel like someone dropped a bomb on us. We are shell shocked. We can't think. We don't know what to do. We walk around in a daze. We need a place to rest, we need a peaceful place. To recover our sense of balance to decide how to proceed. To wait for the all clear signal.

General George S. Patton was one of the great leaders of the Second World War. Actually, he commanded the first tank battalion in World War I with great distinction at the Battle of the Argonne. In World War II, he distinguished himself as general of the Third Army storming across France and chasing the Nazis back to Germany.

He is particularly remembered for his forced march in the dead of winter to relieve Bastogne right in the middle of the Battle of the Bulge. His incredible maneuver and courage finally cracked the German army and victory was only several months away.

But he sullied his record by striking a soldier across the face. Patton was visiting the wounded in a hospital. Blood he could understand. Broken bones he could understand. But one soldier appeared unscratched. Why was he in the hospital? Why was he taking up a bed? Patton called him a coward and slapped him. The great general failed to grasp the concept of shell shock. Battle field trauma. That poor infantry man had been on the front line too long. He had seen too many of his buddies die. He had heard the crash of too many shells. He was in shock. He needed a quiet place. He needed to be by himself. Undisturbed. He needed to get his wits together. Otherwise he wouldn't be able to function. He needed a miklat, a place of refuge from the horror of battle. But Patton didn't understand. We understand.

In the early 1970s, the first golf course in Israel was built at Caesarea, right on the Mediterranean. As you can imagine, not too many Israelis owned golf clubs in those days, or had the leisure time to play 18 holes. Beautiful homes were built on the golf course, and the club became quite an attraction for visiting tourists.

When my father heard that the Caesarea Golf Course was open, he was determined to play the only Hebrew golf course in the world. He got one of his Israeli friends to take him out one day. On the eighth hole, they begin to overtake a twosome in the distance. My father recognized one of them. It was Chaim Herzog, who had just been appointed Israel's ambassador to the United Nations. My father had met him several times in New York and was anxious to say hello and compare handicaps and maybe to be invited to make a foursome.

Before he could get any closer, two security men appeared out of the rough and told him to stop. My father explained that he only wanted to say shalom. But the security guards explained that they were under strict orders from Herzog not to let anyone approach.

Several months later, my father met Herzog at an Israel Bonds dinner in New York and he told him the golf course story. Herzog apologized and explained, "the golf course is my miklat (using the Hebrew word for refuge). You have to understand that Israel is a very small country and the only place I can be alone and find some peace and quiet is on the golf course. And my security guards are under strict order not be let anyone bother me."

My friends, where are you going to find your miklat, your protected place, your quiet place, where no one will intrude, where you can be by yourself, with yourself?

We don't live in a palace on Kensington. We can't have the Turnberry Golf Course all to ourselves. But we do have a miklat, a refuge where we can hide away from the intruding world.

The first place of refuge has to be your home. When you close the door, you close out all other intrusions. When the lock clicks shut, you shut out all unwanted interference. Then it's just you and the people most dear to you. A husband, a wife, children, a best friend. The people whom you choose to invite into your life. Not those who invite themselves, or even force themselves on you uninvited. Life is too short to spend it with people who bother you, or bore you, or frighten you, or make life miserable for you. The Talmud says that the most important principle that should govern your home is shalom bayit. It means a peaceful home. If you don't have peace of mind in your own home, then you will never have peace of mind. Shalom bayit. Without it a person can literally go crazy. Turn off the TV. Turn off the computer. Turn off the fax and the portable phone and the cellular phone and start speaking to a real live human being. It's bad enough that you are reduced to talking to a machine and selecting electronic menus all day. You don't need that at home. At home, you need a little compassion and understanding. At home you need a little love. You need shalom bayit. Peace.

And the other place of refuge is the synagogue, God's house. Here, the Jewish people come together to draw strength from a shared history and tradition. We shut out the dangerous and often threatening outside world. Here, we remind ourselves of God's law and God's plan. Here, we can transcend the mundane. And if we are properly tuned, we can attain a heightened sense of spirituality.

If no one else will protect us and take us under His wings, certainly God will. We have only to call upon Him with sincerity. If no one else can show us the way, He can. If no one else can encourage us, He can. If no one else can calm our fears and soothe our anxieties, He can.

King David summed it up so well in *Tehillim: Yastireni beseter ohalo.* God offers us refuge in the tent of His divine presence. We say this prayer all during the holy day season. It is a time when we realize how badly we need a place of refuge, a quiet place, a peaceful place.

I called a friend of mine who is a Rabbi in New York. His secretary said, "the Rabbi cannot be disturbed. He is meditating." Usually, I get he is in conference, he is visiting the hospital, but never "he is meditating." Well its a very good thing. He is either talking to himself or to God. And if he is talking to himself, I wouldn't worry.

Aileen's grandmother used to talk to herself, and when we asked why she is talking to herself, she would answer, "I like to talk to smart people."

So be alone once in a while. Talk to yourself once in a while. You would be amazed what you can learn.

Diana, the princess of Wales, died searching desperately for her place of refuge. It was denied to her in life. She found it only in death. What a shame. What a waste. We can do much better.

Find that place of refuge; it's there, in a corner of your home or in a corner of your soul. Take the time to breathe, to think, to plan, to recharge your spiritual batteries. Listen to your inner voice. Listen to God's quiet voice.

And when you emerge, may you have the calm, and the confidence, and the courage to go on with your lives.

May the New Year bring you shalom, peace of mind and tranquility of the soul.

THE PRAGUE CEMETERY

Inscribed on the gates to the ancient Jewish cemetery in the Jewish quarter of Prague is the following phrase: *Zedaka tatzeel mimavet*. Charity will save us from death. Is it really true that charity will save you from death? Because we would certainly like to know. If this is true then I am sure every one of you is ready to write another check out to the synagogue immediately. Well, not immediately—after Yom Kippur. Who wouldn't be ready to buy even one more day of life? Even one more minute or second? None of us is ever ready for the Malach hamavet, the angel of death.

A man in his middle 70s was left all alone in a shtetl in Poland before the Second World War. All his children had immigrated to America. He had a hard time securing shelter and food. Every morning he would pick up sticks and put them in a burlap bag, and just before sunset he would take this bag to the wood merchant who would buy it for a kopek or two and sell it to the villagers. One hot July day, he trudged from morning to night picking up sticks. As he was putting the last stick in his bag, the burlap broke and all the sticks fell to the ground. Tired, frustrated, and disgusted, he looked up to heaven, and said: "God, what do I need this for? Send me the Malach hamavet, the angel of death." Instantly, the angel of death appeared at his side. The angel looked at the man and asked, "What can I do for you?" The man looked at the angel of death and replied: "Help me pick up these sticks."

Hope is a great gift from God. None of us should reject it. Hatikva is not only the national hymn of the Jewish people, but should also accompany every Jew during his or her lifetime.

To tell you the truth, I am not sure what that phrase means on the gate of the Prague synagogue and, incidentally, on dozens of zedaka boxes I have seen.

But one thing I do know, the giving of zedaka has a magical quality. It automatically makes you feel that you are part of the Jewish community. It saves you from the death of isolation. It means that you personally participate in all the good things that we do. You don't always have the time to come to the minyan. We pray every morning and we have you in mind. You can't come every Shabbat, we mention your name at the Torah so God won't forget you. You can't attend our Torah classes, we study for the whole community.

Now, please don't misunderstand. Of course, I would like you to come to shul more often. And, of course, I would like you to study. But you might have some pretty good excuses why you can't always be here. But for giving zedaka, there are no good excuses.

So, once a year, we ask you to reconnect with us in a tangible way. Help us to continue to pray for our people and to teach our people and to do all the good things we do for the Jewish community.

And for your generosity, may God grant you and your family a good year.

IF THERE IS A WILL

In the city of Basel, on the border of Germany and Switzerland, is a hotel called the Drei Koenig, the three kings. It has rooms with balconies overlooking the Rhine River. I had my picture taken on the balcony this summer. Just 100 years ago, Theodor Herzl had his picture taken on the same balcony. He had come to Basel for the first World Zionist Congress. It was the crowning success of his career. I wondered what was going through his mind 100 years ago as he prepared to address the members of the Congress. The most prominent Jews in the world had assembled to consider the idea of Zionism, and every one of the delegates had a different idea of how to proceed.

Theodor Herzl was a lawyer by profession. A graduate of the University of Vienna Law School. He soon left the legal profession to pursue his first love, writing. He wrote a number of successful plays, which were produced on the Austrian and German stage.

Eventually, he became the Paris correspondent for the liberal Vienna newspaper, the *Neue Freie Presse*. And as you know, it was in Paris in 1895, that Herzl witnessed the trial of Alfred Dreyfus, the innocent Jewish officer publicly humiliated and condemned to Devil's Island. Herzl heard the mob shouting "Morte aux Juifs," death to the Jews. He became convinced that the only solution was a mass exodus of the Jewish people from their anti-Semitic surroundings.

"Der Judenstaat," an independent Jewish state, was the only answer. And he spent the rest of his life trying to fulfill his dream for the Jewish people of a political state.

The details of his accomplishments are well known. This distinguished man with the luxuriant jet black beard and the piercing eyes was the founder of modern Zionism. He himself said that he doubts that it would happen in five years, but surely in 50 years. And in 1948, exactly 50 years later, there was indeed an independent Jewish state. And this year we are celebrating the fiftieth anniversary of the State of Israel.

How did Theodor Herzl manage to organize the entire Jewish world? Two Jews, three opinions. How did this one man set the foundation for the modern Jewish State? Surely, there were other capable people who were equal to the task. Was he stronger or smarter then they were? Was he more convincing?

The secret lies in what he himself wrote. *Im tirtzu ayn zo agada.* If you will it, it is no fairy tale.

The difference between success and failure, between life and death, often depends on the will. How bad do you want it. How hungry are you? Herzl was literally obsessed with the Zionist idea. He felt that the very existence of the Jewish people depended on an independent Jewish state. And he was right. And if the state had come into existence just ten years earlier, millions of Jews could have been saved.

Herzl's will was able to overcome any obstacle in his path. All things being equal, a person with the strongest will is the one who will succeed.

The basis of Herzl's plan was to enlist the support of the wealthiest Jewish financiers of the day. With the help of the Rothschilds and the de Herschs, he would found a financially powerful bank, the Anglo-Palestine Company. He would then enter into diplomatic negotiations with the Sultan of Turkey. Turkey was in a terrible financial state and needed an infusion of capital. In return, Herzl hoped to receive permission to establish the Jewish State in the territory controlled by Turkey, the land of Israel.

Baron Edmund de Rothschild rejected the plan. It would be impossible to organize the Jewish masses. But Herzl didn't give up.

Kaiser Wilhelm II of Germany agreed to sponsor a Jewish Land Company for Syria and Palestine and to recommend the Zionist organization to the sultan of Turkey. The kaiser changed his mind when he heard that the Jewish bankers weren't supporting the idea and that the German liberal Jews were against it. But Herzl didn't give up.

The sultan suggested a Jewish homeland in Iraq. Lord Rothschild suggested a homeland as part of the British empire, perhaps Cyprus or Sinai. Britian decided on El-Arish and the Sinai, but it was opposed by Egypt. Herzl became more and more frustrated. But he refused to give up.

The Kishinev pogrom in 1903 reminded the Jewish people that they were in a crisis. Chamberlain of Britian offered to settle the Jews in Uganda, and Herzl brought the idea to the Sixth Zionist Congress.

He was misunderstood and misrepresented. Herzl never had any intentions of creating a Jewish state in Uganda. He just needed a safe place for the Jews of Europe until Palestine could be secured. They could not safely stay in Russia and Poland anymore. Half the Congress walked out on him. It took a superhuman effort to bring them back and all of his powers of persuasion not to split the movement. And still he didn't give up. He had the will.

On top of everything, Herzl suffered from a heart condition. His doctors told him his activities would kill him. And they would have killed him much sooner, if not for his will to live to see his dream fulfilled. Sometimes life can be extended just on will.

He had no support from his wife; she thought he was crazy. His daughter, Pauline, became a drug addict and died in a Bordeau hospital. His son, Hans, was a manic-depressive, who converted to Christianity several times and eventually shot himself. His younger daughter, Margarethe, was hospitalized many times.

She was killed by the Nazis in Theresienstadt. Her son, Herzl's only grandchild, was a British captain in World War II, and visited Palestine. He served in the British mission in Washington after the war. He jumped off a bridge in the Potomac.

This was Herzl's home life. This was Herzl's family. A weaker man would have collapsed. A weaker man would have died. But Herzl had the will. The will to live, the will to achieve his dream, the will not to let anything stop him. Not cantankerous Jews, not myopic diplomats, not snobby financiers, not anti-Semitic governments. Nothing—nothing could stand in his way.

Because, if you will it, it is no dream.

We often speak of God's will, Besiyata diShmaya. Observant Jews write at the top of their letter bet samach-daled.

On Rosh Hashana, we often make reference to God's will. Yehi ratzon, may it be God's will to grant our hearts desire. For health, for success, for nachas from our children and our grandchildren. But before God can will it, we have to will it. We have to want it; we have to want it bad enough to go out and work for it. We have to want it bad enough to invest all our energy.

You know the line that all the landsman from Vilna like to quote. Vilna is the birthplace of the famous Gaon of Vilna, Eliyahu ben Shlomo Zalman. In the second half of the eighteenth century, he was the leader of the Misnagdim, the Jewish intellects who opposed the Chassidim and their emotional, nonintellectual approach to Judaism. In other words, the Hasidim suggested singing and dancing in place of serious academics.

The Vilna Gaon was one of our greatest scholars. All the boys in the yeshiva wanted to grow up to be like him. And their parents would say, "if you want to be like the Vilner Gaon, VIL NA," which in Yiddish means you just have to want it badly enough.

Now, I don't mean to imply that all you need is will in order to succeed. I once mentioned to you that I learned to play the violin as a child. All Jewish children had to learn to play the violin or the piano. Our parents thought that it was the cultured thing to do. Probably Theodor Herzl himself had to take lessons. At any rate, I dutifully went to the teacher once a week and I practiced everyday in between baseball games and the Milton Berle show.

I really wanted to be a great violinist. I was so impressed by Jascha Heifetz. He was my musical hero. He had perfect technique; he never made a mistake. I, on the other hand, always made at least one mistake. I never got through the first movement of the Mendelsohn without making a mistake. I had the will to be great. But it didn't do me any good. Because I didn't have the talent.

But all things being equal, the desire and the will make all the difference. Jascha Heifetz had many young students with him in the same studio in Russia. They were also quite talented. But no one knows their names today. They didn't become famous. Only Heifetz and Mischa Elman and one or two others did. Because they had the will. The burning desire to succeed. And the others didn't.

I also wanted to be a great basketball player. I wanted to be good enough to make my college team. I was tall enough, I was fast enough, but the coach said I would have to come to practice every night. Now my classes at Yeshiva University finished at 5 or 6 in the evening. I had homework to do, double the homework of any other university because we had a double program, Talmud and Chumash, as well as English literature and organic chemistry. So I didn't have the will to spend hours every evening shooting foul shots and executing fast breaks and then to come home and first begin my school work. So I never got to play at Madison Square Garden. I didn't have the will.

But I like to watch the games. Under my daughter's influence, I have been following the new women's basketball league. And since there is no Miami team, we root for the New York Liberty. They have some very talented players.

Among them is Teresa Weatherspoon. She is close to 31 years old. That's usually too old for a basketball player. She's been playing professional basketball for ten years. Where? I never heard of her before. In Italy. In places like Bologna and Rome. Did you ever see a Black person in Italy? Did you ever see a Black woman professional basketball player in Italy? Weatherspoon spent 10 years waiting to fulfill her dream of playing professional ball in America. All that pasta. All that time trying to learn a foreign language. All that time away from her family. What drove her? Why didn't she quit? Why didn't she give it up as a hopeless dream?

Because she had the will. Ratzon. Desire. Or as she says, attitude, or "tude" for short.

And now she and her teammates inspire every young woman in America. Ratzon. It takes will. Im tirtzu ayn zo agada. If you want it bad enough, you can turn a dream into reality.

This is the first day of the New Year. The first day of the rest of our lives. What do you want; what do you really want? You want to live a healthier life? You want to lose 20 pounds? You want to cut 3 strokes off your handicap? You want to be closer with your family? You want the respect of your children? You want to draw closer to Judaism? You want to feel more spiritual? What do you want? What do you really want? Have you decided? Now just do it! Don't make any excuses. Just do it.

Im tirtzu ayn zo agada. If you will it, it is no dream.

ORANIENBURGERSTRASSE SYNAGOGUE: THE FACADE

In East Berlin, on Oranienburgerstrasse, stood the biggest synagogue in Europe, the Neue Synagogue. When it was built in 1866, it had permanent seats for 3,200 people. The women sat in two balconies. There were more than 100,000 Jews in Berlin. And they had attained some measure of affluence. They were proud of their accomplishments in industry, in business and in the arts and science. Their new Synagogue would become a symbol to all of Berlin that the Jewish people had arrived.

No expense was spared. The Moorish style building was breathtaking. It dominated the skyline. The golden domes glistened in the sunlight and could be seen for miles around.

The Jews of Berlin felt themselves to be Germans first and Jews second. They called themselves Germans of the Mosaic tradition. Led by the renown, Moses Mendelssohn, they developed a philosophy of integration and assimilation into the mainstream culture. This, of course, was the beginning of the Reform movement.

What was so reform about the new synagogue? The Rabbi spoke in German. One or two prayers were read in German. And organ music was introduced. Everything else remained the same. Even the men and women sat separately; the men on the main floor and the women in two balconies. The men wore hats or yarmulkes. I saw a photograph of Albert Einstein participating in a concert in the synagogue in 1930. As you know, he was an accomplished violinist. He was wearing a large yarmulke out of respect to the holiness of the place.

As you can imagine, the introduction of the organ created quite a controversy. In the end, the old synagogue remained for the traditionalists, and the new synagogue for the liberals.

A great choir was assembled by the most famous liturgical musician of the day, Louis Lewandowski. The music he wrote is still used by cantors around the world. The music was spellbinding.

In the synagogue archives, I found that the Berlin Jewish community council encouraged the city Rabbis to preach and to officiate at all the city's synagogues on a rotating schedule. With the completion of the new synagogue, permanent rabbis were assigned to each synagogue. The Neue Synagogue, now the largest institution in Berlin, had three Rabbis.

According to the membership lists that I saw, the Neue Synagogue was filled with the movers and shakers of Berlin, important people from the arts and sciences, from politics and journalism and finance; as well as Jews from all walks of life, young and old. The Rabbi and the elected officials of the congregation sat at the side of the steps leading to the aron hakodesh that held the Torahs. And it is reported, and I find this so difficult to believe, that there wasn't a whisper heard during the service. 3,200 people filling the synagogue and not a whisper. Incidentally, the cost overrun was seven times the original budgeted amount. Sound familiar?

All this came to an end on the night of November 9, 1938. Kristellnacht. The night of the broken glass. Synagogues and Jewish businesses throughout Germany were vandalized and burned. In Berlin, the Nazi thugs set fire to the Neue Synagogue. But an amazing thing happened. The district chief of police appeared with a drawn pistol and chased off the thugs. Wilhelm Kruetzfeld prevented any serious damage. And he was honored as a hero by the community.

But there was no holding back the Holocaust. When World War II broke out, the Nazis demanded that the great golden domes of the synagogue be painted gray, protection against air raids. The work was done precisely on the first day of Rosh Hashana, exactly 58 years ago to this day, while the Jews were praying inside.

The synagogue was officially closed in 1940. Soon Berlin would be Judenrein. In 1943, British Lancaster bombers over Berlin heavily damaged the synagogue building. When the war ended, it was a wreck. The Berlin Jewish community that remained or returned after the war had more to worry about than the expensive reconstruction of a synagogue. In 1958, the East Berlin Jewish community gave permission to destroy most of the remains of the synagogue. It was in danger of collapsing. The front part was somewhat preserved as a commemoration and reminder. Actually, it was the Jewish community that was in danger of collapse and needed preservation.

And that's how it remained until 1995, when the building was reconstructed by the postcommunist growing Berlin Jewish community.

So we arrived in Berlin this summer anxious to see the New Synagogue; the rebuilt New Synagogue, and to pray there on Shabbat.

We reserved a hotel room in East Berlin that would be within walking distance of the synagogue. On Friday morning we walked over to Oranienburgerstrasse to visit the synagogue museum. I had an appointment with the archivist. We planned to return Shabbat morning for services. We would participate first hand in the ongoing resurrection of the Berlin Jewish community.

We turned the corner onto Oranienburgerstrasse and there it was: golden and glistening in the sunlight. The gorgeous domes, the beautiful entrance. The sight was breathtaking. It dominated the entire neighborhood. We couldn't wait to go inside, to sit in the seats where Otto von Bismarck and Albert Einstein and Lewandowski once sat. We walked into the lobby; which is a historical museum. And then we passed through the doors that led to the synagogue itself in great anticipation.

But there was no synagogue. There were no Torahs, there was no bima, there were no seats. There was no shul. There was only a big empty space enclosed by glass where the synagogue once stood.

Everything was just a facade. A remembrance of a synagogue that once was the most glorious in all Europe.

I was stunned. To this day I am in shock. You see this magnificent golden dome in the distance; you walk up to the entrance with gold letters across the front: Pitchu shearim (Isaiah). Open the (gates of righteousness). You pass through the beautiful lobby and then—nothing.

I expected to join in the Shabbat prayers with the Berlin Jewish community literally rising from the ashes of the Holocaust. Instead, we were faced with a facade, a front, with a big empty space behind it.

The Mishna suggests: *Al tistakel bakankan elah bemah sheyesh bo*. Don't look at the container, rather look at what's inside. In other words, be careful about the facade. Reserve your judgment until after you've seen what's inside, what's behind the fancy front.

In the world of marketing, packaging is all important. Companies hire experts just to advise them on the design of the package. How big, what color, whose pictures to put on the front. My little nephew had a box of Wheaties on the table the last time I had breakfast with him. But he was putting frosted flakes in his bowl. "Why did you ask Mom to buy Wheaties if you're not even eating it," I asked. "Because Michael Jordan was on the box," he answered. Everything is in the packaging. But it can't make up for what's inside. It can't change the fact that Wheaties taste, like cardboard. Its perfectly kosher, but it tastes like cardboard.

We tend to judge people also according to their facade, by their exterior packaging.

Last year a lady by the name of Anne Scheiber tried to call Dr. Norman Lamm in Manhattan. Dr. Lamm is the president of my alma mater, Yeshiva University. Actually, Anne Scheiber's lawyer tried to call Dr. Lamm. He was afraid to take the call, thinking that a lawyer's call only meant trouble for the university. Finally, he got a handwritten note from Anne Scheiber. She wanted to talk to Dr. Lamm about donating some money to the yeshiva. $22 million dollars. Well, you can imagine how quickly Dr. Lamm got in touch.

They met. Anne Scheiber lived quietly, by herself, in a rent-controlled studio apartment on 56th Street. The paint was peeling, the furniture was old, and dust covered everything. She walked everywhere, in the same black coat and old hat. When she went out, it was only to see her broker. If you saw her on the street, you would think she was a poor New Yorker one step away from the Salvation Army shelter.

She worked for the IRS until retirement in 1944. The $5,000 dollars saved from her professional career, she invested in the stock market. For the next 50 years, she carefully studied company reports, earnings statements and management philosophy, and made many smart purchases. $5,000 became $22 million in 50 years.

The IRS never promoted her. She was a talented estate auditor, but she was the victim of discrimination against women. 50 years later, she was determined to give more women a chance to succeed in the professions. She had observed the women at Stern College near her apartment. I'm sure they never gave her a second look. And if they did, it was because she looked like she needed charity. But her holdings in Paramount Studios and Coca-Cola and more than 100 other stocks will benefit the women of Yeshiva

University. Al tistakel bakankan. Be careful of judging people by their facade. Look into their hearts.

Every now and again, people come off the street and ask to speak with the Rabbi. And invariably they present a hard luck story. The end of the story is always the same. They need some money. The car broke down and they need to repair it to get to work. They have to buy a car to get to work. They have a job but they need money to rent an apartment. They have an apartment but the landlord raised the rent. Their new job doesn't start until next week and they need money for food. And on and on. All good reasons, if they are true.

If I would judge a person by his shabby clothes and dirty hands, I would conclude, he's a bum. But what if I am being tested. The Messiah is coming. Maybe by the new millennium. It says so on the bumper stickers and billboards. What if one of these people is Elijah the prophet in disguise? Testing me to see if we deserve to have the Messiah come. Testing me, the Rabbi of this great Jewish community, to see if we understand the concept of Zedaka, of Gemilus Chasadim. What if I turned away Elijah himself? What if the Messiah canceled his ticket to Aventura because I was in a bad mood that day and told my secretary to get rid of him? We have to be careful about looking only at the facade.

A tattered coat says nothing about a person's heart. And an Armani suit says nothing about a person's soul. We have to look past the surface to see the truth.

And, by the same token, a glistening golden dome tells us nothing about the nature of the congregation inside, not in Berlin and not in Aventura.

If you want to know who we are, the congregation of Aventura-Turnberry, look into our hearts. We were moved to build this beautiful synagogue, our Neue Synagogue, so that our people could gather for prayer and study. We were moved to build a magnificent school so that we could educate the next generation, thus preserving our continuity. We were moved to surround ourselves with the finest teachers and educators and administrators and executives so that we could strengthen our ties to our ancient tradition. And we were moved to build a real Jewish community, not just a facade. There is a dome that glitters above us. But there is also a bima and Torahs and prayer books and Bibles and tallisim and all the accouterments needed for a real synagogue. And there is the sound of prayer and study. And most of all, we have our people, who are imbued with Yiddishkeit and strive to live Jewish lives. We are not a museum to the past. We are not a facade. We are a living, breathing, thriving, and vibrating Jewish community. The Great Synagogue of Berlin is gone. Only a museum remains.

Only ghosts haunt the old space on Oranienburgerstrasse. The magnificent Berlin community is gone. Into smoke and ashes.

But we are here. We are alive. We are vibrant; and we carry forth Jewish history. We are no facade. We are the real thing.

GOOD FOR THE JEWS

So my friends. I ask you: Is it good for the Jews. Or as my grandmother would say: "Iz es gut far Yidden?" Had my grandmother been watching the Democratic convention as Senator Joe Lieberman accepted the nomination for Vice President of the United States, that's what she would have said. Is it good for the Jews?

Tens of thousands of Protestants and Baptists and Episcopalians screaming "Go Joe Go," for a Jewish guy from Connecticut. Can you imagine? Can you imagine this happening in Poland, or Germany, or even France, or England? Just decades ago, in Europe the mobs would have been screaming for our blood; shouting and cheering to see synagogues burning and Jews dying. They would have applauded the Nazis and the fascists and the Ustachi and the

Chetniks. This was barely 50 years ago. And now look at us.

Jewish people haven't been so excited about a political leader since Franklin Roosevelt. You know that many people in America thought that Roosevelt was Jewish. The Jewish people adored him. They used to say in the 1930s, the Jewish people believe in three worlds (velt in Yiddish means world) "De velt, yenne velt, and Roosevelt."

And when Roosevelt died, the Jewish people all cried. Of course, they didn't yet know about the Holocaust, and Roosevelt's indifference. But that's a different story. And 60 years ago, the idea of a Jewish Vice President, a heartbeat away from becoming President of the United States, was a dream. An impossible dream. Do you know something of the history of the Jewish people in America?

Just before Rosh Hashana in 1654, 23 Jews arrived in America in New York from Recife, Brazil. It was called New Amsterdam and it was a Dutch Colony. Recife had been a Dutch possession but it was under attack by Portugal. With Portuguese dominance of Brazil would come the Catholic Inquisition. The Jews weren't about to form a welcoming party for the Inquisition, so they sailed for New Amsterdam. Holland had always been a safe haven for Jews and all religious minorities. A tolerant and progressive government and likeminded citizens.

But the 23 Jews were met by the first mayor of New York, Peter Stuyvestant, who tried to refuse their entry at the port. He protested to the Dutch West India company against this "deceitful race" (his words) who professed an "abominable religion" and who "worship at the feet of Mammon." He claimed that the Jews would threaten and limit the profits of the company. But Peter Stuyvestant didn't know that some of the major stockholders in the Dutch West India Company were Dutch Jews. They contacted the company officers and convinced them that the Jews would be good for business. Peter Stuyvestant was over ruled and the Jews were given equal privileges. They could even have their own cemetery. But they couldn't build a public synagogue. That would come later after the hubbub had died down.

They continued to fight Stuyvestant successfully because the Dutch traders understood that the Jews were good for the new colony. And they had no use for small anti-Semitic minds.

P.S. In 1655, just one year after they began arriving, the Jews were 2 percent of the population. According to the records of New Amsterdam, they paid for 8 percent of a public works project called "Waal Street": that has to be one of the best investments we ever made. It's just too bad that Rudy Giuliani wasn't the mayor when they came. He would have put on a yarmulke and made them a big party.

So look how far we have come. We are still not much more than 2 percent of the population, but look what we have achieved in America. For ourselves and for the country. In science, in education, in medicine, in law, in the arts, in philosophy, in sports. The list is so long I would be reading the names until Yom Kippur. And it could happen only in America.

I have said it many times. America didn't guarantee us anything. America only gave us opportunity. And that's all we needed. That's all we wanted. The "Goldeneh Medina" wasn't paved with gold. Only golden opportunities. A chance. The chance denied us in Warsaw or Heidelberg or Budapest or Moscow.

The opportunity to make it in America. The opportunity to fulfill the American dream. Never mind your religion or your race, never mind your color or your creed. What counts, the only thing that counts, is your ability and determination.

And here we are talking about Joe Lieberman, who could be the first Jewish Vice President of the United States. And not Jewish in name only. This man is a proud, clearly identified, unashamed, traditional Jew. And so is his wife, Hadassah, and so is his daughter, Chani. On the first Saturday after his nomination, he went to shul. On the second Saturday, he got off the boat in Mississippi for the Sabbath. This is amazing even in America.

Joe Lieberman is not the first Jewish Senator. And until recently I thought he wasn't the first Jewish Vice President. I was taught that Judah P. Benjamin was Vice President of the Confederate States of America during the Civil War. He was second in command to President Jefferson Davis, but he was really Secretary of War. And when the war went badly, the anti-Semites blamed "that infamous Jew." But Jefferson Davis refused to cave in. Judah P. Benjamin, Yale graduate, Senator, and leader of the Southern rebellion was the most prominent Jew in nineteenth century America. But he took no interest in Jewish affairs. He never supported a Jewish cause or charity. He never belonged to a synagogue. In short, there was nothing Jewish about him except his name. Senator Joe Lieberman has been active in Jewish affairs all his life. He belongs to two shuls, one in Washington and one in Connecticut. He is strongly committed to the Jewish people and to Israel. And he is proud to be identified as a traditional Jew. He is proud of his name and proud of his heritage.

Joe Lieberman is not the first Jewish Senator in America. In 1845, David Levy was elected to the Senate from the State of Florida. But he changed his name to David Levy Yulee (his wife's name) and turned away from his people.

Joe Lieberman is not changing his name. On the contrary. His wife's name is Hadassah. And she is the daughter of Holocaust survivors. Her mother survived Auschwitz and Dachau, and her father, a lawyer and Rabbi, escaped from the Nazis during a forced march to Auschwitz. The Liebermans send their daughter, Chani, to an orthodox Hebrew day school. They keep kosher; they walk to shul on Shabbat. And the Senator tries mightily to balance his passionate commitment to Judaism with his responsibilities as a political leader.

Joe Lieberman is an example for us all. You can be a committed Jew and live in the real world. You don't have to retreat behind the walls of a Williamsburg or Boro Park or B'nei B'rak. Nor do you have to wear a black hat or long "payis." Suddenly, in America it's okay to be a clearly identified Jew. It's okay to have a real Jewish name.

When Joe Lieberman showed up in shul on the first Shabbat after his nomination, it was quite a scene. At Kesher Israel in Washington, it was Senator Lieberman Day. 20 secret servicemen trailed them to shul along with the media. 10 were women. To sit with Hadassah in the women's section behind the mechitza. The shul gave out a statement welcoming the media to observe but not to bring recording equipment into shul and not to interview the shul members. Everyone respected the dignity of the Shabbat service. Secret servicemen were in shul but everyone knew who they were; they were wearing the white yarmulkes left at the door in the box.

Senator Lieberman got an aliya and the whole shul started singing "siman tov and mazel tov."

The Rabbi quoted a sentence from the Sedra, which was Va'etchanan:

"Observing and studying God's law brings a person wisdom." And wisdom gains the respect of the nations of the world.

And indeed this is exactly what the reaction has been. An outpouring of respect and admiration for Senator Lieberman, a Jewish American, not an American who happens to be Jewish.

Is it good for the Jews. Iz es gut far Yidden? Absolutely. Not only is it good for the Jews, but it's good for America. For every immigrant who reached these shores. For every refugee who dreamt of a better life. For every political exile who yearned for freedom. And if the Internet is inundated by anti-Semitic remarks. If there still is a lunatic fringe, even in America, who would like to see us all back in Auschwitz, it will not change a thing. We are here to stay. We have achieved the American dream. God has blessed all of us. We live in the greatest country in the world at the moment of its greatest success in a time of unprecedented prosperity and progress. We live in America, where people are more interested in what you think than where you come from.

And if Joe Lieberman's candidacy brings out some of the anti-Semitism hidden under the surface, then so be it. A Jewish Vice President will not eliminate anti-Semitism in America. But it will accomplish one thing: it will finally allow us to stop obsessing about it; it will allow us to stop worrying about it all the time. It will no longer be a factor in our lives. It will be reduced to the category of an annoyance. A mosquito that has to be swatted every now and again.

One day soon there could be a Jewish Vice President. And maybe even a President. Just 50 years after Hadassah Lieberman's parents sailed past the Statue of Liberty and passed through Ellis Island, her husband is nominated to be the Vice President of the United Stated. This is a symbol for all immigrants; the embodiment of the American promise.

This is a great moment for us, the Jews of America. The moment when we put aside our fears and anxiety about being a minority. The moment when we stop worrying about the anti-Semites. The moment when we realize that we don't have to change our names or our noses to be accepted in America. The moment when we American Jews finally grow up and take our places in the mainstream of American life.

There is a little known custom for the Rosh Hashana festive meal. Sephardic Jews customarily begin the evening meal by eating the head of a fish or a sheep. And then they recite the following blessing: May it be God's will that the Jewish people rise to be the head of society and not the tail. Well, my friends, after tailing along in so many societies, at so many moments in our past history, we have finally gone to the head of the class. In honor of this Rosh Hashana, we have arrived at the rosh.

I don't know if Joe Lieberman will win the race for Vice President, and lest you get the wrong idea, I am not telling you to vote for him, but for me, he is already a winner! He is the man who changed Jewish life in America forever. And we, the Jewish people, are already the biggest winners.

We have been blessed with so many things; success, influence, power, respect, and pride. Let us all pledge that in the coming new year, we will give back to our beloved country, America, as much as she has given to us. America has honored us. And we in turn honor America. As did Jefferson and Franklin and Hancock and Hayim Solomon, we, too, pledge our lives and our fortunes to the one country in the history of the world that brought a Lieberman to the door of the Vice Presidency. Who knows what great things the future will bring. Iz es gut far Yidden? Thank God, it's very good for the Jews.

SACRIFICING OUR CHILDREN

Every year we read the same story: Abraham hears the voice of God. Take your son Isaac, your only son, the son you dearly love, and sacrifice him. And every year, I am bothered by the story. Not bothered, actually horrified.

What kind of a God could be so cruel to ask Abraham to sacrifice his son. To tie him into an altar and stab him to death. Every year I think, what father in his right mind could do such a thing? What father could even think of doing such a thing? Abraham should have been arrested for attempted homicide.

God himself is a bit hesitant to make such a demand on Abraham. He speaks elliptically, not coming directly to the point.

"Take your son." Which son? Abraham also had Ishmael. "Your only son from your wife." But Abraham had two wives. Sarah and Hagar. "The son you love." Abraham loves both of his sons. And finally God says "I want you to sacrifice Isaac." And suddenly, it becomes very clear what God is asking. Abraham now realizes the price of being God's chosen one. The cost of being Jewish. He knew that adopting the new religion wouldn't be easy. That declaring himself to be an Ivri, a Hebrew, meant that he placed himself in opposition to everyone else. On the other side. In opposition to the religious and political currents of the day. In opposition to the culture of the Assyrians, the mightiest empire of the day. All this he was ready to do. To leave his own parents and strike out for himself. To leave the luxury and comfort of a great cosmopolitan center and go off across the desert to find, what? A promised land.

It was a test for Abraham. Of his courage, his strength, and his faith. And he passes the test. In the new land of Canaan, later to be the land of Israel, he becomes a wealthy, powerful and respected leader. Local kings consult with him. They join forces with him to repel invaders. They seek his advice and counsel. They admire and respect his faith in God; the way he attributes everything to God's blessings. A powerful man, yet humble, a wealthy man yet generous, a successful man yet thankful. Obviously, God's chosen one.

And then this shocking new test: take your son Isaac and sacrifice him. Abraham and Sarah became parents at an older age. It took a long time to have a child. They prayed for years to have a son. And now Abraham is about to sacrifice him, because that's what he thinks God demands.

This can't be the story. How could the God of the people of Israel do such a thing? How could he crush his loyal servant Abraham? How can He be so cruel? How can we read this story and still be expected to believe in this God? To love this God? Every Rosh Hashana, I ask myself these same questions. This year I have an answer.

For several months last year, the whole country talked about a little boy from Cuba named Elian. Elian Gonzalez washed up on the shores of Florida. Actually, he was rescued off the coast by a fisherman. The refugees with him, including his mother, were lost at sea. His relatives in Miami, in Little Havana, took him in and made him part of their family. A wonderful heart-warming ending to a terrible tragedy. All of America rejoiced. A desperate attempt to reach freedom. A furtive escape from communist Cuba. A terrible tragedy at sea. The rescue of a little boy. A family to take him in. He finds a new home. He finds people who will care for him. He finds love. A script for Hollywood. It brought tears to our eyes.

And then we heard that Elian had a father. In Cuba. And he wanted his son back. Suddenly, there was no happy ending to the story. It went on for months. Many of us were disturbed and confused. In the Jewish community, some of us were reminded of the Kindertransport; Jewish children sent out of Berlin and Hamburg as the Nazis closed in on the Jews. Some of us recalled the last ships leaving Germany with hundreds of Jews aboard only to be turned back. The St. Louis sailing from Hamburg to Havana and back again in 1939. Most of the 900 Jews aboard were eventually caught and murdered by the Nazis.

We looked at this little helpless boy, about to be returned to Cuba and our hearts were torn. We saw visions of that little boy in the Warsaw Ghetto, that frightened little boy, standing in front of the storm troopers with his little hands in the air. We thought of a million Jewish children who were murdered in concentration camps because no one would take them in. No one would even give them a piece of bread. No one cared. We saw Elian Gonzalez in terms that we could understand. In terms of the Shoah. And we hoped that he could stay with us.

But we were wrong. We weren't thinking correctly. We were seeing concentration camps in Cuba. We were seeing Nazis in Havana. We were seeing Elian Gonzalez being returned to Cuba and condemned to be machine gunned by a firing squad.

Of course, we are opposed to the communist regime of Fidel Castro. Of course, we await the day when the people of Cuba will rise up and throw off the shakles of dictatorship. But the case of Elian Gonzalez really wasn't about democracy and communism. It wasn't about politics. It was really about a little boy and his father. A father back in Cuba who wanted him. A little boy in Miami who needed him. And well-meaning relatives who confused the issue for all of us. Who were ready to sacrifice little Elian on the altar of politics.

And I thought of Abraham, up on Mount Moriah ready to sacrifice his son Isaac because he thought it was the right thing to do. To sacrifice his son because of some idea, some misguided idea. That somehow God wanted the life of his son.

What happens at the end of the story. God says stop. You have misunderstood me, terribly. I don't want your son. I want you to have your son. I want you to learn that nothing in this world is more important than your son. Take him. Take care of him. Love him. And never think that any idea, or philosophy, or political agenda or even religious principal is more important that that. And if anyone, or anything demands the life of your son than reject it. Because that idea is false.

And at that point, God instructs Abraham to free his son and give him a big hug. The nearby ram is sacrificed. And the ram's horn (shofar) is sounded on every Rosh Hashana to remind ourselves: nothing is more important than our children. Nothing is more important for our children than the love of their parents.

Abraham thinks that Isaac is better off with God's family with God the father. God says that Isaac is better off with his own family, especially with Abraham, his own father. No one can take the place of your own father, not even God himself. There will be time enough in the next world to be with God, the father of us all.

So Elian went home to his father. He was not sacrificed on the altar of politics. It was not a perfectly happy ending. It never is except in Hollywood. Elian's mother died trying to bring him to freedom. Isaac's mother Sarah died of shock. But the son was reunited with his father.

And the love between them will survive long after the walls crumble and the politics are forgotten.

JONAH & COLUMBUS

Yom Kippur coincides with Columbus Day for the first time in memory.

Columbus was Jewish. I hereby claim him as our ancestor. Especially for all of us who love to go down to the sea in boats. All of us who fish, all of us who like noisy powerboats, and the aristocrats of us all, those who love to sail. We are related to Christopher Columbus.

Christopher! What kind of a name is that for a Jewish boy? And therein lies the tale of a Jewish boy born in Genoa, Italy, to the family Colon, or Columbo. Not the Columbo you know from New York of Rikers Island. Columbus was born into a Marrano family, refugees from Spain who had to hide their Jewish identity or be tortured by the inquisition.

Ferdinand and Isabella of Aragon financed his expedition due to the influence of Luis de Santangel and Gabriel Sanchez, who were hidden Jews or New Christians as they were called. Columbus sent them the first copy of his account of his success when he returned. On his voyage he used the nautical instruments and tables perfected by the Jews Joseph Vecinho and Abraham Zacuto. His interpreter was Jewish: Luis de Torres. And de Torres was actually the first one to step on shore at San Salvador. Columbus was ready to leave on August 2, but he postponed his voyage by one day to August 3 because he didn't want to sail on the ninth of Av, the day of mourning for the destruction of the two temples in Jerusalem. Sailors are superstitious. The day was a bad omen.

Columbus referred to the Second Temple calling it the Second House (we say Bayit Sheni in Hebrew); and he connected himself with King David. All this I have seen with my own eyes in the archives of the Indies in Seville. I held his documents in my own hands, and read them with the help of the librarian.

So what does this historical account of Columbus really have to do with Yom Kippur? It has everything to do. Today, this afternoon at mincha, to be exact, we will read about another Jewish sailor, perhaps the most famous Jewish sailor of all time: Jonah.

According to the book, Jonah is called upon to travel to the city of Nineveh and charge them to repent. Otherwise, the Lord will destroy them for their wicked ways.

Jonah is not interested in the job. He has no intention of leaving his farm to make the long and arduous journey across the desert all the way to Assyria on the Tigris River. And who is Jonah to tell the people of Nineveh how to lead their lives. Imagine if you got up on a chair in the middle of

Times Square and announced to the passing people that
God sent you to tell them to repent? No one would pay attention to the meshuggener. And inside of five minutes, Rudy
Giuliani's police would cart you off to Bellevue for making a
public nuisance of yourself. So Jonah does what we all
would do. He says, "no thanks."

But you can't ignore God so easily. If God has a task for
you, then, sooner or later, you are going to have to carry it
out.

Jonah decides to run away. He goes down to the port of
Jaffa and books a passage on a cruise through the
Mediterranean to the Riviera. Not the French Riviera but
the Spanish Riviera, the Costa del Sol. Even the resort
where he has hotel reservations is mentioned in the Bible.
Tarshish. Not far from Malaga.

If you had a choice between going to Iraq or going to the
Spanish Riviera, where would you go? Do you think you can
play 18 holes in Baghdad? Jonah is no fool. So off he goes to
the Western Mediterranean.

And you know what happens. A great storm comes up in
the sea. The sailors are frightened to death. The ship is taking on water fast. It is about to sink. In those days, there
was no radar or sonar. There wasn't even a compass or a
lifeboat. If a storm came up, you tried to reach the nearest
shore. Otherwise, you took your chances. All along the coast
of Israel are ancient ports where ships could put in during a
storm. I saw one Phoenician port on the northern coast of
Israel called Dor where the skeletons of ancient ships are
scattered on the floor of the harbor. Ships that went up on
the rocks while trying to find shelter from a storm.
(Incidentally, Haifa University is in the process of salvaging
the wrecks and preserving them in its new maritime museum.)

At any rate, the sailors decide that Jonah is the problem.
They have already thrown the cargo overboard to lighten
the load. And Jonah is going to be next. It is clear to the
sailors that Jonah is a curse on them. And when Jonah
admits that he is trying to run away from God, they know

he is the cause of the storm. Over he goes, and the storm miraculously stops. The ship is saved. But Jonah is swallowed by the sea monster. But since the sea monster prefers to eat sea algae (fortunately he is a vegetarian) he spits Jonah out on the shore. Jonah is saved. Jonah learns his lesson. He goes to carry out God's will. End of story.

But not the end of our story. What is Jonah really running away from? What is he really disturbed about? So disturbed that he becomes a fugitive. So depressed and aggravated that he almost dares the sailors to throw him into the sea. It can't be the people of Nineveh. He hasn't even been there yet. He has no idea if his mission could be a success. Something else is bothering him; from the past. Some recent failure that is making him afraid to even try again.

Hidden in the pages of an obscure midrash, I found the answer. Jonah's first task as a prophet was to go up to Jerusalem and remind the people of the absolute importance of a united Israel with its united capital in Jerusalem. Jonah lives during a time of terrible division in Israel. The nation is split into two entities: the southern kingdom of Judah, with its capital in Jerusalem, and the northern kingdom of Israel, with its capital in Samaria. This state of affairs cannot be tolerated. Not politically, not religiously, not militarily. A nation wracked by competing monarchies; by a fractious religious authority, and by a military divided against itself would be easy prey to powerful enemies. Only a reunion of the two kingdoms into a united nation with one united capital in Jerusalem could ensure the future of the people of Israel.

Jonah had already carried the same message to the people of the northern kingdom. With powerful words, he reminded them of the terrible cost of civil war. Surely, the people of Israel can find a common ground to unite once again, as in the days of David and Solomon.

Jonah seems to be successful. The Kings listen to him. The people take his words to heart and a process of reconciliation seems to begin. But the negotiations go on too long.

The politicians are too narrow-minded, the people grow tired, and patience is at an end. The final result is that Judah and Israel remain divided; Jerusalem never becomes a united capital of the Jewish people; and ultimately both Jewish kingdoms, divided and therefore weakened, are destroyed by more powerful enemies. Jonah's mission is a failure. He doesn't live to see the destruction of the Holy Temple, and of the Holy city Jerusalem. But he understands what's coming.

This is what disturbs Jonah. This is why he is so depressed. This is the real problem that he is running away from when he boards that ship in the port of Jaffa.

And I believe that this is the problem we are running away from. This is the issue that we Jews would rather not face. The issue of Jerusalem.

From the day that Jerusalem was put on the negotiating table, we have been hiding our heads in the sand. Every Israeli leader who came to speak to us, from Labor or Likud, always said the same thing: Jerusalem will always remain the undivided capital of the Jewish people. And we would all applaud and cheer. The Golan could be given back to Syria. Judah & Samaria would be given back to the Palestinians. The Jordan river would become an open border. All the strategic and tactical commandments of the past 50 years could be broken. Everything that every general and every prime minister believed about security, military prepared-ness, and geographical depth was suddenly all wrong. A new reality took hold of the popular Israeli imagination. The all powerful State of Israel could will a peace upon its neighbors. No cost was too high for peace. Just Jerusalem was untouchable, nonnegotiable.

But it was not true. Jerusalem was negotiable. The deal in the back room was already on the table.

And we, like Jonah, find it easier to run and hide from the truth. Do you believe that Jerusalem must remain the united capital of the Jewish people? Then, if you do, why haven't you said so? Why hasn't there been a ground swell of opinion from the Jewish people around the world, begging, demanding that Jerusalem be taken off the negotiating table. Do you understand what our silence will mean?

Every Passover we conclude the Seder with Leshana habaah beYerushalayim. Next year in Jerusalem. And before 1967 when Jerusalem was divided, we used to say Leshana habaah beYerusalayim hashleyma. Next year in the united Jerusalem. Because, in case you have forgotten, before 1967 no Jew was allowed to go to the Western Wall. No Jew was allowed in the old city of Jerusalem. No synagogue existed in the old city of Jerusalem. Every one of them, and there were dozens, was dynamited by the Jordanians. Until 1967, old Jerusalem was "Judenrein."

And when the Jewish flag was planted on the Temple mount on Wednesday, June 7, 1967 at 10:45 AM, the entire Jewish people vowed that Jerusalem would never be divided again. That it would remain the united capital of Israel forever. We took an oath. Im eshkachech Yerushalayim. If I forget thee Jerusalem, let my right hand fail.

That day in 1967 was the greatest in our lives. Maybe the greatest moment in the last 2000 years of Jewish history. I will never forget the pictures of generals Moshe Dayan, Uzi Narkiss, and Yitzchak Rabin (alav hashalom) coming up to the Western Wall for the first time. I heard the voice of Chaim Herzog broadcasting Dayan's words as he put a kvittel into the wall: "we have come home to this holy place, we will never leave it again." He was surrounded by battle weary troops, tough young men who had just survived the greatest battle in Israel's history. They stood and cried. David Ben-Gurion looked up at the Kotel and called upon the Jewish authorities to tear down the walls dividing the city. 33 years later we have no intention of letting anyone divide the city of Jerusalem, ever again.

Every day, three times a day, Jews face east to Jerusalem. And we pray: "Return to Jerusalem. Rebuild it. Reunite it, as it was in our history." These are more than words, even more than a hope or a prayer. They are a plan of action. A solemn promise. A declaration, that every Jew makes. That when it will be in our power, we will reunite and rebuild Jerusalem, the heart of the Jewish people.

Now it is in our power. We just need the will.

Every Yom Kippur we conclude the service with Leshana habaah beYerushalayim. Next year in Jerusalem. We are the first generation in 2000 years to be able to say "this year in Jerusalem." Not next year. Not a vague hope, not a prayer, not a distant dream. This year; now; today you can get on the plane and be at the Kotel, the Western Wall, in 11 hours. Tomorrow you can show up at Ben-Gurion Airport and tell the authorities you are coming home. And you are automatically a citizen. You want to live in Jerusalem; no problem. You want to spend your days breathing in the air of the Holy City, no problem.

Is there another city in any other country where a Jew is automatically and officially welcomed as a citizen? No visa, no passport, no green card required, no immigration quotas, no guard towers, no machine guns. Just a Siddur or a tallis or a grandfather from Minsk or a grandmother from Lodz. Just someone who is proud to be a Jew. Who wants to live in the Jewish homeland.

The holy city of Jerusalem is not up for negotiation.

It is our historical capital. Only our historical capital. Not one conquering empire ever made it their capital. Not Rome, not Babylonia, not the Saracens, not the Ottoman Turks, and certainly not the Arabs. Only the Jewish people made it their capital, 3,000 years ago.

Our Bet Hamikdash, our holy Temple stood on the Temple Mount, in the heart of Jerusalem. It was the religious focal point of the Jewish people from all over Israel, and from around the world. It is our holiest place. It is the very foundation of the holy of holies. The Kotel is only a wall, a remnant of the exterior retaining wall of the Temple platform. We went there to pray because we had nowhere else to go. The Muslim authorities didn't allow us to go up to the Temple Mount. So we made do until

1967. And when we were finally in control, what did we do? Did we bar all non-Jews from coming into our holy place? No. In the most magnanimous gesture for peace, we gave control over the area to the Muslims. To worship in peace at their Mosque. But never did we declare, or expect that the Temple Mount would be off limits to Jews. "Judenrein." In the holiest place in the Jewish religion, no one may bar a Jew from entering. We have shared our holy places with others. Always. Magnanimously, to the amazement of the world. But no one may dare tell us we cannot enter. Every Jew is welcome. As is every Muslim and every Christian.

It has been said that it was the wrong time for Ariel Sharon, the hero of every war in modern Israel, to visit the Temple Mount. The week before Rosh Hashana was the wrong time. So when is the right time? Last week? Last month? Next month? Next year? There will never be a right time unless we assert our rights. Not to the exclusion of anyone, but to the inclusion of everyone. And everyone begins with the Jewish people.

Do we bar Christians and Muslims from the Kotel? Do guards check your religion or passports before they let you into the Kotel Plaza? The only thing they check is if you have a gun or a bomb, and if you are wearing a kippa and are modestly dressed. The last I looked, half the people at the Kotel looked Arab. They were Sephardic Jews. Did anyone stop them because they appear to be Arabs?

You and I have a responsibility to the next generation and to the next hundred generations; to see to it that Jerusalem is never divided again. Every Jew is a citizen of Jerusalem. Every Jew has an address in Jerusalem. Every Jew says Leshana habaah beYerusalayim. And every Jew had better mean it.

Yerushalayim means city of peace. But the city has had more conflict than peace over its 3,000 year history. On this Yom Kippur, our holiest day, we pray for Jerusalem, our holiest city. We pray with all our hearts, with all our fervor, with all our might, that God will share his wisdom with our leaders. That God will sharpen their vision, so that we can find a way out of the shadows of violence and into the sunshine of peace.

"Sha'alu shalom Yerushalayim." Shana Tova.

MORAL RESPONSIBILITY

There was a man who rose to great prominence. He became the leader of his people. He was tall and handsome, and so charming. He could talk anybody into anything. He was ruddy looking, with wavy hair. He was a talented musician. He married a fine woman with talents in her own right. But, they never could establish a solid relationship.

His roving eye got him into trouble on several occasions. But each time, he managed to talk his way out of any serious consequences. Then, one day, he went too far. He took up with a young woman. And it became a public scandal. His family was embarrassed. The country was embarrassed. He teetered on the brink of a personal disaster.

I am speaking of a man called David, king of Israel, some 3,000 years ago.

David was the golden boy of the people of Israel. He was a brave warrior. The man who united the twelve tribes into one solid nation. The man who conquered Jerusalem from the Jebusites; and established it as the capital of the State of Israel for evermore. The man who composed the famous Psalms, the most sublime and moving prayers in our Siddur. The man who became King by popular acclaim. The man about whom they wrote and sang epic poems. A man who was larger than life, too good to be true. And the man who was almost brought down by his infatuation with Bathsheba.

It was a hot afternoon in Jerusalem. David was just getting up from a siesta in the heat of the day. He walked out onto his roof terrace and noticed a woman bathing a few houses away. He was immediately smitten. "She was very beautiful." He sends his messengers to find out who she is. She is an aristocrat, married to Uriah the Hittite, an officer in the army, a convert to the Hebrews. David is so infatuated that he disregards the fact that she is a married woman. He carries on an affair with her and she becomes pregnant.

David becomes desperate. Now everyone will find out. It will be a headline in the *Jerusalem Post*. His whole career will be jeopardized. His place in history will be lost.

He comes up with a desperate scheme. The Israelites are in the middle of a campaign against the Amonites. David orders his general to send Uriah to the front lines. And, of course, he is killed.

David can now sleep easier in Bathsheba's bed. No one will be any wiser, after all, David has magnanimously married a poor grieving widow.

But David knows the truth. And God knows the truth. And one fine day, the prophet Nathan,knocks on his door. He confronts David with his terrible secret. Nathan draws himself up in front of the King and he begins his charge, "I anointed you King over Israel; I delivered you from the anger of Saul; I made you master over Israel and Judah, and look what you did. You took a man's wife and you had him killed. Now you will live the rest of your life by the sword. You will never have peace till the end of your days."

Now, David was a very powerful man. He could have called for his guard and had Nathan executed. He could have continued to deny his sin until the end of days. Who could have proven otherwise? His general was loyal to him. He wouldn't talk. There was no Ken Starr to lead an investigation. Who was going to challenge the word of the king?

But this was not David's way. He was not only the King, but a truly great man. And it is the mark of a great man, that when he is confronted by his sins, he immediately accepts the moral responsibility for his actions. Everyone sins. Kings and commoners alike, presidents and plebeians. Big people and small people. All human beings sin. It is our nature. None of us are perfect. That's why we have Yom Kippur. That's why we say Al chet. That's why we ask for forgiveness.

David doesn't try to protest, or to deny, or to read the latest polls on his approval ratings. When David is confronted by the prophet Nathan, he immediately answers:

"I have sinned before God." David broke three of the ten commandments at once. "Thou shalt not covet your neighbors wife." "Thou shalt not commit adultery." "Thou shalt not murder." All because of an adolescent infatuation. And, yet, he doesn't try to slip side away. No denials, no cover up, no obfuscation. I did it. I have sinned. I am sorry.

The Torah is not a script for a soap opera. It is not entertaining us with vivid details of the royals. The Torah tells this story of King David so that we might learn from it. That a human being, even a king can sin, is not news. Anyone made of flesh and blood can be tempted. Anyone with normal hormones and normal conditioned responses can, at times, go astray. Yes, we are expected to be able to control ourselves. That's what "mind over matter" means. That is the essential difference between a human being and a "behema," as my grandmother used to call people who acted like animals in the street. Animals act by instinct. They can't control their behavior. But, a person, a "mentch," is supposed to control himself. That's why God gave us intelligence. And that's why he gave us the Torah to guide us.

And, yet, now and again, we lose our way. Our negative impulses, our yetzer hara take over. And we do something foolish, or ridiculous, or even worse, something hurtful or even criminal. But our lives don't end there. We have a way to come back, to return, to our families, to our God, to ourselves. It's called teshuva, penitence; and it's exactly what we are doing today on this Yom Kippur. And the process of teshuva begins with admitting that you did something wrong. Be a big boy. Own up to what you did. Try to set it right. And, don't do it again.

And no one should think that he is so powerful that he is above the law. That the law is only for little people; the people who pay their taxes to the penny; the people who never cut the line at the supermarket. For the people who say "please" and "thank you" and "have a good day," and mean it.

But I am not the appointed one to chastise kings or presidents. I am not here to read their list of indiscretions, their Al chet. I have my own to worry about, and you have your own. The president will have to make his own decisions. And he will have to face the consequences of his own actions.

The focus of my address today is not the kings or the president. The focus is you and me.

On this Yom Kippur Day, our holiest day, I wish to remind you that we are all here to ask forgiveness. From our family and from our friends and ultimately, from God. How sincerely we do this job determines what happens to us in the New Year.

"On Rosh Hashana, it is written who shall live and who shall die." This is serious business. Everything we do is noticed, if not on earth then in heaven. If not by men's eyes, then by God's eyes. And everything is recorded. David's life, warts and all, was recorded in the chronicles, Divrei Hayamim. You can read it to this day. Matter of factly recorded: his adulterous affair with Bathsheba. His murder of her husband Uriah.

The Rabbis of the Talmud were so eager to put a positive spin on the story. They write, that legally speaking, David had every right to take Batsheba as his wife. Because by custom, every soldier in David's army going to war was expected to write a bill of divorce, a Get, for his wife in case he would be missing in action. In case he would be killed in battle and his body would never be found, and his death was not witnessed by his comrades. Without a document of divorce, and without witness to the death, she would never be able to remarry. Interestingly in the modern army of Israel, the same procedure is followed as mandated by the Chief Chaplain.

But this was all political spin. David was a powerful man from the most influential tribe in Israel, the tribe of Judah. To some extent, he controlled the media of the time, the official court documents and scribes. He was the darling of the priestly class and the religious leaders. The prophets presented him as a veritable messiah, and continued to support him throughout his personal troubles. He extended the territory of Israel through military conquest to its largest borders. He was good for the country. He was a hero.

However, the religious leadership could not ignore what David had done. They couldn't erase the sin. They dutifully recorded the basic facts. But in just a few sentences. Not in ten boxes of transcripts. And they carefully omitted the salacious details. It would be demeaning to the office of the king. It would be harmful to the future of the country.

But as a moral force, David would never again be effective. He had failed in his personal life. With his women and with his children. His son Absalom tried to lead a revolution against him. He was killed in the process, before he could kill his father. David was a total failure in his private life, both as a husband and a father. Even though he was one of our greatest national leaders, he is held strictly accountable for his moral failures. And it is written in the Chronicles and in the Book of Samuel for every one to read, and learn from that no one can escape the eye of God. That, sooner or later, we will all have to answer for our actions. Accountability. That's what it means: "On Rosh Hashana, it is written, and on Yom Kippur, the record is sealed." And the indictment will be handed down. And we will be held accountable.

I read that Dan Quayle may run for president. Surely, you remember when he suddenly was lifted from obscurity a number of years ago to run for Vice President. Perhaps you don't remember the press conference at the announcement. Someone dug up the story that Dan Quayle had used his influence to get into the National Guard instead of having to go into the army. And one of the reporters asked him why he did it. His answer was very simple, and very touching. Later on, he backed away from that first answer and tried to evade the question, but this is what he said the first time; he said simply: If I had known back then that I would be standing here today, I wouldn't have done it. Believe me. That's what the prayer is all about. That's what it means. It means nothing goes unnoticed. Everything gets recorded. And it all comes back someday to haunt you.

My first-grade teacher taught me something about accountability. She stood in front of us on that first day of class. I remember it like yesterday because it made such a strong impression on me. She said: Behave yourself or it will go on your permanent record. Did your teacher tell you the same thing? I believed her. I believed that there was a permanent record that they kept on you somewhere in the principals office and that it went with you for the rest of your life. Otherwise, why would they call it permanent? Entry: "Konovitch, kept after school for failing to hand in homework. Entry: Konovitch, suspended for two days for cutting homeroom class to play basketball."

I imagined that when you wanted to get married, you had to go down to City Hall and they looked up your permanent record, and if you had behaved in first grade, they gave you a license, and if not, you were out of luck. It was only years later that I realized that there was no permanent record, not in that sense.

But there is a permanent record. It says so in the prayer. What we do, everything we do, is written somewhere. And the truth will be known.

Yes, everything is recorded. All our sins on the permanent record. And we come to God on Yom Kippur, hat in hand (yarmulke on the head), to ask his forgiveness. Why should He? Because we are contrite, because we sincerely want to change; because we are also ready to forgive others. Forgiveness is the basic theme of Yom Kippur.

And even a president deserves forgiveness. I heard him with my own ears admit his guilt. I saw him realize that he had to own up to what he did.

After trying to hide from his guilt, and hide from his responsibility, he finally confronted the truth. How long can we be angry at him? He is only a man. Made of flesh and blood. Not an angel, not a superman. I am deeply saddened by it all. Perhaps we have felt hurt, and maybe betrayed. But none of us is free from sin. And, as I said, all of us pray for forgiveness. So it is appropriate that we pray for William Clinton. And it is proper that we learn to forgive him. Because it is the only way we will unite as a people, and take our place once again as the leaders of the free world.

Several weeks ago, I came across this sentence in the Bible dealing with the president of the tribes of Israel: "When the President will sin." A discussion of how to deal with presidential wrongdoing. Not "if a president will sin, but WHEN a president will sin." It is assumed that if you are human, you will sin. And, the bigger you are, the greater the temptation to sin, as the Talmud says.

The only question is will you atone? Will you come back? Will you do teshuva?

Furthermore, the Bible discusses punishment for sin. In ancient times, people were stoned to death for capital offenses. And it says, "Those who came forward to accuse; those who bear witness against their neighbor, let them throw the first stone." As if to say, if you yourself are not free of sin then you had better not be casting stones.

Who is ready to throw the first stone at Bill Clinton? Who is so perfectly free of sin that he can pillory the president?

Rather, let us do the Jewish thing. Let us not judge. That we leave to the congress and ultimately to God. Let us feel sorry for a man who has so much talent and so much potential, but is still in the grip of his yetzer hara, his baser instincts. Even the people of Israel were not so quick to be offended by David's actions. Nowhere is it recorded that they demanded his resignation from office. In the very next paragraph of the Bible, it tells of the birth of Solomon. Apparently, God forgave David and gave him a son who would become the wisest King of Israel. And the people continued to follow him. They gathered together to be led by David's brilliance once more. Apparently, the people eventually forgave him. But make no mistake about it. King David had committed a terrible sin. He was to be severely punished. His personal life was in shambles. His reputation was permanently tarnished. The Talmud records that for the next 22 years, until the moment he died, David repented every day for what he had done. And the Prophet Nathan chastised him in front of all the nation. The great King David reduced to an apologetic prodigal son.

But David refused to slink away from Jerusalem and run home. He refused to give up. He assessed the situation and realized that what was done was done. There was nothing he could do to change the fact that he had sinned. He couldn't call it back.

The only thing left was to counterbalance his sins with good deeds. And for 22 years, he tried to be a real leader for his people.

And ultimately, the people forgave him. And they began to follow him once again. But why? Why didn't the people turn their backs on him? Why weren't they permanently ashamed of him?

Because I think the people recognized in David their own shortcomings. Their own tendency to occasionally slip. And they admired the way David handled the situation. "I sinned," says David. "I will try to do better. Please forgive me. I am ready to take my punishment."

King David is every man. Every man confronted by sin, agonizing about moral failure. I would like to know if there is anyone in the congregation who didn't commit a single sin this year. Raise your hand. I will personally nominate you for zadik of the year. What, no hands? The point is that none of us lead perfect lives.

People come through my office every week with terrible problems. And the problems are usually of their own making. And some of them can rival King David's problems.

The one thing I don't do is judge. I don't tell them how bad they are. I try to show them a way to come back, to atone. To get out from under the burden of sin and begin again. I teach them the words of the Torah. The same words I offer you today. You did something wrong, have regret, charata, and say so, al chet. Try to make it right, and promise to do better in the future, Kabala leatid. It is the same formula for kings and commoners, presidents and paupers. In front of God, we are all the same. We all are tempted. We all stumble on the road of life. No one's life runs straight and smooth. But, as the wise man said, fall down nine times, but get up ten.

We all lose our way now and again. But God always holds a light in the window, waiting for us to find our way home.

So, my friends, on this Yom Kippur, let the power of forgiveness flow through our souls. Let us forgive each other. Let us join hands and hearts and together. Let us find our way back, back to the Torah, back to God, and back to a happier life.

SAVE IT, USE IT

When a person passes away, and if they wish to observe the tradition, then they are buried in tachrichim. Tachrichim are a white linen uniform. Simple and dignified. All white. Because we stand before God, our creator, and we present ourselves as pure.

The tachrichim have no pockets because you can't take it with you. The way you come into the world, with nothing, so you leave this world with nothing. There is no point in saving it; you might as well have the mitzva of giving it away while you are alive. Because when God takes you, you can't take your stock portfolio with you.

What you can take with you are mitzvas. The mitzva you get from honoring your parents, respecting your teachers, giving zedaka.

Several years back, one of our people called me with the bad news that her father had passed away. Several weeks after the funeral and the shiva, she called me again. It was time to go back into the apartment to empty out all the closets. It is one of the hardest things to do. But it had to be faced. The apartment had a buyer and everything had to go.

Her question to me was, "What about my father's shoes?" She had heard that no one could wear the shoes of the dead. She had seen her grandmother throw the shoes in the river. She was about to throw her father's shoes in the canal behind the building.

An old superstition that the spirit of the dead remains to occupy the shoes.

I wasn't satisfied with this answer. It can't be just an old superstition. In our religion, there is a reason for everything. Finally, I found a reference in the Talmud: If the deceased was ill, and often times it is a disease that strikes down a person, then the shoes might transmit the bacteria of the disease. Certainly makes good sense, even to our modern scientific minds.

In another reference to shoes, the Talmud talks about dreams and their meanings. You'll be amazed how many people come to me troubled about dreams and asking me what they mean. And my name isn't even Joseph.

The Talmud says (Berachot 47), If you dream of your deceased ancestor, it is a good *omen*.

If however the person in the dream takes shoes out of the house, then it is an evil omen that someone is about to go on the long journey. Of course, a nice way of saying the final journey.

So there you have it. Shoes connected with the dead, as a bad sign. So we certainly wouldn't want to wear them. And we might want to throw them away. We might want to be rid of the evil omen.

I said, No. Rather give them to a poor person with the rest of the clothes. The Talmud warns us against destroying property, especially clothing. Why waste a good pair of shoes? And to me, they looked brand new!

And then she added, "The shoes were practically brand new. He only wore them once, to my wedding. And when I would ask him, why he wouldn't wear them, he said he was waiting for a special occasion. And he added in Yiddish, 'Ich shalive.'" My grandmother used to use the same word. "shalive." It means a person who can't bring himself to use something. Like those shoes that still have the brown color in the soles of brand new leather. Like the suit I bought last year.

I hate to shop. I have about a 20-minute attention span for shopping, and then I give up. But I went to buy a suit. I found one. A very nice suit. I am wearing it today, but you can't see it under my gown. But take my word for it. It's a very fine suit. But, this is the third time I wore it all year. I am saving it. "Ich shalive." Do you think I could ever wear this suit out? If I wore it every Shabbat, do you think it would be used up? Of course not! The suit will last for 30 years. But I only wear it on special occasions. Ich shalive. And I'm not sure why.

Many of us still remember when you only had one good pair of shoes and one good suit. It was your Shabbos suit. Or your Shabbos shoes. And that's what it meant; they were only for special occasions! The rest of the time, they were tucked away in the closet. You shalived that suit. And if you hadn't outgrown it, you might still have it hanging in your closet.

And the day we go to meet our maker, the shoes will still be in the closet, shining as if new, and the suit will be in the closet, with its original perfect creases. And someone will give it all away to the poor and we will go out in white linen tachrichim, shrouds.

Do I think I will never afford such a fine suit again? Do I think my mother will never take me shopping again? My mother used to buy me blue jeans. Only then, we called them dungarees. She bought them a few sizes big. Because I was going to grow into them very quickly. You rolled up the cuffs so you wouldn't trip. A Jewish fellow by the name of Levi Strauss invented blue jeans. He made tough pants for miners and prospectors in the California gold rush.

I was allowed to wear my new jeans only on special days. Did my mom think I was going to wear them out? Levi's are indestructible. Even the California gold miners couldn't wear out a pair of Levi's. Did she think I was going to wear them out playing baseball? I was being taught to "shalive." To save things. Not to use them out too quickly.

In Yankee terms, shalive meant saving for a rainy day. Our parents or grandparents came from Eastern Europe with the clothes on their back, and maybe a battered valise. It was all they had in the world. They had to work terribly hard, day and night, seven days a week just to survive. And if they lived through the Great Depression, they never forgot what it meant. The children went to school in patched and tattered clothing, because there was no money to buy new clothes. There was barely enough money to keep from starving.

So they developed the ethic of saving for a rainy day. Because you never know what could happen tomorrow. The Cossacks could reappear, even in East New York. The factory could close even during the best season in the garment industry.

So they worked hard and saved all of their lives. And finally, they took their first vacation; and finally, they decided to enjoy a little of what they had. They bought a condominium in Florida and moved down to enjoy their golden years. Inside of two years, she was gone and he was alone; wondering what did they shalive for. Why didn't they enjoy life sooner?

So stop shaliving, stop saving it for a special occasion. Today is a special occasion. Yesterday was a special occasion. Rosh Hashana is a special occasion.

Do you understand the significance of Rosh Hashana? It is the beginning, a New Year. You made it. You made it to another year. Don't you think that's an occasion? Celebrate. I hope you put on your best dress today, and your best suit and your best shoes.

You got up this morning. You got out of bed. Both feet worked. Your fingers moved, your head worked (more or less). You were alive again. Last night, did God guarantee that you would wake up? But, you did. Give thanks. Say Modeh Ani. Celebrate. Put on that new hat and smile. Don't save it in the hatbox for a special occasion. It may never come. Today is the occasion. Don't shalive.

And, by the way, I notice that some of you are shaliving your seat. You're saving your seat for special occasions. You seem to use it only for Rosh Hashana and Yom Kippur. Now, it's very nice of you to worry about wearing out the synagogue seats with overuse. But I checked with our interior decorator. The material is first class. You can sit in it every Shabbat for the next 20 years and it still won't wear out. Try it.

But more important, let's talk about the more important things that you're saving for some special occasion that will never come. Never mind about shoes and suits and dresses. Let's talk about you and me. When we are born, we are given the capacity to love. I'm not sure how you measure love. Is it pounds or quarts or cubic feet? But I have come to the conclusion that we have unlimited amounts to spend. No matter how much you give, you still have more to give. I never heard about anyone that ran out of love. Even people who live to be 90.

The Torah writes a few things about love. You will all recognize the line. "And you shall love the Lord will all your heart." It means that when you love, use your whole heart, your whole being. Don't hold anything back. You won't use it up. Your heart won't stop beating. Nobody's heart ever stopped from loving. It might have stopped from the lack of love. But not from too much love.

I read that scientists discovered that a person who loves, who is happy and positive and optimistic because of love, will live longer. They have a better chance of recovering from coronary bypass surgery and their immune systems were stronger. They got sick less and if they got sick, they recovered faster. That's what love can do.

And you don't have to shalive your love. Don't save it. Because as much as you give it, you will still have more to give. I know that God gives us this unlimited capacity to love. And by the time we go back to God, we are supposed to have used up all our love. It's the first thing He will ask us. And if we didn't, if we shalive, then we are committing a crime against our maker.

So I have heard that you are angry at your son. You sent him to medical school. He dropped out to be a musician, in a rock band. You refused to support him in his ridiculous venture. You cut him off. He moved away. You don't talk to him. It happened 20 years ago. Now, you have saved 20 years of love. You shalived 20 years of love. You are expected to use it. God is waiting for you to shower your son with 20 years of lost love.

So . . . what are you waiting for? Do you want to appear before God and admit that you pigheadedly refused to give your love to your son for 20 years?

I told you, you have to spend it. You have to use it. You can't take it with you. So it is time to pick up the phone.

So it might be you, brother, or your mother, or your sister-in-law. It doesn't matter who or what the details of the story are.

You are supposed to love with all of your heart, or your heart will suffer an insufficiency, as my doctor says.

On the other hand, your anger you can shalive. Save your anger. Don't use up your anger. Leave it where it belongs. Near your gall bladder, at your bile duct. That's why we call it bile. Anger saps your energy. It makes you tired. It wears you down. It destroys your heart. The heart is supposed to love, not hate. It was made for love, not for anger. Anger will only give you a heart attack. So the choice is yours. It's Rosh Hashana. Time to start over. Time to pick up the phone. Time is running out.

Another thing you don't have to shalive are compliments.

The easiest way to make a person happy is to give them a compliment.

Last month, one of the ladies in our Sisterhood came into the office looking completely different. I wasn't quite sure what it was. Lost some weight, a new dress, a face peel? Then it suddenly struck, a new hairdo. A lot shorter than usual. A bit daring. She looked a bit concerned. You know how it is? You walk into the beauty parlor and you never know what you're going to walk out with. It makes no difference what you tell the hairstylist. They say yes. But they're not really listening. They are going to do what they want to do. Every hair stylist thinks they are the Rembrandt of hair. They know better than you. Just sit back and let them create. Well, you want a hair cut, not a creation. But it's too late.

So this lady went in with long hair and came out with short hair. A lot shorter than she was expecting. And she was concerned how people would react.

I didn't hesitate. I said, "New hairdo?" She said yes, waiting for the bomb to drop. And I said, "Looks great!" She broke into a great smile; she looked so relieved." Do you really think so?" And I said "absolutely."

Maybe I made her day. Did it cost me anything? Did I use up my daily quota of compliments? What did it hurt?

Now to tell you the truth, that lady looked just fine in her old hairdo. Why did she have to experiment with a new look? And, actually, I preferred the old look. But I immediately sensed that the situation needed a compliment. So I gave it.

When I was younger, I gave out compliments like thousand dollar bills. Not very often. It had to be something very special. Unusual. Extraordinary. Perfection. The dinner had to rival Chef Allen. The essay had to approach Hemingway. The performance had to match Isaac Stern. Now, I realize that something can be good without being perfect. Now, I save perfection for God. And I compliment all the good around me. It doesn't take anything away from me to tell the president that she made a fine speech. It doesn't take anything away from me to tell the cantor that he sang a beautiful piece. It encourages them to do even more and even better. They feel appreciated. They feel good. And isn't that the purpose of a compliment? And no matter how many compliments I give, I will never use them up.

I find that if you look hard enough, you can always find something to compliment a person about. It is certainly better than always finding fault. I naturally begin to avoid people who never have a good word to say, who are always critical of what you do. Who needs them; they depress you, they lower your resistance. They make you sick.

So who did you compliment lately? Who is sitting next to you? Your wife? Tell her she looks elegant. Your friend? Tell him you're happy that he is in shul with you today. Your daughter? Tell her you're proud of her work at college. Your son-in-law? Tell him you couldn't ask for a better son-in-law. You get the point. So start spending your compliments. Don't shalive. Use them up on earth. And when the time comes to speak to God, don't worry, He doesn't need your compliments.

Now I have one thing more to do. To practice what I preach.

Friends, you are the finest congregation in the country. What we have accomplished in the last half dozen years would take another congregation 25 years to accomplish.

There is a great deal more for us to do in the coming years. To continue to raise the Jewish consciousness of our people, both young and old. To make our synagogue the central address for Jewish life in South Florida. We do it by taking no one for granted. We do it by listening to you and saying "toda." Thank you. For being here; for doing such outstanding work for our community; for being so generous whenever we ask you; for accepting the responsibility of being Jewish. I love you all. My prayer for you is that God didn't learn from my grandmother to shalive. May he shower you with his blessings. May he bless you with good health, tranquility of the soul, and exciting days in the new year, Amen.

RUNNING AWAY FROM YOURSELF

On the walls of the Pinkas synagogue in Prague are inscribed thousands of names. They are the names of the Jews of Prague whose history came to an end in the Theresienstadt concentration camp and the gas chambers of Auschwitz. The curator of the museum, because the Pinkas synagogue is only a museum to the past, was anxious to show me one name.

I thought he would point to the Loew family, descendants of the famous Rabbi Judah Loew, the Maharal of Prague, who was the Chief Rabbi in the late 1500s. Rabbi Loew was a brilliant Torah scholar as well as being expert in mathematics and astronomy. He was often invited to speak with the emperor, Rudolph II, who thought that the Rabbi was also a magician. You see, it was Rabbi Loew who was reputed to have created the Golem, the first superhuman robot in history to defend the Jewish people from attack. But the Golem ran amok and Rabbi Loew had to destroy it. They say that it still lies in the attic of the Alt-Neu shul; but I couldn't find it.

But it wasn't the Löew name that I was shown.

Neither was it the name of the Landa family, descendants of the renowned Talmudist and Chief Rabbi in the eighteenth century, Rabbi Yechezel Landa, whose great, great, great grandson is our chairman of the board, Bill Landa. Rabbi Landa was one of the greatest intellects of the classical Ashkenazic period and was a direct descendant of Rashi, the greatest of all biblical commentators. He represented the Jews before the Austrian government. His legal responsa, bold, innovative and lenient, are studied to this day in the yeshivas. They attempt to reconcile the Jewish tradition with the modern world.

But the Landa name was not the one I was asked to look at. The curator was pointing to the name Koerbel. The Koerbels died in Auschwitz. But you may not recognize the name. But if I mention the name of their granddaughter, you will know them immediately. The granddaughter of the Koerbels is Madeleine Albright, our Secretary of State. She had been visiting the Pinkas synagogue the day before, looking at her grandparents' names, listed with all the other Jews of Prague. I wonder what she was thinking.

Since it was revealed in the press that Madaleine Albright came from a Jewish family, I have tried to understand. Madeleine Albright's father, Josef Koerbel, married his high school sweetheart, Mandula Spiegel. Josef Koerbel served as a Czech diplomat in England, even as the Germans marched into Prague. But he was safe; or at least he thought he was safe, because the Koerbels had converted to Christianity even before Kristallnacht.

A Jew in Prague wouldn't get too far in the diplomatic corps in the 1930s. Just a few decades back another Jewish Prague lawyer was trying to get a job. His name was Franz Kafka. The insurance company wasn't open to Jews; and only after pulling strings through a powerful friend, Kafka got the job. Franz Kafka was a world-famous author, but for the anti-Semites, he was only the Jew.

Josef Koerbel had no desire to be a Jew, humiliated and abused, or to be held back in his chosen profession. And he had no strong connection to his Jewish roots. The family was mostly assimilated anyway. So he was baptised. He and his family became Roman Catholic. And little Marie (who later took the name Madeleine) was brought up as a normal Catholic Czech child.

Joseph Koerbel was naïve enough to think that he could wash away the sin of being Jewish in the baptismal font. He was foolish enough to think that his family would be safe from the Nazis under the cross of the church.

Madeleine and her parents remained safe enough from the Nazis in London. But her grandparents were turned to ashes in Auschwitz. And their names appear on the walls of the Pinkas synagogue.

And even after Madeleine Albright looked at those names with her own eyes, she still couldn't explain why she hid the truth all these years.

Madeleine Albright ran away from her identity; and to this day, she refuses to accept the fact that she is Jewish. If I push myself, I can begin to understand why her parents would run away from being Jewish. During the Nazi period, being Jewish was fatal. A Jewish identity was a terrible handicap. Secular Jews who had no real connection with Jewish tradition, could easily cut all ties and begin again with a new identity. They would be like everyone else.

And yet, most of Europe's Jews refused to turn their backs on the Jewish tradition. They went to their deaths, probably trembling in fear, but secure in the knowledge that they never betrayed their heritage, as tempting as it might have been. I'm sure many Jews tried to hide the fact that they were Jews. Who wouldn't to save themselves? And after the war, they once again took their seats in the synagogue and their places in the Jewish community. But very few of them blamed their suffering on the fact that they were Jewish. After all, that would be blaming the victims for being victims, instead of blaming the Nazis.

But there were some who were afraid to face the world again as Jews; who did blame themselves for being victims. And they ran away from themselves. And Josef Koerbel was one of these Jews. And Madeleine Albright chose to stay with him and his decision.

She chose not to come back to us. We would have welcomed her with open arms. Room would have been made for her in any synagogue. She would be received with all due respect. But she chose to remain outside. She could not accept who she really was.

We are in no position to be judgmental, and I am neither condemning or condoning. I am merely expressing my sadness at a Jew who is terrified of coming home.

I stood on the mass graves in Theresienstadt this summer. And I tried to see my self as a Jew in 1942. Of course, I would try to hide the fact that I was Jewish. I would do anything to escape the clutches of the Nazis. Anything. I would steal food. I would break into buildings. I would kill a Nazi with my bare hands if necessary. I would do anything in my power to stay alive. I would make believe I was an Aryan. I would go to church. I would kiss the cross. I would drink the wine and eat the wafer. All to stay alive.

I don't look Jewish. In Europe, people automatically speak to me in German. Europeans assume that my family is Aryan. Even some of my congregants will remark, you don't look Jewish. One of my congregants enjoys telling me that I look like a Protestant minister. To me, it's not such a compliment, but for some of our people, it is considered an advantage not to look Jewish, whatever the Jewish look might be. But if I was running for my life in 1942, I would say anything and do anything to keep my family alive.

So I can well understand Josef Koerbel pretending to convert to Roman Catholic. I can see Josef Koerbel pretending to baptize his little daughter Madeleine. But what I can't understand, is what happened after the war? When the Nazis were destroyed and Hitler was a corpse in the bunker, it was safe to come back. It was safe to become a Jew in the open. But Josef Koerbel decided to remain Catholic. He never came back. And when his daughter, Madaleine, found out who she was, she never came back. And there is where I have trouble with the story.

On Yom Kippur afternoon, we read the book of Jonah. If we change the names, it could almost be the story of the Albright family. Jonah is given marching orders by the good Lord. Go to the city of Nineveh, call a meeting of the citizens and announce that the whole city will be destroyed unless they immediately repent and change their ways. It was the equivalent of asking Rabbi Abba Hillel Silver to travel to Berlin in 1938 and announce to Hitler and the assembled Nazis in the Reichstag that they have to stop immediately. That same day, he would find himself in Dachau.

Jonah doesn't have that kind of courage or conviction, so he takes off. He goes down to the port of Jaffa in disguise, boards a ship bound for the other end of the Mediterranean, as far as he could possibly get.

In the course of the voyage, a storm comes up. The sailors begin throwing the cargo overboard to lighten the load. Nothing helps. The ship is about to sink. They draw straws to see who is responsible, who God is angry at, that He brought this great storm. Sure enough, the lot falls to Jonah. They grab hold of him and are about to pitch him overboard. They ask him "Who are you? Why is God angry with you?"

He answers, *Ivri Anochi*, "I am a Hebrew." In that moment, and with those two words, Jonah achieves salvation. *Ivri Anochi*. With those two words, Jonah stops running from himself. He stops hiding from who he is. He comes forward for all to recognize. Whatever the consequences, he must face them. If he has to die, then at least he will die at peace with himself and with his God.

And the storm suddenly stops. The rest of the story is not so important. Jonah carries out his task. The main thing is that Jonah comes to a point in his life where he realizes he can't run away from being Jewish. Even if it means hardship, even if it means putting his life on the line, he has to be true to himself and to his heritage. You can't escape your destiny (even Luke Skywalker knew that).

Madeleine Albright is not the only Jewish child to spend the war years as a Christian. Felicia Bryn lives in our community. She is married to a Rabbi, and as you would guess, lives a rather traditional Jewish life. When she was four years old, the Nazis were rounding up Jews in Poland. Her father got her out of the ghetto and gave her to a Polish couple who lived on a farm. Before they parted, he said to her, "Forget that you are Jewish." Felicia Braun, the daughter of a Jewish doctor, became Felusia Garbaczyk. She learned the prayers of the rosary and she went to church every Sunday. Her real parents disappeared. She grew up as a Polish Catholic. She had no recollection of her Jewish past.

In 1959, a visitor from Israel showed up at her home in Poznan. It was her cousin; and for the first time, she found out who she was. She was Jewish.

Eventually, she put away her cross, and moved to Israel. She met and married a concentration camp survivor, Rabbi Nathan Bryn. They moved to the United States and became an important part of the Jewish community.

Why didn't she remain a Roman Catholic? Because once she knew who she really was, the pull of Jewish tradition was too strong to deny. How could she continue to live a lie?

Madeleine Albright, Secretary of State, is a great woman. But a tragic figure. What really was going through her mind as she stood in front of that memorial wall in Prague and read the names of her Jewish grandparents? Do you think that maybe, just maybe, she might change her mind? Maybe the journey of Madeleine Koerbel Albright isn't finished. Could it be that, one day, as Jonah of old, she will get up at a press conference and announce *Ivri Anochi*, I am a Jew. I will be the first to give her a kiss and welcome her home.

The basic theme of Yom Kippur is Teshuva. We usually translate it as penitence. But it really means to come home, to come back. From the Hebrew *lashuv*.

So many of us are in the process of running away. Like Jonah, we go down to the port, and we get on a boat. We get on the Carnival Cruise Line, and the Holland America Line, and the Royal Victory Line, and off we go to have a good time.

Don't get me wrong, I am all for having a good time. We deserve to enjoy ourselves. But when we get back, we still have to deal with the same problems. The faucet is still leaking; the air conditioning still doesn't work! My brother still doesn't talk to me. My mother is still angry at me. I still don't come to the synagogue during the year. I still haven't decided to close my office for Shabbat. I still haven't taken that trip to Israel. I still haven't taken a step closer to the Jewish people and to the Jewish traditions.

You can go all the way to Singapore or Bali or Timbuktu; but eventually, you have to come back. Eventually, you have to face your responsibilities, eventually you have to accept who you are.

Maybe Madeleine Albright is not coming home. But you, Moshe and Rachel, and Chaim and Sara, you can come home. You must come home, in the best tradition of this High Holy Day season.

And when you do, when you come through that door, on a Shabbat morning, I will be the first to give you a great big hug and welcome you home.

GOING HOME

Where is your home? I don't mean your address on Country Club Drive. I mean "der Alter Heim," your old home, as we say in Yiddish. And I don't mean Brooklyn or Highland Park or Squirrel Hill. I mean the place where your grandfather was born. The shtetl. The town in Poland or in Russia or in the Austro-Hungarian Empire. Did you ever have the curiosity to go back to Vilna or to Lublin or to Warsaw, and find the address of the apartment they lived in? Did you want to knock on the door, look inside, and feel the spirit of your zaide and bubbe, your aunts and your cousins?

Well, I have gone back to the Bronx from time to time; and Aileen has gone back to Brooklyn. But that's all recent history. We wanted to see where our grandparents really came from. We wanted to stand in the old market square where they did business. We wanted to see the address number on the door of the house where they lived. We wanted to find them. Some trace of their presence. Some whisper of their lives. So we did.

I must tell you that when I told my parents that we were going to find the house they were born in, they had no interest in coming with us. "Damned Poles. They can all rot in Gehenana. I wouldn't set foot in that 'cursed' country."

This I understand. Three million Polish Jews were murdered in Birkenau, in Majdanek and in Ponar. Polish Jews who survived, went through hell for three or four years. Some came home to start life again in their little towns and cities of their birth. They were murdered the day they came home by their neighbors who had already stolen their property. So I understand.

But we went anyway. And we knew we would be passing through forests fertilized by Jewish bones and we knew that the beautiful flowers of the field were watered by Jewish blood. We knew all this. But we went anyway.

In the little town of Rutki, some 20 kilometers from Lomza in North Eastern Poland, I found an old lady who remembered my family on my mother's side. She lived on the main square opposite the church, in an old apartment building. She lived upstairs and she owned the grocery store below. She remembers the Jewish family that she bought the store from. And she remembered the four other families that lived in the building and who owned the stores below. And one of those families was my family.

There it was. The connection. From my mother, I knew that the family owned a windmill that ground flour. And the flour was sold from their store. And here it was. The circle of my family history could be closed.

I walked up and down the street, trying perhaps to absorb my past. Maybe it would travel from the sidewalk up into my shoes and into my bloodstream. I walked in the footsteps of my ancestors. They had been here. Part of them remained here, and now I had come to collect it, and take it back with me. I didn't want to leave anything in Poland.

But the old lady had more to say. My family left in the 1920s. They sold the store and sold the house and set out for America. Because they had enough. Enough of the Polish cavalry rampaging through the streets. Enough of the Russian Cossacks looting and burning the stores, enough of the drunken Poles celebrating by murdering a Jew. My grandfather fought in the Russo-Japanese War. Aileen's grandfather fought in World War I. They weren't going to war again, and they weren't sending their sons to be slaughtered for Czar Nicholas, or Franz Joseph, or Pilsudski, or Anders, or anyone. They packed up and left. Thank God they left.

Thank God they had the foresight to understand that there was no future for the Jews in Eastern Europe. Maybe they felt in their bones the coming catastrophe of the Shoah. Maybe not. But the important thing was that American visa, and that boat ticket from the port of Gdansk to New York.

But not all of my family left Rutki. Some uncles and cousins remained behind. It was too difficult, too painful to leave. It was too hard to contemplate beginning all over again in a foreign country, in a foreign language, in a foreign culture. So they stayed. The windmill kept turning in the wind. They sold the same flour to the same townspeople; life went on. Until the day in the fall of 1939 when the Nazis marched in.

The old lady had a lot to tell us. It was pent up inside her for 60 years. She started to cry. The names came tumbling out. Her childhood friends: Pesha, Sarah, and Rochel. The little girls she went to school with, the little girls she played with.

The Nazis lined them all up in the town square just where we were standing and listening. They stripped them of all their belongings.

A few townspeople pointed out any Jews who were making believe they were Christians. And they marched them away into a nearby forest and murdered them. Everyone. Every man, woman, and child. And Pesha, Sarah, and Rochel.

"What could we do?" she cried. If we tried to help, they would have murdered us too. And she sobbed and sobbed as the memories flooded back.

But my grandparents came to the United States in the 1920s. They didn't come after the war as survivors of the concentration camps. We were fortunate. We were not the children or grandchildren of survivors. So we thought.

But we were wrong. Aileen and I were wrong.

In a box of old photographs we found a picture of a young girl. Maybe 16 or 17. Who was she? Where was she? And an old man with a beard. Who was he? We put them on our desks last year. And we began to search for them. That young girl with the brown hair and the searching eyes, what was her name? What happened to her? No one was sure. All we knew was she stayed in Europe. All we had was a postcard. Mostly blacked out by the German censors. An address in the ghetto of their old town. But our family in America got the message with the Nazi swastika, with Hitler's head on the stamp. It read: We eat like Passover and we live like Succos. This the Nazi censor didn't understand. But we did. Eating like Passover meant no bread; probably not much food. Living like Succos meant cramped into a hut, cold and miserable. And that was the last anyone heard from that young girl. For 60 years.

And now we found her. At least, we found a trace of her. Like the old lady said, the Nazis marched in, rounded up the Jews, and murdered them in the nearby forest. I even know the name of the forest: Radzimin. We even walked in the forest. Looking: for what, I don't know. Listening: for voices, for ghosts from the past. For the voice of a 17-year-old girl who never made it to America. Our cousin, a third or fourth cousin, our blood, our flesh. So we are also children of the Shoah.

Several days later, we stopped in Lublin. The great yeshiva of Chachmei Lublin is still there on Lubartowska street. The building now houses the Lublin medical school. Avigdor lived on Lubartowska Street at number 31. I took a picture. Shmuel lived in Lublin. A number of our people lived in Lublin. There is no synagogue today in Lublin. Not even a museum. There are no Jews on the streets of Lublin. Where did they go?

Most went to Majdanek. Majdanek is a pretty suburb of Lublin. From Majdanek, you can see the entire city. In Majdanek you will find the Jews of Lublin, some 45,000 of them, together with 300,000 more. Only they have been burned to ashes. Collected into a huge bowl 25 feet high and 150 feet across. Filled with the ashes of the Jews of Lublin.

So we stood in front of that huge pile of ashes and I began to recite the El Moleh Rachamim. As I had done just a few weeks before in Ponar forest, where the Jews of Vilna were all murdered, and in Treblinka and in Auschwitz just a few days before, where the 3 million Jews of Poland disappeared into smoke and ash. I began the all too familiar words, El Moleh Rachamim and I couldn't say another word. My throat choked. It was too much. Too much to comprehend. Too much to consider. The sheer horror of it. And worst of all, I was looking into hell itself, in that huge bowl of ashes. And I was looking at Chaim's family and Shmuel's family and Avigdor's friends. Chaim and Shmuel and Avigdor are sitting here today in the congregation. I have spent many hours listening to their stories. About aunts and cousins and sisters who were sent to Majdanek. And here they were in front of me. Reduced to white ash. I even knew their names. And I had promised to recite the memorial prayer. And I couldn't say another word; I couldn't even make another sound. I stopped breathing. My body seemed to come to a halt. I felt dead in the presence of this pervasive death all around me.

I felt a hand on my shoulder. A young man in the uniform of the Israeli army. To my complete amazement, a delegation of 30 or 40 officers of the IDF had arrived in Majdanek to place a wreath. It was an official delegation visiting the concentration camps of Poland. Their cantor stepped forward. And he completed the El Moleh Rachamim that had died in my throat.

With the Israeli flags waving in the breeze, and the familiar prayer floating over the barracks of Majdanek, we all came back to life. Even the ashes took on a new existence. Like Ezekiel watching the dry bones come back to life. The young men and women of Israel who brought our people back to life. It was the perfect moment.

Had these men and women, officers of the army of Israel, been with our people 60 years ago; had this blue and white Magen David flag waved in the wind 60 years ago. Had the power of the State of Israel been manifest 60 years ago, we would not be standing in front of the ashes of the Polish Jews barely able to speak. But it didn't happen that way. They said shalom and they marched away. And we were left to contemplate.

We are all children of the Holocaust, the Shoah. Not only the survivors of the Ponar forest and the ovens of Auschwitz. I mean all of us, you and me, whose grandparents came to the Lower East Side and to the South side and the West End in the 1920s or at the turn of the century. We who were born here, who were never called greenhorns, "greener," who never spoke English with an accent. We who consider ourselves dyed-in-the-wool Yankees. We all left part of our families in Europe.

Under the rubble of the Warsaw Ghetto. In the pits of the Ponar forest. In the ghetto of Kovno. In the ashes of Majdanek. An aunt, a third cousin, a great uncle, a sister. Some member of the family. Flesh of our flesh; blood of our blood. We who came from Chicago and Detroit and Cleveland; we also come from Poland and Russia and Slovakia. We are all connected to those little shtetlach and bustling cities where Jewish life thrived for a 1000 years and suddenly went up in flames. And we all left behind a part of our family. And we all mourn our losses. And we all are pierced to the heart by the words of the Kel Moleh Rachamim.

But what is given is given. Ma she'haya haya. What was, was. It's past and gone. Our purpose is not only to cry over the past. Our purpose is to rebuild for the future. Remember that every one of us has been terribly diminished by the Shoah. Six million missing people means that every single Jewish family lost someone. An uncle who would have become a great Rabbi. A sister who would have discovered a cure for cancer. A cousin who would have endowed a new university. We are all the children of the Shoah. And we have to replace all those people, all those wonderful minds, all those beautiful souls. We have to collect all their ideas. We have to pass on their great legacy.

The city of Kovno had a world famous school, the Slobotka Yeshiva. It is today a warehouse, with a little plaque at the entrance to remind tourists that here was once the great Slobotka Yeshiva. The city of Lublin also had a world class school, the Yeshiva of Chachmei Lublin, the school of the scholars. It is a physics laboratory for the Lublin Medical School. It also has a little plaque to remind Jewish tourists.

Every Jewish community in the world needs to transfer a little bit of the Slobotka, or the Mir, or the Volozhin. When the Nazis rolled into Kovno, they broke into the house of the Chief Rabbi. He was studying the Talmud. They murdered him on the spot. His blood spread over the page.

Where the Rabbi stopped his study, we have to continue. On the same page, the very next word. That must be our answer to the Shoah. That is our answer to the loss of the Jews of Europe.

Let the Polish government rebuild Majdanek as a remembrance and a memorial. We don't need it; the Polish anti-Semites need it. Let the German government build a Holocaust memorial in Berlin. We don't need it; the anti-Semite Germans need it. What we need is to build Jews. Intelligent Jews. Committed Jews. Sensitive Jews. "Shayne, Yidden." We will find them. We will inspire them. On the 17th floor of Del Vista. On the ninth hole of the Turnberry golf course; in the swimming pool of the Marina Towers. We will enlist them in our holy work. One new Yiddishe Neshama for every Neshama that was snuffed out in Majdanek. One new member of our synagogue family for every cousin that we lost in Aushwitz.

Proud Jews. Strong Jews. Jews who will remember that the future belongs only to the courageous and the brave.

That the miracle of our existence is a partnership between God's inspiration and our determination.

And then the question of the prophet Ezekiel will be answered: "Will these ashes ever come to life?"

And the answer is yes. I will breathe a new spirit into these bodies and they will come alive. My friends, we will breathe new spirit into our people. We will fill minds and hearts with the power and beauty of our heritage and a new generation will come alive to ensure the future of our people.

MASKS

Last year, as I listened to Kol Nidre, I heard Yom Kippur referred to as "Yom Kippurim."

I was struck by the fact that Yom Kippurim sounded like another holy day, like Purim. And Yom Kippurim would mean a day like Purim. Imagine the holiest day of the year described as a day like Purim. Where is the connection? Certainly not in eating and drinking and merry making.

Perhaps the connection is in the drawing of lots. On Purim, Haman drew lots, Purim, to see which day the Jews would be exterminated. The 14th of Adar. On Yom Kippur, the High Priest, the Kohen Gadol took two goats, and by lot pur, he chose one to be sent out into the wilderness as an atonement (symbolically) for all the sins of the people. A kapara.

And on Yom Kippur in a sense we all draw lots. We hope to pick a lucky number. A number that will give us one more year of life. "A Chai." We hope and pray that our number isn't up.

Or perhaps the connection between Yom Kippur and Purim lies in the masquerade. On Purim we wear masks and dress up as Mordecai or Esther or Roy Rogers or whatever. We hide our real selves behind a mask. On Yom Kippur we come to shul, also behind a mask. But we are expected to take off the mask and reveal our true selves to the Lord our maker. We admit to our true nature. We admit to our sins. We stand unprotected. And we ask for mercy.

A mask is a defense mechanism. In our daily lives we protect ourselves by putting up a false front. We are suspicious of people. We don't want them to see us. Our real selves. We keep up our guard. We hide behind a mask. We don't want to appear vulnerable. But on Yom Kippur we know that God can see right through us, x-ray vision. As we say at Kol Nidre:

"Nothing can remain hidden from God."

Now if the average person goes around with a mask all year, if the average person hides his real self, then we can never know who we are dealing with. And if we are not sure of who we are dealing with, then it is a good policy to give all people the benefit of the doubt. To judge them positively. Because you never really know who you're dealing with behind the mask. First impressions are often the wrong impressions.

A gruff looking, tough acting guy could be a real pussycat. A giant of an athlete with huge muscles who routinely knocks people around the court could be the most charitable and kind person off the court. The fellow driving a new Bentley in the 3 thousand dollar suit, with the 2 million dollar apartment in Porto Vita who seems to be totally and exclusively into himself, suddenly turns out to be a major benefactor of the shul. So don't be so quick to judge. Try to look past the mask.

Have you ever heard of Miracle Max? Miracle Max was Robert Maxwell who died in London in 1991. After WWII he established Pergamon Publishing. It became one of the world's largest media empires. He took over the British printing Corporation, then the Mirror group of newspapers, and even the New York Daily News. He named his empire, appropriately, Maxwell Communications.

He was a very wealthy man, as you can imagine. His 2 sons worked with him, Ian and Kevin. They were also wealthy men. But something was not quite kosher with their business.

Although the Maxwell's were fabulously wealthy, their business was largely unprofitable. And every time a reporter would begin sniffing about, they would be threatened by a libel suit. This threat and the way British law is written was enough to hide Maxwell's real business.

And his real business was a huge scandal. Robert Maxwell and his sons were busy looting the company's huge pension fund. At the end it was discovered that Maxwell took over one billion dollars from the pension funds to boost the company's stock worth. And between Maxwell's Mirror Group of Newspapers and the New York Daily News, 91 million dollars was embezzled. Maxwell was an M.P. and elected member of Parliament who was a highly respected member of the London community. He was a tremendously wealthy man. Then the scandal hit, his empire collapsed, and Robert Maxwell killed himself. He disgraced himself, his family, and the Jewish Community. End of story.

At around the same time, a funeral took place in Israel; a state funeral with full honors. Buried by an Israeli guard was a survivor of the Holocaust. A hero of the Jewish people and the state of Israel. His name was Lev Hoch, a Czech Jew. He came from a town not far from Sighet, Romania, where his cousin Elie Wiesel was from. In 1938, as we all remember, Neville Chamberlain handed over to Hitler Czechoslovakia as a bribe for "peace in our time." Young Lev Hoch joined the French underground and operated out of Budapest. He was arrested by the Hungarian Fascists. He beat his guard to death and escaped to Istanbul and then to Syria. There he joined the French Foreign legion and was shipped back to France. The Nazis were rolling across France and Churchill offered to evacuate to Britain all Czech units that wanted to fight. The Nazis got to most of them first. They were shot on sight and the Jews were handed over to the Gestapo for special treatment. Lev Hoch was one of 4,000 Czechs who made it back to England.

The British put Lev Hoch into a prison camp. There he became friends with a Czech Communist and former member of the Parliament. They never forgot each other.

Eventually, Lev Hoch was released and assigned to the British Army to participate in the D-Day invasion of Europe. He did very well. The British made him an officer, and an army spy. He had a highly successful career during the war, interrogating highly placed Nazis such as Rudolf Hess and Martin Borman. After the war, the British were eager to have him continue in the MI6, the British Secret Service. His job was to identify German scientists for recruitment. He did this by setting up a series of scientific publishing companies. The British loved him. He was their kind of man: ruthless, clever, a war hero, stereotypically British, always eager to please his superiors.

But what they didn't know was that Lev Hoch was secretly an ardent Zionist, since the age of 12. Lev's old friend from the British prison camp became Foreign Minister of Czechoslovakia in 1948. Lev Hoch, the British spy, had learned that the British were going to back the old Nazis in the Czech Civil War, against the social democrats. The British suspected the social democrats of being communist, and pro Stalin. He told his old friend and they broke the scandal publicly. The result was that the Czech Socialists came into power, and the old Nazis were out. Stalin was furious at an independent Socialist Czechoslovakia, more Western oriented than even Tito's Yugoslavia. It took him 3 years to take it over.

But in the meantime, Lev Hoch had engineered the greatest deal in modern Jewish history. In return for his secret information, he asked his old friends in Czechoslovakia a favor to quietly begin exporting arms to the new State of Israel.

The British were busy arming the Arabs to the teeth, At the same time it was illegal for the Jews of Palestine to own weapons. Ben Gurion traveled around the world, desperately trying to purchase weapons. Truman and the US were enforcing an arms embargo against Palestine, but France, Britain and the US were arming the Arabs. Jewish blood was cheaper than Arab oil.

But Lev Hoch funneled privately raised dollars to his friends in Czechoslovakia and they began arming Israel. For the first time in 2000 years, the Jews would have a fair fight. American cargo planes were smuggled out of the US and flown to Czechoslovakia. There they were loaded with artillery, tanks, ammunition, and rifles; and the cream of the old Nazi airforce BF109 Messerschmitts built by the Czech arms industry. The planes were taken apart and packed into US cargo planes.

I don't have to tell you what the effect was on the new Israeli army.

On the afternoon of March 29, 1948 the first 4 Messerschmitts were unpacked and assembled. There were the very first of the Israeli airforce. They took off and bombed a huge Egyptian column of tanks and infantry moving up the coastal road to Tel Aviv, just 25 miles away. Only one Israeli plane returned, but they halted the Egyptian convoy. Tel Aviv was saved to the amazement of Ben Gurion and his staff.

American airmen flew the cargo planes from Oklahoma to Czechoslovakia, (code named jockstrap). Then to Israel code named Oklahoma. A C-46's normal range was 1500 miles. If you were forced down in Greece, they would impound the plane. If you were forced down in an Arab country, they would torture and hang you.

But the real hero of the story was Lev Hoch. It was Lev Hoch who in 1991 was wrapped in a Tallis and buried on the Mount of Olives, the holiest place in the Jewish world. A hero of Israel. And most people didn't know that Lev Hoch had another name. It was Robert Maxwell. Robert Maxwell had single handedly saved the State of Israel at the moment of its birth.

So if you were quick to judge Robert Maxwell, you would have concluded that he was a major criminal, a thief, an embezzler, a disgrace to the Jewish Community. But if you took the time to look beyond the mask, you would have found a totally different man, a Jewish hero.

Maxwell himself wrote: "I have constructed during my years of exile a glittering surface as a kind of protection." There you have it. He lived behind an elaborate mask. He protected himself, his true self behind a mask.

How many Robert Maxwell's are sitting in the shul this morning right next to us? People who we have written off as ostentatious, uncaring, uninvolved, shady, questionable, selfish, ruthless. Have you ever attempted to penetrate behind the mask? Or do you judge superficially?

The President of Yeshiva University, my alma mater, had a visitor last year. An old lady in a shabby old coat. She wanted to see the President. He had his secretary shuffle her around. He had more important things to do than talk with shabby old ladies, off the street with no appointment. But she insisted and persisted. Eventually, Dr. Lamm met with her. End of story, she made a 10 million dollar contribution to the university. It's a good idea to take the time to look behind the mask, to find the real person.

Maybe you are that person. Maybe the next major benefactor of the Jewish Community is sitting next to you. Maybe the doctor who is going to find the cure for cancer is sitting at the end of the row. Maybe the teacher who will motivate the next Albert Einstein is sitting in the last row of the synagogue, all the way back there, quietly praying, hardly in sight of the Bima. Maybe the next political scientist who will forge a final peace between Israel and her neighbors is here. Maybe Eliyahu Hanavi is in the corner over there wrapped in an old tallis dressed in a shabby suit. And no one gives him a second look. No one will look beyond the mask.

Well, take a good look my friends. Take a close look at your friends. Show some appreciation. Some interest. Because you might be looking at the man or woman who will save the world.

THE OLD MAN AND THE MOON

Old friends came down to Florida for the winter and we went over to visit. I looked at them and was amazed at how good they looked. They are about 10 years older than us, but suddenly they seemed 10 years younger. I thought they joined a gym, lost weight, took vitamins. But it wasn't until the next day that it dawned on me. Face-lift. She went; then he went. She looked so good, he also wanted to look good. She looked 10 years younger; he had to drop a few years also.

Aileen and I had such a good chuckle, and then we looked at each other. It took a few moments before we agreed that we looked fine, for the moment.

Publicity Photo—cantor: "The lights are wrong. We have too many wrinkles. Are you sure it's the lighting?"

In our society everyone wants to look younger. People can't seem to deal with growing older. Actually, we don't mind growing older as long as we don't have to look older. Or even more important if we don't have to feel older. The most frightening part of growing older is the threat of sickness. It's a wonderful thing to be able to celebrate our 80th and 90th birthday, but only if we are well.

I had an uncle who always used to say "if you have your health you have everything." You had the same uncle. It is only now, decades later, that I understand and appreciate what that means.

One of the most moving and poignant moments in the Rosh Hashana and Yom Kippur service comes when we recite Shema Koleynu. Everyone stands up as the ark is opened. And then that terrifying line of the prayer:

"Lord do not cast us aside in our old age. When we lose our vigor and our strength do not abandon us."

We don't pray to stop the aging process; because it isn't possible. We never pray for the impossible, the unnatural. We can't pray for permanent youth. Although the Fountain of Youth is supposed to be located in Florida, and we think in Aventura, even the great explorer Ponce de Leon couldn't find it.

So we pray for what is possible. That as we grow older, we should be spared debilitating sickness. That when we need help, someone should be there for us. When we have to face a crisis, we should have someone to lean on, to help us, to guide us, to encourage us, to strengthen us. This is what we pray for to God. For the strength and the courage to face difficulty and the wisdom to make the right decision. And the power that will heal us, and make us healthy once again.

Just as I was writing these words, I got a call from one of our people. He is going to celebrate his 90th Birthday and 65th Wedding Anniversary. I asked him how did you do it? Help and love from my wife. "I love people and people like me." And I keep active helping others in our synagogue.

Essentially he had it right. The same ideas were expressed by a professor of gerontology in a recent study. That's a fancy word for people who study the aging process. He suggested that if you want to live longer, you need love and intimacy in your life. A devoted wife or husband, good friends, a caring family. Then he added a very interesting statistic: members of synagogues and churches recover faster from operations and survive longer.

Now how's that for a bonus in your membership. What is that worth to you? How's that for a CHAI membership, a membership that actually gives you life, that adds years to your life. Can you put a price on that?

And the professor had more: The more love and support we have from our wives and husbands, the less blockage is formed in our arteries. And you thought it only had to do with less fat in your diet and more exercise. I would put it this way: when you give your heart, you receive a stronger heart.

What I am trying to tell you is that you can take charge of your own life. You can make yourself healthier. You can put yourself in a better frame of mind. You can slow down the aging process. You can't stop aging, you can't be 25 again. But you can improve the quality of your life dramatically. So many people do it. So many so called senior citizens are out playing tennis, and running marathons and climbing mountains, and going to graduate school and learning to play the violin, and looking good and feeling great.

And one senior citizen this year blasted off into space. The most amazing senior citizen of the year has to be John Hershel Glenn.

At age 77, John Glenn was strapped into a space shuttle and was rocketed up into space on a pillar of flame, going 18,000 miles per hour. At age 77.

But John Glenn's chronological number of 77 doesn't tell us anything about his real age. Where does a man in his seventh decade of life have the chutzpah to think he can blast into space at 18,000 miles an hour sitting on the top of millions of tons of liquid explosives? I think that driving at 70 MPH on I95 with a tank full of gas up to Boca and back in between huge double trailer trucks, is an adventure in survival. And John Glenn is rocketing into space; for the second time in his life.

As I followed the smoke trails of the shuttle as it disappeared into the stratosphere, I suddenly realized that John Glenn had discovered what we have been looking for all our lives: the fountain of youth, in Florida. Somehow he beat the odds. Somehow he remained healthy and vigorous and able to keep up with people half his age.

So I began to pay close attention to him. What exercise did he do. What vitamins and organic supplements did he take. Did he experiment with growth hormones? Was he able to eliminate the stresses in his life? (Actually, what could be more stressful than blasting off into space on a fireball of a rocket? I would be so frightened I would probably stop breathing.)

First, I noticed he didn't take himself too seriously. Someone asked him how he felt before taking off. His worst fear was that he would catch a cold and they would go without him. Then he added, "how would you feel if you were sitting on top of a million tons of explosives that was made for government contract by the lowest bidder?"

Addressing the fact that he is a little older than the average astronaut he said that space is the ideal place to go for retirement, there is no gravity so you can drop your food and it won't land in your lap.

The rumor was that they wouldn't let him go out on a space walk, because he might wander off and get lost.

[He joked he was the first person to leave Florida, not in a Winnebago. And finally he said the only life support system he wants to be hooked up to is in the space capsule.]

But a good sense of humor is only part of the picture. Yes he kept himself in fine physical shape. And it takes great discipline and hard work to do it. And surely he had the good fortune of having the right parents and grandparents. We call it good genes. And yes he was determined and ambitious. His old high school teacher said he wasn't the most outstanding science student, but he was he most determined.

So how do we do it? John Glenn doesn't need to look young, he is young. John Glenn doesn't need a face lift. He had a space lift. For the rest of us mortals who don't have the option of traveling into space to find the fountain of youth, where do we look?

We can look in the same direction that John Glenn looked, to the heavens. During a news conference in space, he was asked about his religious faith. How it affected his life. He said, "I pray everyday. And my belief was strengthened by seeing the earth from up here." "I felt closer to God. I felt I was literally in His hands." How wonderful to feel protected in God's hands.

John Glenn took courage from the great power that created the vast universe and had the time and the interest to watch over him, guide him, protect him. And so it can be with all of us who travel on our way through dark passageways and terrifying landscapes; who need God's help to make it through to the other side. We can also reach out and touch God's fingers.

So faith in God helps; and faith in ourselves and the love of family and a good sense of humor and taking good care of ourselves: all these factors may serve to keep us young, in spirit and even in body. But there is yet another factor, perhaps the main factor in finding the fountain of youth. It is the search itself, the journey. You don't have to find the fountain of youth; you just have to keep searching for it no matter how old you are.

When Abraham set out on his journey to the promised land, how old was he? When God told him to pack up his tent; load it all into the u-haul and take off down the road, how old was he? He was 75. He had a family, he had grandchildren; he had an established business; he had plans to sell and retire. He was about to close on a condominium in downtown Babylon. And God says lech lecha, go.

Abraham lived to be 175. He had great grandchildren, he built a new house, he made new friends, he got involved in a new synagogue. He made a whole new career for himself in the hospitality business. Hachnasat Orchim.

I believe that he stayed young, because of the challenge of something new. The excitement of the journey got his blood moving again. I believe that he lived a long and healthy life because he continued to search when everyone else was happy to stop.

John Glenn was 77 when he also heard the call "Lech Lecha," go.

John Glenn has a son.

His son was against it. He thought the old man was "meshugga." His fellow astronauts from 1962 called it crazy. But as John Glenn put it, he was going to reignite the meaning of achievement. I like that. Reignite. Light the old fire once again. Enjoy the excitement of the journey. Not for him the rocking chair on the front porch. Not for him living off of old memories. He set out on a new journey; to make new memories.

And this is what I want to suggest to you. All of you. All of us who are looking to be younger.

Don't be afraid to travel a new path. Begin a new jour-

ney. Make your plans. Pack your bags. Put one foot out the
door. And the good Lord will help you on your way. He
guides your path. He will keep you safe. He will keep you
healthy. But you have to make the move. You yourself. You
have to strike out in a new direction. You have to go in
search of your fountain of youth.

So you always wanted to play the violin. So find a
teacher, buy an instrument and begin moving the bow
across the strings. What are you waiting for? Until you can't
move your fingers because of the arthritis? So you won't
sound like Isaac Stern. But you sure will enjoy yourself. You
will play the same notes that Johann Sebastian Bach
played; the same concerto that Vivaldi played. You will connect yourself with the immortality of music. You will lift
your spirits toward the heavens. You will never be old. Not
as long as you can be part of the eternal beauty of music.

So I exaggerate a bit. But do something. Do something
different. Do something new. It will make you feel young
again.

So you never finished cheder, because the Nazis rolled
into your town when you weren't yet Bar Mitzva. And you
spent the war years behind barbed wire, barely staying
alive. Come to us; we will teach you. Come and sit with us
at the minyan one morning. Sit quietly and meditate on the
ancient words of King David. Connect yourself to the magnificent history of the Jewish people. Consider that we are
the eternal people, and all who share our history are themselves eternal. How is that for an idea that will keep you
young? Never mind young. We are offering eternity. And it
doesn't come in a bottle. And you can't buy it in Nieman
Marcus. But you can have it in this holy place. Everyday at
8:30 in the morning and 5:30 in the evening. You can say the
same words spoken by King Solomon. You can study the
same ideas taught by Rabbi Akiva. You can sit next to God,
just the way the Kabbalists did. Lech Lecha. Just Go; and do
it.

I met a fellow a few weeks ago whose wife died last year.
To say he has been depressed is an understatement.

Nothing his friends could say to him seemed to make a difference. This man looked ten years older than his real age. He was aging right before my eyes. He had one foot on the other side. I met him a few weeks ago and he was transformed. He had a bright smile, he had a spring in his step. His wrinkles were gone. And he didn't even have to tell me: I could guess. A certain lady had come into his life.

He has two sons and a daughter. They voted two to one against it. So what. It's not their life. It's his life. I said to him, "people rarely get a second chance in life. Don't think twice. Go. Lech Lecha. Begin your new exciting journey. Recapture some of your youth. Don't grow old before your time. Go and Mazal Tov."

A new road, a new journey, a new man.

The Vishnitzer Rebbe went to the doctor complaining: "It hurts me here, it hurts me there." The Doctor said: " I can't make you younger." The Rabbi answered: "Golem; I don't want you to make me younger; I just want you to let me get older."

Abraham lived to be older, to 175 because he wasn't afraid to set out on a new journey. So you decide. 30 different vitamins and supplements a day. Good. The cosmetic surgeon, maybe. Growth hormone injections. Experimental.

Just believe that your journey ends only when you say it does. Just believe that God will give you the strength. As he did for John Glenn. As he did for Abraham. But you have to light your own rocket. You have to decide where you're going and by the grace of God you will get there. Youth is in the search. Vigor is in the journey. Lech Lecha my friends. GO. And may the good Lord be with you.

A LITTLE THING

The prayer in our Machzor describes a typical average person:

"Man comes from dust and will return to dust." That's our beginning and that's our end. But during our lifetime, we are compared to a vessel that is cracked. Not smashed into pieces, but pretty much one piece, with a crack here and there. A good description. None of us is perfect. Whole. All of us have a little crack here, a little dent there. We all need a little repair. Not such a big deal, a little epoxy here, a little glue there; and we will be OK again.

That is my definition of what Rosh Hashana is all about. We call it an internal inspection if you will. An inspection of our holy soul. To see if we are whole, if we are in good spiritual shape. To see if there are any cracks or holes that need repair. Because if you don't repair a crack, then it gets bigger and bigger until the whole vessel cracks apart, falls onto the floor and shatters into a hundred pieces and then it's almost impossible to repair.

The Israel museum in Jerusalem houses some of the Dead Sea Scrolls, at least the most famous ones. They include the Isaiah scroll, and the so called Thanksgiving hymns. They face each other on opposite walls of the room. In my conversations with the scholars and archeologists over the years, I learned that both scrolls were written about the same time, at the end of the second temple period.

But the condition of the two scrolls is totally different. The Isaiah scroll looks as if it was written yesterday. The script is precise and clear. The parchment is smooth and almost undamaged. It was written almost 2000 years ago, and yet it has been perfectly preserved. On the opposite wall the scroll is badly disintegrated. The letters are worn away, whole sections are missing, and if you touched the scroll it would probably turn to dust.

Both scrolls were found in the same caves at the Dead Sea above Kumran, both written at the same time, yet they are so different in condition.

Why? The curator of the scrolls explained: Both were found in the same cave in identical clay jars. The jars both had sealed lids. So at first the archaeologists could see no difference. Then one day, as they examined the jars with high intensity lights in the lab, they found the answer: one jar had a tiny hole in its side. It wasn't noticed by the scientists until they shined a light into the jar; and then a pin point of light shone out from the tiny hole.

That was the reason for the tremendous difference in the scrolls. That tiny hole let air into the jar. And over the centuries it disintegrated the parchment. No big thing, no huge crack, no missing lid, just a tiny hole, and the scroll was destroyed.

All of us have little flaws in our personality. Not one of us is perfect. But we have to notice our flaws, the little cracks in our personalities. And we have to make the necessary repairs. Before they get worse. Before they destroy us.

That's what we are doing here on Rosh Hashana. Searching for our flaws. Looking for the cracks in our personalities. It is called CHESHBON HANEFESH. Taking stock. Examining our faults. Shining a light on our Neshama. Making corrections. Making repairs. Before it is too late.

That ancient scribe in the Judean desert 2000 years ago: had he noticed the little hole in that clay jar, he would simply have taken a bit of clay and sealed it up. So easy, so simple, but so important. One little repair could have saved that scroll. One little drop of clay could have preserved the scroll forever. Be he didn't bother to inspect. And the scroll disintegrated.

A small thing can make a difference. Like that missing small piece of clay. I always stand up when an older person comes into my office. I always hold the door open for them. I don't have to. I am the Rabbi. But I do it to make them feel good. To show that I value them, their knowledge, their experience. That I follow the law of the Torah. "Bifnei Sayva Takum." Rise before one older than you.

I make it a point to say hello to everyone I meet during the day. A small thing. But it means a great deal, and it encourages people to feel closer to us. It is part of the Jewish value of mentchlachkeit: being a proper human being.

Just after Pesach, the work for the Wilner Pavilion began. Our most recent addition, in the courtyard area, will add a beautiful reception room to our synagogue, a place to celebrate simchas. Zoll Zayn Simachas Bayidden. Which means may God grant us many celebrations in our lives.

A crew of workers showed up one day with jackhammers and shovels, and the noise began. It was constant and deafening. Four huge holes had to be dug out for the concrete piers. For hours on end that noise continued until we ran out of aspirin in the office.

Each day I would pass the construction site many times. Five men were hard at work. They dripped with sweat. They struggled with those jackhammers in the hot sun. They went home. The jackhammers fell silent and the next morning started again.

I watched each day as people passed. No one spoke to them. No one waved. No one even acknowledged that there were strangers in our midst. It was as if we were looking at 5 black machines.

So one morning, I walked out into the construction site and said hello. I asked them their names, where they were from, what their plans were and how much money they were making.

They were from Jamaica: Courtney, Richard, Davis, Oneil and Bryce. Trying to make some money; and then to return home. The cost of living in Jamaica is high. Here they can earn enough money to start a business back home. Even at six dollars an hour.

So from that day on, every time I came by I waved, and they smiled from ear to ear. It was as if I had announced to them a hefty pay increase.

Now what was the big deal? It was such a little thing on my part. A few words exchanged; a wave; a smile. But it signaled that I saw them as human beings, fellow human beings, not just inanimate machines, not just automatons to be ignored. And by the way, I know what it means to work like that. When I came to Israel for the first time, I was a student. I volunteered to work on a kibbutz before the start of university. I thought it would be a good experience. I wanted to be chalutz, work the land, sweat and labor for my people. And I certainly did. I got more than I bargained for.

So I appreciated what these five Jamaicans were doing. I showed my appreciation by sharing a few words, by a gesture of humanness. Just a little thing. Sometimes the things that mean most are the little things.

The preliminary work came to an end. It was time to pour concrete. There was a knock on my door. In came the work crew. They stopped to say goodbye. I wished them well. We shook hands. And we smiled at one another again. And in that touch of hands, and in that smile we acknowledged that we were fellow human beings, fellow travelers on the same road.

A little thing but it made all the difference in the world. It repaired the connection between us. It underscored our common humanity. Without that handshake, without that smile they would have come and gone with no human connection between us. I wonder what they would have thought of us, of the synagogue, of the people. Certainly "Mentschlachkeit" is a little thing, but it is the glue of humanity. It holds us together.

During the summer, as many of us go on vacation, our daily minyan is diminished. One day we were waiting for a 10th person at 5:30pm. I went outside to search the parking lot. I was even tempted to bring in the policeman on duty. Odds are a policeman in Aventura is Jewish. And suddenly a class of Tauber School students came by on the way to practice for graduation from kindergarten. Again, I was tempted to bring them in and add their ages together to make 13 years old. Finally, one person arrived, late and out of breath. And now we could pray. Now we could say Kaddish. Just one little person makes us a community. A complete community. A whole prayer group, instead of just separate parts, each forced to pray alone. A little thing.

I am often called upon to give a eulogy. And sometimes it is very difficult to find something nice to say about a person.

Recently, I was officiating at the funeral of a retired sergeant major of the US army. Those of you who were in the service know that the sergeant major and the master sergeants are the ones who run the army. This fellow was the commanding sergeant major of the Port of Antwerp during WWII. That means that every piece of materiel for the war in Europe came through his office. He was in charge of the war. And when the Germans counter attacked through the Ardennes in the famous Battle of the Bulge they were intent on seizing the Port of Antwerp. They could have stopped the allies cold. That's how important the Port of Antwerp was to the war effort. Every gun, every bullet, every tank came through Antwerp. And one Jewish sergeant major who was now lying in a casket in front of me draped with the American flag, was in charge.

I was very impressed. But his two children weren't very impressed. It became clear very quickly that they didn't like the man. He had treated them badly like lowly recruits; pushing them around, giving orders, making himself obnoxious to his own children. The "Great Santini" come to life. Dragging them around from one military base to another, destroying their childhood, a cold unfeeling man.

So I got up in front of the assembled family who had nothing good to say about the old man and I said:

I am sure it never occurred to you that across America there have been tens of thousands of young men who blessed your father every day of their lives; and they looked up at me in amazement. And I continued: during the winter of 1944, every soldier who got a new pair of wool socks blessed your father. He saved them from frost bitten toes. Every soldier who got a new warm jacket blessed your father. He saved them from freezing to death. Every soldier who got a warm meal. Every soldier who got a new supply of ammunition who could defend himself for another day blessed your father. And I added, "your father was responsible for every loaf of bread and every bullet. And thousands of soldiers survived because of him. And they blessed him for the last 50 years. And so should you. And they were proud of him and so should you be proud of him."

And I watched their faces. Just one little idea. And I could see I had transformed their thinking. A father could rest in peace because of my one little thought. Children could rest at ease with their father's memory because of a few little words. Sometimes, all it takes is a little thing to change the world.

The things that bring us down. The things that make our lives miserable are the little things. At least they all begin as little things. And the things that can make us whole and healthy again are also little things. A little patch here, a little repair there, before things get out of hand. Before we crack apart altogether.

Today is the day for repairs. This shul is Home Depot for the soul. Get out your hammer and nails, get out your caulking gun and epoxy mix. Take your flashlight and shine it into your souls. Find the cracks and close them up. Find the tiny puncture holes and repair them, before it is too late.

On this Rosh Hashana let us stand before God as complete human beings; whole in body and whole in spirit. In Hebrew the word is Shalem, repaired, complete. It is the same word for peace, Shalom. Repair your soul, and repair your spirit, and God will grant you peace.

RED BENDEL

A young woman came to see me about her son's Bar Mitzvah. I noticed she was wearing a red string around her wrist.

So I said, "how nice that you are planning to have another child." She looked at me with a strange look. "Where did you get the idea that I am interested in having another child. I already have 3 and they are quite enough.

Her mother-in-law was sitting next to her and she pointed to the red string. "The Rabbi is looking at the red bendel."

I proceeded to explain. There is an ancient custom of our people. Women who experience difficulty in giving birth visit the Tomb of Rachel in Bet Lechem. (Nowadays you take your life in your hands). The elderly women who sit and pray there daily, show you which prayers and psalms to say. Then they stretch a red thread all the way around Rachel's tomb. They cut the thread into the pieces, and they tie a piece around the wrist of a young woman who wishes to give birth. And the woman wears the red string until the blessed event takes place.

I have seen women wearing a red string around their wrist; and they were a bit past child bearing age: 70, 75. And I ask them about the red bendel. "Do you know what that means." One woman quickly took off the string when I explained that she was about to have a baby, at 70, with 3 great grandchildren.

The young mother proceeded to tell me that she got the red string at her Kabbala class. The leader gave it to her, for enhanced spiritual energy; to put her on the right path. I'm thinking Madonna goes to a Kabbala class, Madonna wears a red string. Just the perfect example for spiritual strength and enlightenment. Exactly the role model for our young women.

The young doctor who comes to our daily minyan walks in one morning with a red string on his wrist. Why? He blames his wife. Like Adam. She got involved in the Kabbala class. They told her it was for more power. And he has a big bandage on his finger. "I cut myself," he says. Even with a red string. A doctor operates with his hands. The next day, there was no red string..

And yet, we all know about the red bendel from our grandmothers. They had some interesting beliefs. Call them superstitions if you will. But are you willing to take a risk? Are you willing to have a stranger in the mall come up to your little granddaughter and say "what a beautiful child and you won't say under your breath, KE NAYN NE HORA and maybe even "TOI TOI." Are you willing to risk an evil eye? Of course not. And a real Yiddishe grandmother would make sure to put a red bendel on the little girls stroller, or maybe pinned inside her dress.

When my sister was married, my mother made sure to pin a red bendel inside her wedding dress. This strategically placed red bendel would ward off the evil eye and keep her safe. Nobody ever pinned a red bendle on me. Maybe it's not supposed to be used for men. Because originally it is connected to fertility, to pregnancy. So men shouldn't be concerned about wearing such things.

And yet, the prayer for these holydays refers to red in a negative way.

"If your sins be as scarlet they will become white as snow." If your sins be red as crimson, they will become white as wool. Red is sin, white is purity. Red is evil, white is good. Hence the custom of not wearing red to shul on Yom Kippur. The appropriate color to wear is white. Some wear a white Kittel—a robe. All a reflection of our hope for forgiveness and state of purity.

When Nathaniel Hawthorne affixed the mark of sin on Hester Prynne, it was the scarlet letter. The ultimate mark of sin.

And we go around with a red mark on our wrists.

It has been suggested that the color red has magical power because it is associated with the blood of sacrifice. As a sacrifice, it appeases the powers of evil.

This red symbol was used by many religions and many cultures throughout history. And it was tied around the neck or around the wrist of people from London to Segovia. It has no specific Jewish meaning, except the meaning we choose to give it.

So you want to tie something around your wrist that will make you feel good? Take your husband to Tiffany's and have him tie something around your wrist. Something in silver, or something in gold. Preferably with a few stones. Red stones or blue stones or even those white stones called diamonds. I assure you that you will feel better.

What is the Jewish connection with diamonds? Well I know many Jewish women named Kimberly. Obviously after the most famous diamond mine in the world, in South Africa.

But I jest. If you are looking for an authentic Jewish symbol to tie around your wrist, may I suggest tephillin? You wind them around your arm seven times, above your wrist, and you wind them below your wrist, on your hand and on your fingers. It spells out the name Shaddai in Hebrew letters. Shaddai is God's name. Shomer Daltot Yisrael. God who guards us and our homes. You will actually wear God's name on your hand. How is that for a good luck symbol? You wear it and God protects you. All day. From bad luck. In your business; when you cross the street; when you drive on the highway; when you rise up and when you lie down as the Shema prayer says.

The seven windings are the Jewish lucky number. Seven symbolizes the creation of the world. And seven symbolizes the creator, God who watches over us and protects us. Tie the tephillin on your hand and tie yourself to God. What a powerful symbol. Connect yourself to God. Connect yourself to God's spirit.

Forget about red strings. Wear something authentically Jewish, something real, something powerful.

Incidentally those same letters of God's name Shaddai, appear on the mezuza, on your door posts, for the same reason. A prayer for God's protection; of our homes, and of our families.

If you don't have one up, or if your not sure if the mezuza is properly placed or if the parchment is authentic, then better see me right after Yontif.

And what of women? Aren't tephillin only for men? And only in basic black, not even in designer colors? Well the Talmud describes women who put on tephillin. Rather unusual. But it is possible.

But you want something more feminine, something authentically more Jewish specifically for Jewish women.

Let's go back to that red string. And another woman attached to a red string. The story comes from the Book of Joshua. The name of the woman was Rachav; and according to the Bible, she hid the spies that came to Jericho from the Israelite camp. Joshua sent spies to see how strong the people of Jericho were. The Israelite invasion was underway, and Joshua wanted to minimize casualties. The spies were sent to probe the city's weaknesses. They were discovered in the city; but they manage to hide in Rachav's house. She doesn't give them away. Before they leave, she has a last conversation with them. She understands that the destruction of the city is coming. But she asks that the Israelites spare her and her family.

The spies agree. But they remind her that in the confusion of the battle, it will be hard to find her. They suggest she hang a red cord "CHUT HASHANI" in the window of her house. A sign, a mark, a reminder.

There is that red cord again, associated with a woman again.

The Israelites come back with the entire army. They march around Jericho seven times. The ark and the priests lead the procession. They blow the trumpets. "And the walls came tumbling down." In the mass confusion of the attack, Rachav's red string is noticed in her window. She and her family are saved; as she had asked. She refused to go without her family. They were her most prized possession. Everything was left behind and destroyed in Jericho. But Rachav and her family survived.

She was a single woman. Her family consisted of parents, brothers and sisters.

But she didn't remain single for long. It is written (Midrash) that Joshua himself married her. What impressed him so much? That the leader of the people, inheritor of Moses' mantle, took as a wife, a woman from Jericho.

He was impressed by her devotion to family. Family above all else. Family at all costs. Symbolized by the red thread. The thread that tied Rachav to her family. The cord that bound her to flesh and blood. The red cord that symbolized the sacrifices you have to make to keep family together, the blood that you literally have to give to insure the survival of your family.

The umbilical cord, that is cut, but never fully untied.

In a Jewish life there are always strings attached. The strings that bind us to our God, to our history, to our tradition. The strings that attach us to our children and to our parents, the unbroken chain of tradition. If God forbid the strings are ever cut, we dangle in the air drifting aimlessly, eventually disappearing. Like Chagall's painted figures, teetering on the roof, flying through the air, headed to oblivion.

So my friends, in the New Year, 5762, tie yourself to the Jewish community. Come to the synagogue, double and triple the knot. Tie yourself to your family. It is the most important thing you have. If you have your family, you have everything. If you have your parents, you have direction. If you have your children, you have the future.

Consider this statistic, if I may call it that, from the terrorist attack on September 11th: 1,500 children were made orphans in the space of a few horrible minutes. Thousands of fathers and mothers were killed. Thousands of young people, would-be fathers and mothers were killed. Thousands of children who might have been, will never be.

So consider what is important in your life. Your children, your grandchildren. Never take them for granted. Tie them close to you, with bonds of love and respect. Connect them to you—to their history. Connect yourself to them and to the future.

And may God grant you health and energy, peace and "nachas" in the New Year.

THE COLLECTOR

At the Kotel in Jerusalem you will find the Collector. He collects young people with backpacks who are traveling the world, but are drawn to Israel and to Jerusalem and to the Kotel. The holy place exercises a spiritual magnetism, even for young people far removed from our tradition. Young people in search, not even consciously realizing they are in search. The small, barely flickering spark in their soul, "daspintele yid," attempting to reconnect with the great Jewish flame emanating from the holy place.

They are easy to spot. Backpacks, rough beards, cardboard yarmulkes.

As I wait for Kabbalat Shabbat services to begin, a man with a black hat, long beard and tzitzit flying approaches them. I expect he is looking for zedaka. But they don't have any money. He is handing out cards. An address. A place to go for Shabbat dinner. A backpacker's dream come true. A free meal.

He is called the "chapper." The collector of young Jews. An attempt to bring them back, to invite them in, back in to the Jewish community. To experience the beauty of the Jewish tradition. Perhaps to ignite that fluttering spark in their souls that still remains. He's the "chapper" as he is affectionately known.

I don't know how many young people started on the road back through the "chapper." Young people who went on to learn more. Who took off their backpacks and traded their copy of Jack Kerouac for the Chumash. Who sat and learned at one of the Jerusalem Yeshivas for a month or a year. Who went on their way refreshed spiritually; who came home with a new sense of identity. Who reinvigorated their families and their communities with their new sense of identity and commitment. Who found answers in the oldest religion on earth, our religion, their religion. Young people who sought answers everywhere: from the mystics in India, from the monks in Tibet; from the Buddhists in Nepal. Who finally found the answer, or at least the beginning of an answer from the "chapper" the collector at the Kotel. The collector of Jewish souls.

The use of the term "chapper" is ironic.

Czar Nicholas I (1825–55) [Mendele Mocher Seforim: Emek Habacha]

He ordered the conscription of Jewish boys into the army. They were sent away to special military schools attended by sons of soldiers. Each province had to fill a quota (Lithuania and Ukraine). Of course no Jew wanted to serve in the army because of the appalling inhuman conditions. The Jewish trustees charged with filling the quota had to hire "chappers," actually kidnappers or collectors to seize youngsters. They would have to serve for 25 years. They were supposed to be at least 12 but were often 8 or 9 because the "chappers" had to fill the quota.

They were placed in barracks (cantonist units) and given instruction in military drill and discipline and were given a rudimentary education. The real purpose was to make them into Christians. Their tallis and tephillin were taken away. Discipline was maintained by beatings and starvation. Little Jewish boys from sheltered homes were forbidden to pray or even speak Yiddish. They were cut off from home and family and religion. They were usually from the poorest families whose fathers couldn't pay off the "chappers." Some died in the process. It is estimated that some 40,000 Jewish youngsters were taken from their families never to return as Jews. Many served in the Crimean war when Russia fought the European allies. Can you imagine the possibility that Jews stood against the charge of the light brigade? That it was Jewish artillery gunners who destroyed the finest regiment of British Cavalry? Could it be that Tennyson immortalized the young Jews kidnapped by the "chappers" and didn't even realize it? But I digress.

The "chapper" at the Western Wall was collecting lost Jews. He was trying to make Jews, not destroy Jews. And the tradition of collecting lost Jews is an ancient one.

The Israelites marched in formation in the desert and camped in formation.

The tribe of Dan marched last, they were eating everyone else's dust. A tough position, but very important. They were the lost and found department. Picked up lost objects. (After services you would be amazed what we find in the synagogue: glasses, keys, wallets, jewelry, handkerchiefs, notes.)

Talmud Yerushalmi. Dan was the largest tribe so they marched last to give every other tribe enough room. And they would march in one line across instead of a square phalanx, so they could find any lost object, and return it to its owner when they stopped for the night. They were the lost and found department.

Chizkuni. If an Israelite from another tribe grew tired and couldn't walk, Dan would pick him up and carry him so he wouldn't be left alone. Dan collected all the stragglers, all the tired people, all those who were dropping out and couldn't keep up.

Eged bus has a subsidiary called Dan. They express bus is "mahir." The local bus stops for everyone. It is called Ha'ma'asef. Dan Hama'asef. Dan the collector of all the people.

The Torah has a law requiring us to return any animal that is lost from its master. You have to take it in and feed it and shelter it until its rightful owner can be located. (ki tetze).

If this is the case with animals who are lost, how much more so does it apply to people, to our brothers and sisters, who are wandering, who are lost?

How many Jews do you think live in our area? The recent Jewish Federation study says that 630,000 Jews live in south Florida.

In Aventura, our medina, we have almost 50,000 Jews. Some 20% belong to a shul. 10,000 Jews. That means some 40,000 Jews don't belong to a synagogue. 40,000 Jews are out there drifting around with hardly an interest in the Aventura Turnberry Jewish Center, or any other synagogue.

When I discussed these figures with a colleague at the Federation, I asked if he knew why? And he said the survey even collected the reasons why people don't join a synagogue.

Four reasons:

The shul is too far away. Well I know a fellow who gives me this excuse. Yet he thinks nothing of driving 3 hours down to the Keys to fish for sail, or flying 6 hours to Alaska to fish for salmon.

My children are not yet ready for Hebrew School; or my children were already Bar Mitzvah.

Children learn by example. Makes no difference what you tell them. They do what you do. You never set foot in a synagogue during the year, then you have taught your children that the synagogue isn't really important in your life. But don't be surprised when your young man leaves the synagogue after his Bar Mitzvah and never shows up again until he comes to say kaddish for you. And then he doesn't even remember how to hold the book.

It costs too much. I hear that from people. Yet they think nothing of spending $200 at a restaurant several times a month. There's the membership dues in the synagogue for a year. A woman tells me membership is too expensive. She spends more on one dress in Lord & Taylor than our Chai membership.

And the main excuse, given by most people who won't join the synagogue. I am not religious; I am not observant.

Well neither am I. There are 613 laws in the Torah. The Torah says you shall not harvest the corners of your field; you shall leave them for the poor. I never did that. I never even harvested a field. Just a few tomato plants in my backyard.

The Torah says you shall bring an offering in honor of the holyday to the Temple in Jerusalem. The closest I ever came to that was buying a Bar Mitzvah gift from a difficult store keeper on Ben Yehuda St. The outrageous price I paid I considered an offering to the holy city.

But I do pay close attention to honoring my father and mother. And I take great pains to be scrupulously honest. And I don't go to the beach on Shabbat. I try my best. And so do you. And that's what it means to be religious, to observe the Torah law as best as we can, even if we are not perfect. If we were perfect, we would be saints.

Everyone who came to shul today is religious. Religious is a Latin word meaning to re-connect. That's what we are all doing. Reconnecting to our people, and our tradition. We feel good about it. And so can anyone who will join us.

I hear an excuse that the Federation didn't record. When I ask someone to join us they tell me I used to be a member up north. As if when you retire to Florida you retire from the Jewish people. Sometimes I get the impression that these people think that God lives only in New York and Chicago and Detroit. That He doesn't operate below the Mason-Dixon line. Or maybe after you begin collecting your social security check you no longer need God's blessings; Uncle Sam's blessing and signature are enough.

So how do we convince 40,000 Jews in the greater Aventura area that they need to be here with us? How do we drag them off the golf course, away from their card game and out of the pool? At least some of them.

Today in shul we are 2,000 strong. I am deputizing each one of you to be a "chapper," a collector. A collector of one Jewish soul. Go out and find just one person. Your neighbor, your bridge partner, your doctor, your stock broker, your friend. Just one person.

Invite them to come with you just once to our synagogue to see if they like it. Try it. They will like it. I am sure something here will appeal to them. But bring them through the door. "Chap" one person. Save one Jewish soul.

Can you imagine what another 2,000 members could do for our synagogue? We would have the wonderful problem of figuring out where to put everyone. We would have to raise the roof and build a balcony. With box seats, with closed circuit T.V. to see every detail on the bima. With a small refrigerator stocked with challah, a little schmaltz herring and a little bottle of Schnapps; for kiddush, in case the service ran too long. But not on Yom Kippur, of course.

Even a few hundred new members could make a huge difference in what we can do for the Jewish people, and for the State of Israel.

Do it. Make it your project for the New Year. Make it your New Year's resolution. "Chap" one new Jewish soul. Collect one new member for our synagogue.

Too many of our people have fallen out of the ranks. They grew tired. They couldn't keep up. It is our holy obligation to lift them up. To collect them. To bring them home. To return them to their rightful place in the synagogue.

Collect the widows and widowers, who are alone, and no one invites them because they are one and no longer a couple.

Collect the survivors who are still angry at God and haven't been in shul since Vilna.

Collect the people on the golf course and around the pool who are on a permanent vacation from God.

If you do this. If you take one Jew by the hand and guide him back home to the synagogue; if you collect one Jew, just one Jew, then I promise you that God will remember you.

God will support you when you need help, God will find you when you are lost. And God will collect you and take you to Him after 120 years, when your time comes. Because God Himself said: Ha'mekayem Nefesh Achat. He who saves one Jew, saves an entire world.

THE TALLIS

One day last summer on a Shabbat morning in shul, my attention started to drift. I began thinking of all the missing faces. All the people who are gone. So many of them over the last 10 years. I remember their names; I can even see their faces if I concentrate. I can even remember where they sat in the synagogue. Sol, and Herman, and Charlie, and Phil, and Harry, and Moises, and Sam, and Izzy and Yetta.

Sometimes I think that their spirits are still here. They hover over us. Especially at these holy moments in our year. They did so much for us. They were the pioneers. They built this synagogue. They nurtured it. They protected it; they cared for it. And because of them we grew and prospered and became a recognized and respected Center of Jewish life.

As much as these wonderful people took care of us, we took care of them. They were like fathers and mothers for us all. We respected them. We treated them like kings and queens, like princes and princesses. Nothing was ever too difficult for us to do when it came to taking care of their needs.

But the most important gift we gave them was the gift of being wanted and needed. Everyone of them was an outstanding member of a major congregation somewhere else. In Chicago or Detroit or New York or Toronto. Every major synagogue in North America. They were presidents and members of boards and advisors and consultants. They could have retired from synagogue life as they had retired from business life. But they didn't. They stayed connected and committed to us as strongly as they were in the North. Sometimes the bonds they forged with us were even stronger than any synagogue bonds they had before. And the reason was, our secret was, an ability to make them feel totally at home with us. To feel that we really cared about them. That we needed them; we valued them. We made them feel important, significant, honored and respected. They knew there was nothing we wouldn't do for them. And soon there was nothing they wouldn't do for our synagogue.

But the most important factor was they felt wanted and needed. Sometimes for large projects, sometimes for small projects. But always for something. Sometimes for financial support. Sometimes for moral support. Sometimes for their wisdom, sometimes for their experience. But always for something.

Yetta is one of our missing synagogue family members. She came most every Shabbat and sat right back there on my right in one of the last rows. Modest and unassuming, always ready to offer her apartment and her table to a shul guest.

I found out one day she was an accomplished seamstress. I kept it in mind until one day last year. My weekday tallis was getting a bit worn. Actually, I have a few talleisim. One for Rosh Hashana, one for other holydays, one for Shabbat, and one for weekdays. My weekday tallis was looking a bit yellow. In my mind I associate that yellow tallis with decay and disintegration. I have seen so many of them ready for burial. I have seen so many of those yellow talleisim, draped around a body, in a casket. I'm not ready for that. It makes me uncomfortable so I decided to bury it. I didn't really need a new one; I had plenty. But I wanted to save the collar. Called an "atara." It had my Hebrew name on it embroidered by one of my friends.

I called Yetta, because I knew she could remove the collar and sew it on another tallis. She assumed I would buy a new one.

Weeks passed and I couldn't decide if I really wanted by buy a new tallis. How many talleisim does one person need? It's not like dishes, where you need one set for milk, one for meat, another set for milchig on Passover and yet another set for fleishig on Passover, and yet another set that sits in the breakfront, that is used only for special guests.

Finally, Yetta calls me one morning to ask when I was coming over with the tallis so she could begin work. I explained I hadn't decided and I would call her when I did. She called me every week to ask about the tallis. Finally, one morning she called me and said, you need to bring me the tallis so I can sew it before I go away.

At first, I didn't quite understand what she meant. Where was she going; maybe to visit her sons. Maybe she was going to a hotel for the holydays because it was getting hard to prepare for herself.

Then it dawned on me. She was trying to tell me that she didn't have much longer on this earth. She was about to go away. On the final journey. And before she went, she had some unfinished business. A mitzva that she needed to do for me. A tallis. A part of her soul stitched into my tallis. So whenever I put it on, I would be reminded of Yetta. And whenever I put it on and fulfilled the mitzva, she too would be part of the mitzva. A permanent connection between heaven and earth. Between Yetta and the tallis.

I bought a new tallis. Not because I needed it. But because Yetta needed it. She sewed on the old collar with my Hebrew name, in beautiful, careful stitches. As if she were stitching part of her neshama into it. She proudly presented it to me; and I thanked her.

And then she went away. Three days later, she was dead. I told the story to her sons, when they came to take her back.

Yetta needed to know that she was doing something important, something useful. More than that, she wanted to be part of a mitzva. A mitzva that would endure long after she was gone.

We are all passing through but once. One day we will all be gone. What do you want to leave behind? A three handicap golf score? A corporation listed on the stock exchange? A three car garage? How do we really want to be remembered?

We need to be part of something greater than we are. Something that transcends time. Something that will endure beyond our 120 years. We need to stitch our lives into the fabric of Jewish history. We need to link our lives to the life of the Jewish people. The Jewish people are eternal, we shall be eternal.

Do it with a mitzva. The mitzva of building our synagogue, this synagogue where our spirits will live long after we are gone. Where people will remember where we sat, what our faces looked like and what we did to build the future of the Jewish people. Where people will say our names from time to time, with reverence and respect. Where the pattern of our lives will be stitched into the holy fabric of the Jewish community for generations to come.

LIFE IS THE BEST ANSWER

I can't bear to see another picture of the World Trade Center exploding in a ball of flame. I go to sleep with the nightmare, and I get up with the nightmare. Those pictures never leave me. I will never forget the sisters and fathers and uncles and co-workers desperately searching for their loved ones, walking the streets of lower Manhattan with pictures in hand. Stopping everyone; and asking: Have you seen my son, have you seen my sister?

I am beyond shock, and I am beyond anguish. I am seething with anger. My rage smolders as the fires in lower Manhattan still smolder.

And now, for the first time, we the American people understand. We can empathize, we can begin to see the importance of the war on terrorism. Because we are now its victims also. Our country, America, not just Israel; our cities, New York, not just Jerusalem.

Now thousands of American citizens are dead. In the World Trade Center, in the Pentagon, murdered by Arab terrorists. Now let the sleeping giant awake. Now let us solemnly swear to do our duty. To eradicate terrorism once and for all. To hold responsible every government everywhere who have financed, encouraged and hidden these criminals. Every person who contributed a dollar to their organizations. Every person in Nablus who danced with glee in the streets when the news was broadcast to Middle East. We have seen the dark side. We will find the rats scurrying through the sewers of the world trying to hide. Our light will find them. And justice will be exacted. And our world made safe again.

But until then we worry. We are sick with worry. Because our America, the greatest and most powerful nation on earth is not safe. Now we are afraid to take the subway, we are afraid to go the mall, and we are afraid to go near an airport. Our whole way of life came tumbling down with the World Trade Center Towers. Our feeling of strength and inviolability was destroyed in the explosion of the Pentagon.

And we are sick with worry over Israel.

I don't even want to open the newspaper. I quickly scan for news for Israel. I shudder when I see the word Israel in a headline. It is never something good. Invariably another Israeli citizen is dead or wounded because of Arab terrorists. I don't want to see another picture of the "chevra kadisha" picking up pieces of bodies on Jaffa Road. I can't bear to see another CNN clip of an eight year-old boy from Tekoa standing at the grave of his murdered mother.

A good day for me is a day when there is no news about Israel. No news is good news.

Is there no way out of this nightmare? Is there no apparent path to peace? It is so frustrating to realize that the mightiest army in the Middle East, the Israel Defense Forces, cannot deal with a gang of murdering thugs; because of the political reality? The political reality is that Israel must fight with one hand behind its back. Israel must bleed, and bleed again. Israel must sacrifice its citizens on a daily basis. In the buses, in their cars, in the shopping malls and in the pizza shops. Because a proper defense against terrorists would be a comprehensive offense. Sweeping through the Palestinian territory and eliminating the nests of terrorists. And repeating the operation until it remains quiet. This is the primary duty of the Israeli government, of any government: to protect its citizens from attack.

Unfortunately, these operations are termed by western governments as "over reactions" or provocations. Imagine, 30 young people are killed when an Arab terrorist explodes a bomb in a Tel Aviv nightclub. Blood and body parts are everywhere. Mothers are screaming. Funerals go on all week. That's not a provocation or obstacle to peace. When Israeli jets destroy a headquarters of the Palestinian authority, where the plans are made and the orders issued, the leaders of the free world call it an "over reaction", a provocation.

An Arab terrorist murders 15 Israelis in a pizza parlor in Jerusalem. He calmly sits down next to several children, to be sure he murders Jewish babies. Israel ejects the Palestinians from Orient House, their base of operations in Jerusalem and Western leaders call it an over reaction. How many Israeli citizens have to die before they stop calling it an over reaction? How much Jewish blood has to be spilled before Western governments recognize the legitimate right of the Israeli people to self-defense?

Even worse is refusal of the media to make any distinction between a murdered Israeli citizen and a Palestinian terrorist shot as he prepares a bomb. This equation between innocent Jewish people, and Arab murderers, this false moral equivalent, is the reason why the violence against Israel continues. Is it perfectly right and legitimate to murder Israeli citizens?

I have every confidence that the government of Israel will find a way to secure peace. No one wants to send their son or husband to war. How can you ever relax when your brother is manning a guard post in Gaza or Hebron, or your son is guarding the worshippers at the Kotel? How can you live when you jump at the ringing of the phone? When you are afraid to answer the phone because it could be bad news.

Does anyone know the way out of this nightmare? Does anyone have a good idea? Does anyone know the path to peace? Usually peace comes only after compromise. Difficult compromise. Yet, the offer of significant compromise by the Barak government was rejected. In favor of a violent Arab uprising. The conclusion: We are not wanted in the Middle East. Not only in Hebron or Gaza or East Jerusalem, but in Haifa and Tel Aviv. The solution for peace: Pack up and go back to Warsaw or Vilna where we came from. Or move to

New Zealand or America. Then there will be peace in Israel. When there is no Israel. A Judenrein Middle East.

The other answer is remain strong, and determined until the Arab terrorists and the Arab governments grow tired. Because who ever gets tired first, who ever weakens first, will lose. And God forbid it should be the Israeli people.

There is another way. To go on with life as best as you can. To live a normal life in abnormal times. To live a peaceful life when you are threatened by violence. To choose life even when surrounded by death. But to do this you have to be a special person. To exist this way you have to be an unusual nation. To insist on taking the same bus that exploded last week. To stop for ice cream on the same corner where children died last month. To shop in the market where Jewish blood flowed last Friday, Erev Shabbat. To continue to live even when surrounded by death, to get married, to raise a family even in such difficult circumstances. Because living is the strongest statement that the Jewish people can make. Walking the streets of Jerusalem is a courageous political act. Riding in the bus is an act of faith in the future of the Jewish people. Stopping at the pizza place and ordering a slice is an act of faith in Israel.

The Maccabiah games were held in Israel during the summer. Many Jewish teams from around the world were afraid to come. Many Jewish athletes hesitated to compete in Tel Aviv. By the time the opening ceremonies took place at Teddy Kollek Stadium, there was an American squad in the parade.

I was very proud of our athletes who put their fears, their legitimate fears, aside and came to compete. Who came ready to show solidarity with the people of Israel. To demonstrate to the world that the Jewish people will not be frightened off by Palestinian thugs.

And you can imagine how difficult it was. You are about to begin a race, and in the back of your head, you remember Munich; Arab terrorists, the murder of Jewish athletes right in front of the entire sports world. And the Games going on as if nothing happened. I was so proud of these brave young people.

Let me tell you about my favorite athlete. His name is Todd Schayes. Some of us remember his uncle, Dolph Schayes, one of the greatest basketball players of all times. Todd, of course, plays basketball and he came with the U.S. Masters team. That's a nice way of saying the "over the hill boys." In basketball, "over the hill" is 35.

Todd Schayes wasn't getting any younger and he decided that it was time for tachlis. Which means he needed to find a wife, settle down, and have a family. But as anyone over 35 knows, it's not so easy to find the right girl. It's never easy to find the right girl. But the older you get, the more difficult it gets.

And Todd was very clear that he wanted a young lady who shared his heritage and tradition. He wanted a Jewish wife. The problem was even bigger for Todd because he lives in a city with a relatively small Jewish population. Not a whole lot to choose from. Now Todd isn't exactly Tom Cruise, but neither is he Quasimoto. He has a receding hairline but he's a great guy, according to his mother.

So Todd came up with an ingenious idea: he knew that in the opening parade of the Maccabiah games, the United States team would march in just ahead of the Israeli team, and this being Ramat Gan, Israeli television would spend most of their time focused on the Israeli athletes. So Todd Schayes put himself at the very end of the American contingent. So when Israeli television would begin filming their Israeli teams, Todd would be in the picture because he was walking one step in front of the first Israeli athletes. And he carried a big sign. The sign read in Hebrew: "Single male, American, looking for Israeli wife. Contact Todd Schayes at the Tel Aviv Hilton."

Well you can imagine what happened. That night he had 75 calls from young ladies. The next morning he was on *Good Morning Israel*. Then interviews in the newspapers and magazines. Everyone wanted to interview Todd Schayes, the American Jewish Prince. By the time he went home, he had more than 5,000 calls. Todd spent every evening in Tel Aviv interviewing young women. Each young lady had one half hour. And there were lines up to the elevator. This was serious business to them. Todd's requirements were about 30 years old, interested in having children, beautiful inside and outside, nonsmoker, who would move to Colorado, and would have to work. He told them he wasn't one of those rich Americans.

One mother called Todd and said she had a son, not a daughter. Before Todd hung up on her, she asked for Todd's list of women after he finds his bashert, so she could find a wife for her son. Todd has narrowed down the field, and the last I heard, he is conducting an e-mail relationship with four of the women he met.

Israelis are murdered by Arab terrorists every day. Violence and killing have unfortunately become a fact of life in Tel Aviv. But Todd Schayes has an answer. Nothing will destroy the Jewish people. Nothing will kill the Jewish spirit. Even surrounded by death, life will go on. Young people will marry, children will be born and life will go on. We will eat ice cream on Ben Yehuda Street. We will have a pizza on Jaffa Road. We will picnic in the Kennedy Forest. We will lead as close to a normal life as possible. And one day with God's help, peace will come to the people of Israel. Until that day, we will never give up hope, we will never be frightened off, and we will never lose our courage. Because the best answer to the death all around us, the only answer, is life. Lechaim.

And by the way, I sent Todd Schayes a letter expressing my admiration. He sent me a note. "You will be invited to the wedding."

EPILOGUE

ONCE AGAIN, THE MOUNTAIN

Once again the mountain beckons; only this time, it is in Africa and it is the highest point on the continent. One of the "seven," the highest summits on each continent. Everest is out of the question for normally endowed human beings, but Kilimanjaro, even at almost 20,000 feet, is possible for those willing to prepare rigorously and to suffer.

The stark facts are best left for the trip epilogue: no doctor, no helicopter rescue, no hospital. If something goes wrong, ranging from acute mountain sickness to a broken ankle, the porters will take your body back down. Hopefully, you will still be breathing.

Getting to the trail head for the Machame route up "Kili" is an expedition unto itself. Two overnight flights and a small plane into Kilimanjaro from Nairobi Airport, followed by a rough jeep ride to the assembly point. There are very few miles of paved road in Tanzania, so most trips are by four wheel drive on dirt and mud tracks. In the chill of the mountain jungle forest, already at 5,000 feet, we check our gear, assemble our guides and porters, and off we go.

Jonathan, myself, Danford our guide, and six porters hauling our tents, food, and assorted gear for the six day trek. The porters carry 60 and 70 pound bags and boxes on their heads and shoulders. They wear rubber sandals and torn tee shirts, and they arrive in camp two hours before we do.

I carry nothing; moving my body along with the aid of trekking polls is enough for me. The suggested hiking time per day is five to six hours. We take six to eight ours in the best tradition of *pole, pole* (Swahili for "slowly, slowly"). It becomes immediately apparent to me that I am in for an extremely rigorous trip, one that I will barely hope to survive.

The first day's trek is only a preview of the difficult terrain to come. The wet and muddy trail is treacherous to negotiate. It is criss-crossed by soaking tree roots and rocks, and the footing is slippery. We are soon covered by mud up to the tops of our gaiters. Some three hours into the trek, I pause to hang on my poles, and to glance questioningly at Jonathan. What have I gotten myself into? But there is no going back.

Just before we reach Machame camp at the end of our first day, we pass through the clouds and catch our first glimpse of snow-covered Kilimanjaro. It is magnificent in the beckoning distance. Our tents are set up, hot tea is waiting, and we gratefully sit ourselves down. Before trying to sleep for the night, we spend an hour, in what becomes the daily evening ritual: mixing iodine and assorted chemicals into our boiled water to purify and improve taste. To this vile concoction we add Gatorade. We are well fortified against the assorted African parasites that seek to make a home in our intestines.

Morning finds us out of the wet, uncomfortable jungle and up onto the Shira plateau. Ever gaining altitude, we climb up through a series of huge boulders to Shira camp. I am breathing hard and need to rest now and then. Our porters, with their huge loads and no high-tech boots or clothing, pass us by with ease. We chose to take Diamox to prevent acute mountain sickness, and it seems to work. We have elected to take the longer Machame route (the "whiskey" route as opposed to the easier Marangu, or "Coca-Cola" route) in order to have an additional trekking day to acclimatize. It seems to be working, however, it cannot save us from sheer exhaustion.

At the end of the third day, we camp at the foot of a 250 foot rock face at Barranco Camp. I look up at the cliff and then at our guide in disbelief. He assures me that I am not suffering from altitude sickness and that I will be able to scale the cliff. I have my doubts and explore the possibility of a different way out of here. By sunrise, we are scaling the rock face, slowly and carefully picking our way along a barely perceptible trail that even a mountain goat would have difficulty negotiating. We collapse on top after two and a half hours, congratulating ourselves. We still have another five hours of trekking to go to reach Barafu base camp, where the serious climbing will begin.

We barely have time to put our heads down before we are awakened at midnight. Time to go. Dressed in everything we have to ward off the freezing cold, we stumble along in the thin light of our headlamps, following our guide. I can barely keep my head up from the muscle strain of pole plants and head-down navigation of the last several days. It is now much more difficult to breathe as we approach 19,000 feet and our progress is slowed by the difficulty in finding a solid foot purchase in the loose volcanic scree. My progress slows to a crawl punctuated by rest stops every ten steps. I do manage to notice that the night sky covers us with a veritable blanket of brilliant stars, a sight I have never seen in all my sojourns. It remains my most vivid vision of that last dreadful push to the top.

Sunrise finds us still a hundred meters from the top. I feel the strength and energy quickly draining out of my body. I am pushed and cajoled by Danford in an attempt to extract one last superhuman effort from my quickly deteriorating body. Finally, Stella point, the top of the volcano, and the beginning of the snows of Kilimanjaro. I collapse in total exhaustion, unable and unwilling to take one more step. Jonathan continues on to Uhuru point. I am satisfied; I have had more than enough.

We meet several hours later down at Barafu hut, rest awhile, have a cliff shot and a drink, and pack for the trek down to Mweka camp. Then another day of sliding and slipping though the mountain jungle mud and we are out.

At the Mweka Gate, we sign in: name, address, country of origin and age. I leaf through the back entries and note that trekkers to Kilimanjaro are usually in their late twenties or early thirties. No one my age seems to be listed. The ranger seems to recall one "senior citizen" who made the climb successfully some three or four years previous.

Certificates are signed and presented and we pack the jeep for the ride back to Arusha. We made it, much to our satisfaction and delight, and much to my surprise. This is as high as I will ever go. From now on, it's "down hill."

For the rest of our time in Africa, I try to remain as immobile as possible. Two weeks later, I am still recovering from Kili.

Months later, I have the opportunity to reflect on the climb. I am impressed with our monumental achievement and amazed at the energy, stamina, and discipline we were able to muster in the preparation stage and certainly during the trek. Mental discipline played an integral part in the effort. Probably the difference between defeat and success lies in the simple question of how badly you wish to achieve the summit. Nothing can substitute for the proper training and preparation. But nothing can prepare you for high-altitude stress, and nothing can propel you forward like the internal engine of the will. It is tempting to give up in the face of suffering. But there is no greater satisfaction than overcoming pain in the pursuit of the goal, especially in retrospect. The best place to savor the victory is in the comfort of your own chair back at home. It is also comforting to know that we don't have to do this again; we have nothing more to prove.

Some would question our sanity. Why would you wish to put yourself through such a grueling, even life-threatening experience, for the privilege of standing on top of a volcano in the middle of Africa? The answer is complex: It has to do with a personal vision of yourself, what you can do, what you can overcome, and what you wish to look back on with the personal pride of achievement.

Outdoorsmen often speak of the need for personal testing, to move beyond the confines of comfortable civilization and encounter the natural environment in all its grandeur and all its danger. It is a desire to exchange a safe existence for a precarious, but infinitely more exciting, challenging, although dangerous one.

In addition, it is an ongoing attempt to hold the forces of age at bay. It is quite gratifying to realize that at the end of my fifth decade of life I am able to muster the energy, muscle power, and stamina worthy of "youth." Overcoming perceived limitations brings with it a satisfaction that cannot be achieved in any other way.

I have always referred to "climbing the mountain" as a metaphor for life. Noteworthy is the fact that Moses made his last expedition up the mountain of Nebo. He never experienced the path down; he left this world from the peak of the mountain ascending even higher, in the spiritual sense, to be reunited with his Creator. And, according to the Bible, his energy and power were not diminished by the ravages of old age. Perhaps this blessing is only vouchsafed to a select few, the Mosaic community. The rest of us can only pray that we can maintain our vitality. We will not win the battle against age, but we can diminish, if not fend off, its ravages. We can achieve much more than we think. It is this positive thinking that can make all the difference. The angel of death will not go away, but he can be made to stand in the corner, at least for the time being.